My Neighbor Seki

6

Tonari no Seki-kun

Takuma Morishige

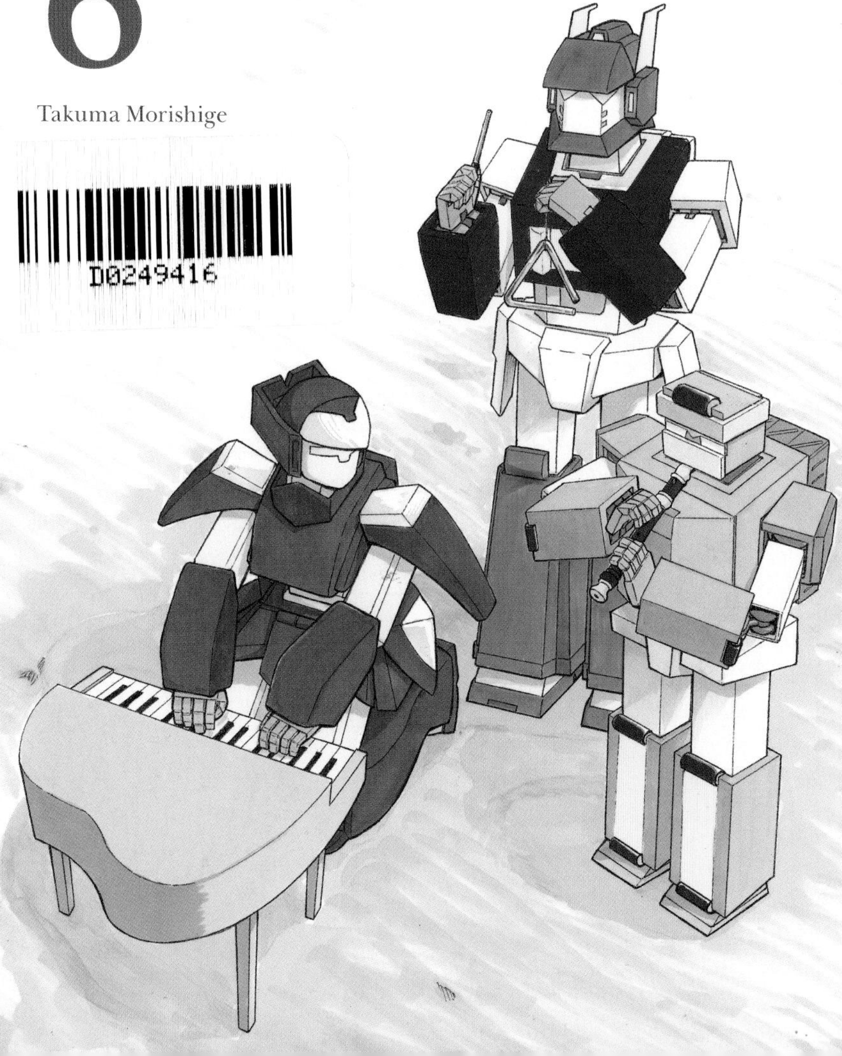

Schedule

My
Neighbor
Seki

6

* THIS IS A WORK OF FICTION. NAMES, CHARACTERS, PLACES
AND INCIDENTS ARE PRODUCTS OF THE AUTHOR'S IMAGINATION
OR USED FICTITIOUSLY. ANY RESEMBLANCE TO ACTUAL EVENTS
OR LOCALES OR PERSONS, LIVING OR DEAD, IS ENTIRELY COIN-
CIDENTAL.

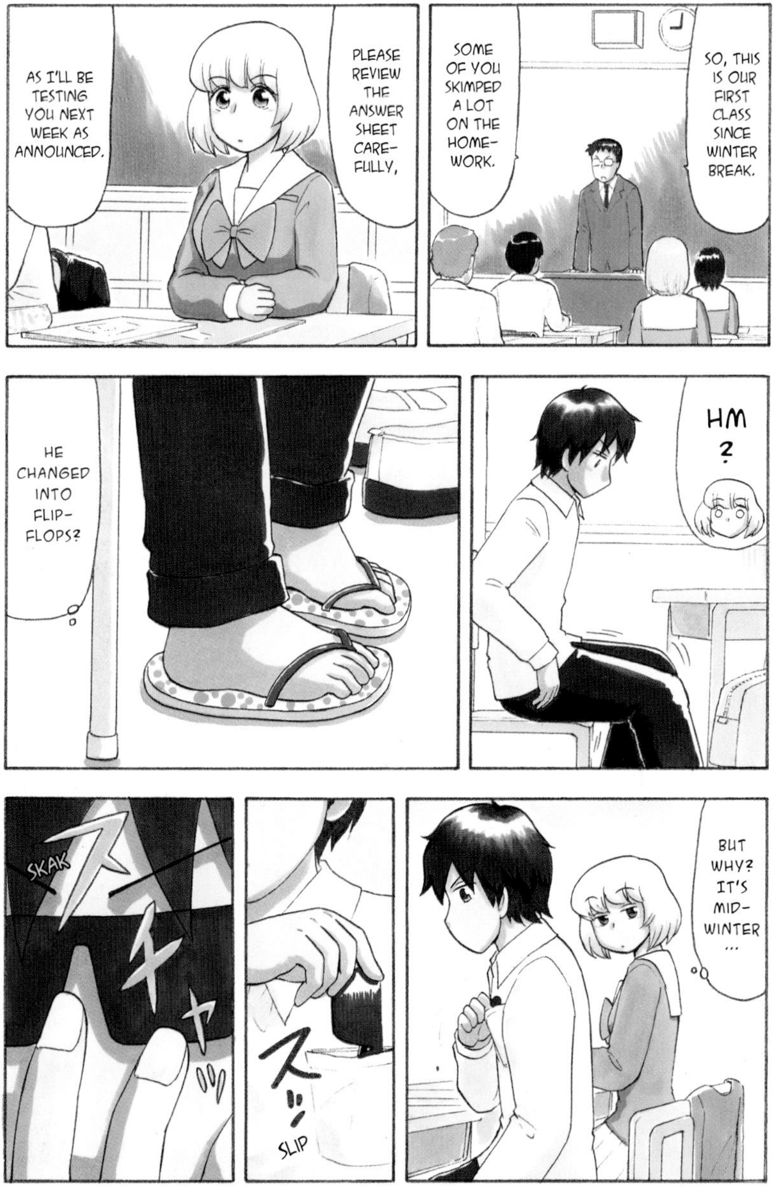
SO, THIS IS OUR FIRST CLASS SINCE WINTER BREAK.
SOME OF YOU SKIMPED A LOT ON THE HOME-WORK.
PLEASE REVIEW THE ANSWER SHEET CARE-FULLY,
AS I'LL BE TESTING YOU NEXT WEEK AS ANNOUNCED.
HM ?
HE CHANGED INTO FLIP-FLOPS?
BUT WHY? IT'S MID-WINTER ...
SLIP
SKAK

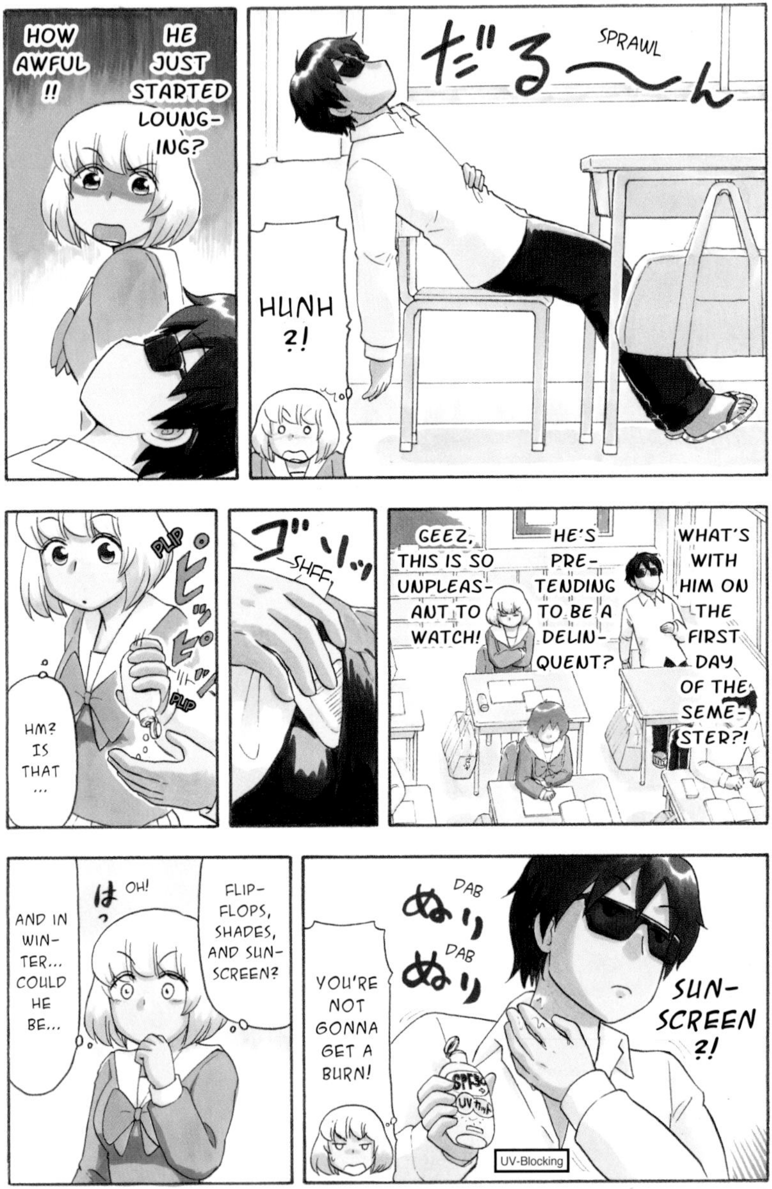
だる〜ん
SPRAWL
HUNH?!
HE JUST STARTED LOUNGING?
HOW AWFUL!!
WHAT'S WITH HIM ON THE FIRST DAY OF THE SEMESTER?!
HE'S PRETENDING TO BE A DELINQUENT?
GEEZ, THIS IS SO UNPLEASANT TO WATCH!
ゴソッ
SHFF
ピッピッ
PLIP
PLIP
HM? IS THAT...
ぬりぬり
DAB
DAB
SUN-SCREEN?!
YOU'RE NOT GONNA GET A BURN!
UV-Blocking
FLIP-FLOPS, SHADES, AND SUNSCREEN?
はっ
OH!
AND IN WINTER... COULD HE BE...

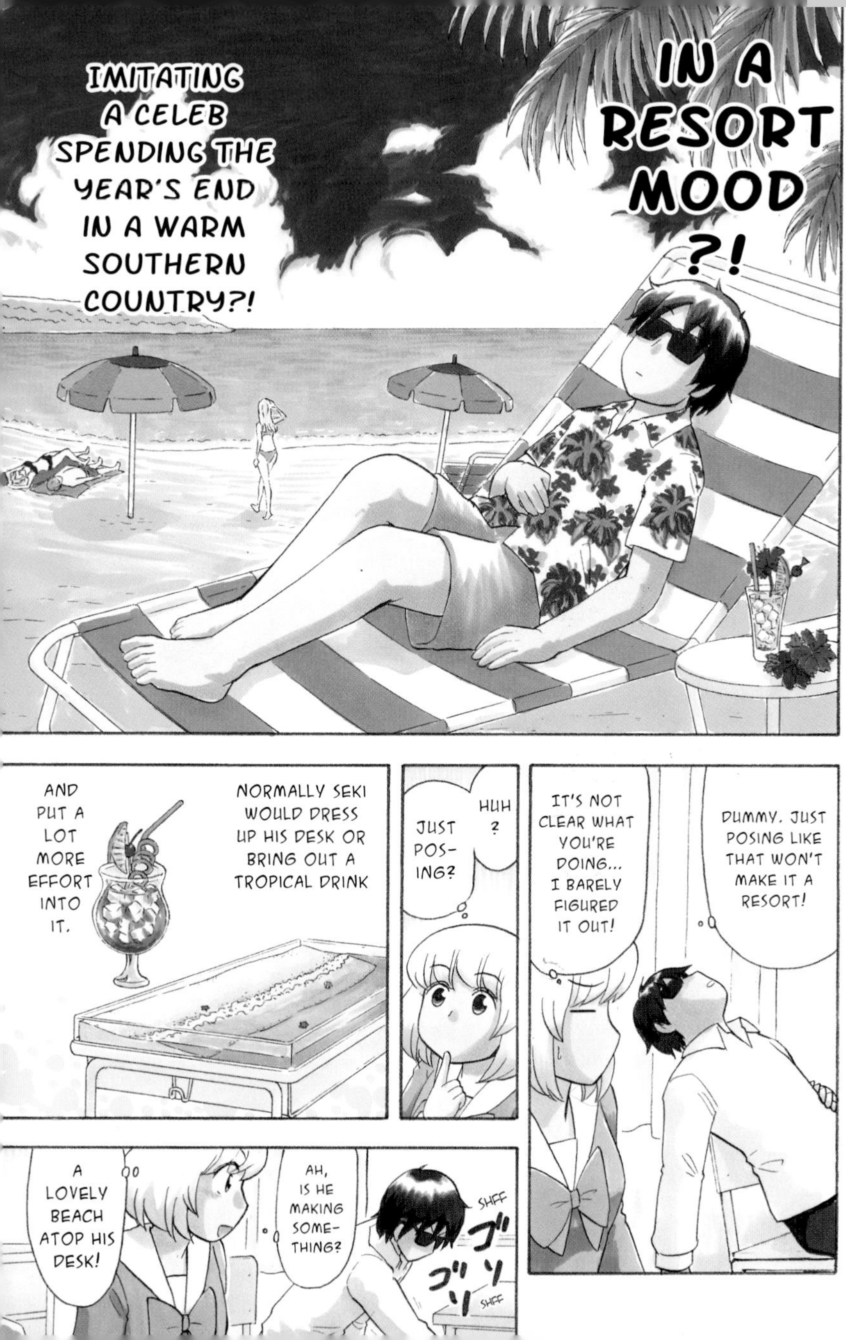
IN A RESORT MOOD ?!
IMITATING A CELEB SPENDING THE YEAR'S END IN A WARM SOUTHERN COUNTRY?!
DUMMY. JUST POSING LIKE THAT WON'T MAKE IT A RESORT!
IT'S NOT CLEAR WHAT YOU'RE DOING... I BARELY FIGURED IT OUT!
HUH?
JUST POSING?
NORMALLY SEKI WOULD DRESS UP HIS DESK OR BRING OUT A TROPICAL DRINK
AND PUT A LOT MORE EFFORT INTO IT.
AH, IS HE MAKING SOMETHING?
SHFF
SHFF
A LOVELY BEACH ATOP HIS DESK!

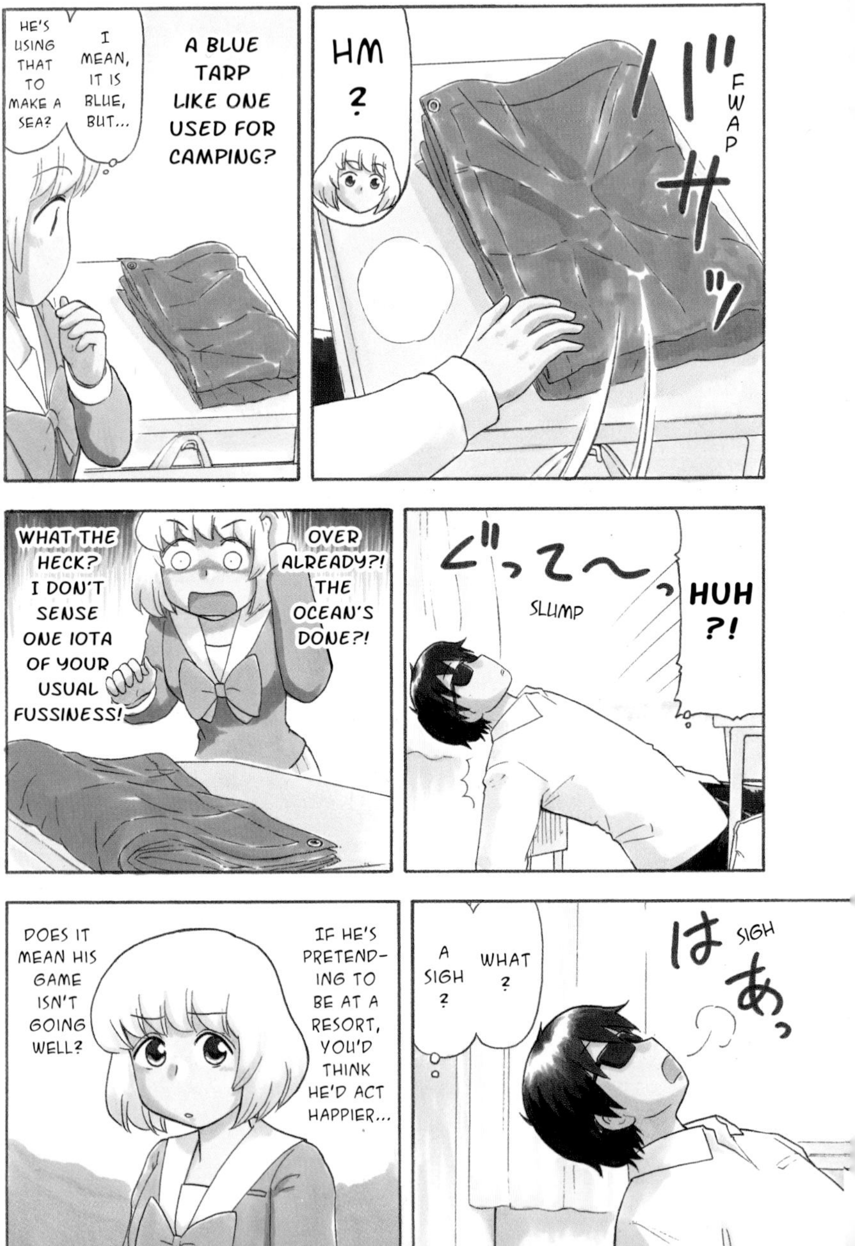
バサッ
FWAP
HM?
A BLUE TARP LIKE ONE USED FOR CAMPING?
I MEAN, IT IS BLUE, BUT...
HE'S USING THAT TO MAKE A SEA?
HUH?!
ぐって～っ
SLUMP
OVER ALREADY?! THE OCEAN'S DONE?!
WHAT THE HECK? I DON'T SENSE ONE IOTA OF YOUR USUAL FUSSINESS!
はあっ
SIGH
WHAT?
A SIGH?
IF HE'S PRETEND-ING TO BE AT A RESORT, YOU'D THINK HE'D ACT HAPPIER...
DOES IT MEAN HIS GAME ISN'T GOING WELL?

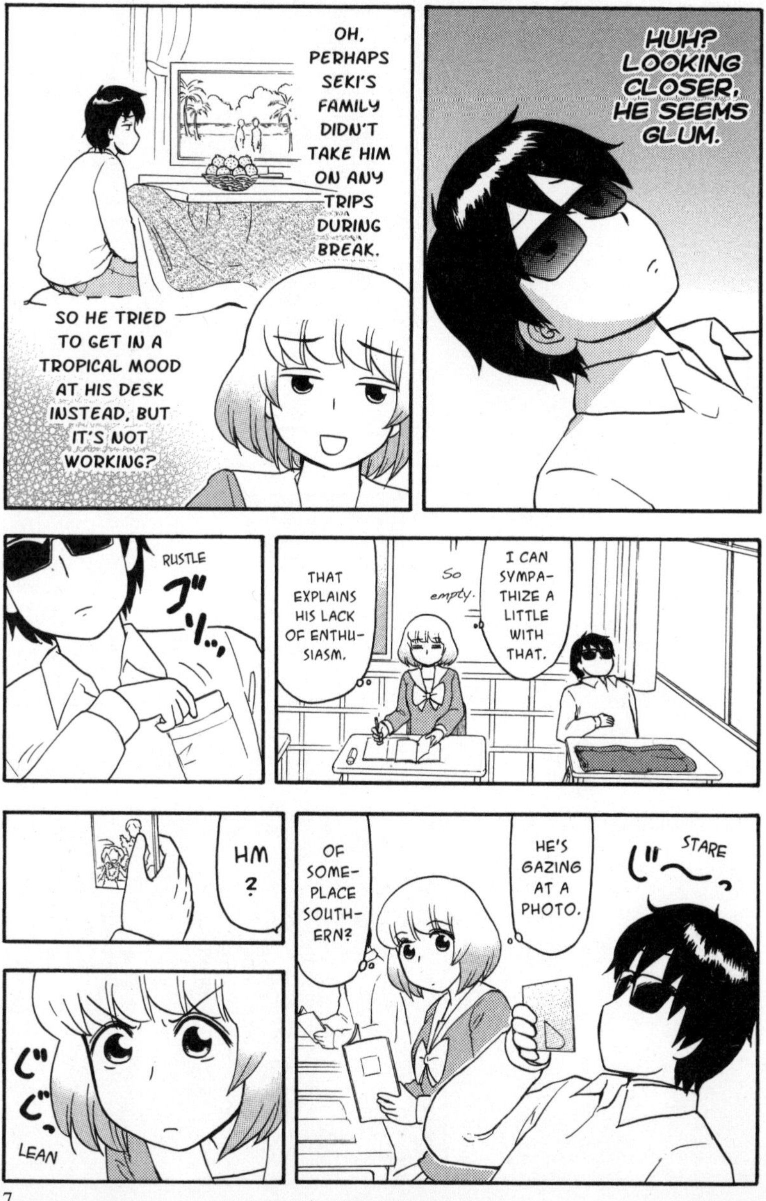
HUH? LOOKING CLOSER, HE SEEMS GLUM.
OH, PERHAPS SEKI'S FAMILY DIDN'T TAKE HIM ON ANY TRIPS DURING BREAK.
SO HE TRIED TO GET IN A TROPICAL MOOD AT HIS DESK INSTEAD, BUT IT'S NOT WORKING?
I CAN SYMPATHIZE A LITTLE WITH THAT.
So empty.
THAT EXPLAINS HIS LACK OF ENTHUSIASM.
RUSTLE
ゴソ
STARE
じ〜
HE'S GAZING AT A PHOTO.
OF SOMEPLACE SOUTHERN?
HM?
じじ
LEAN

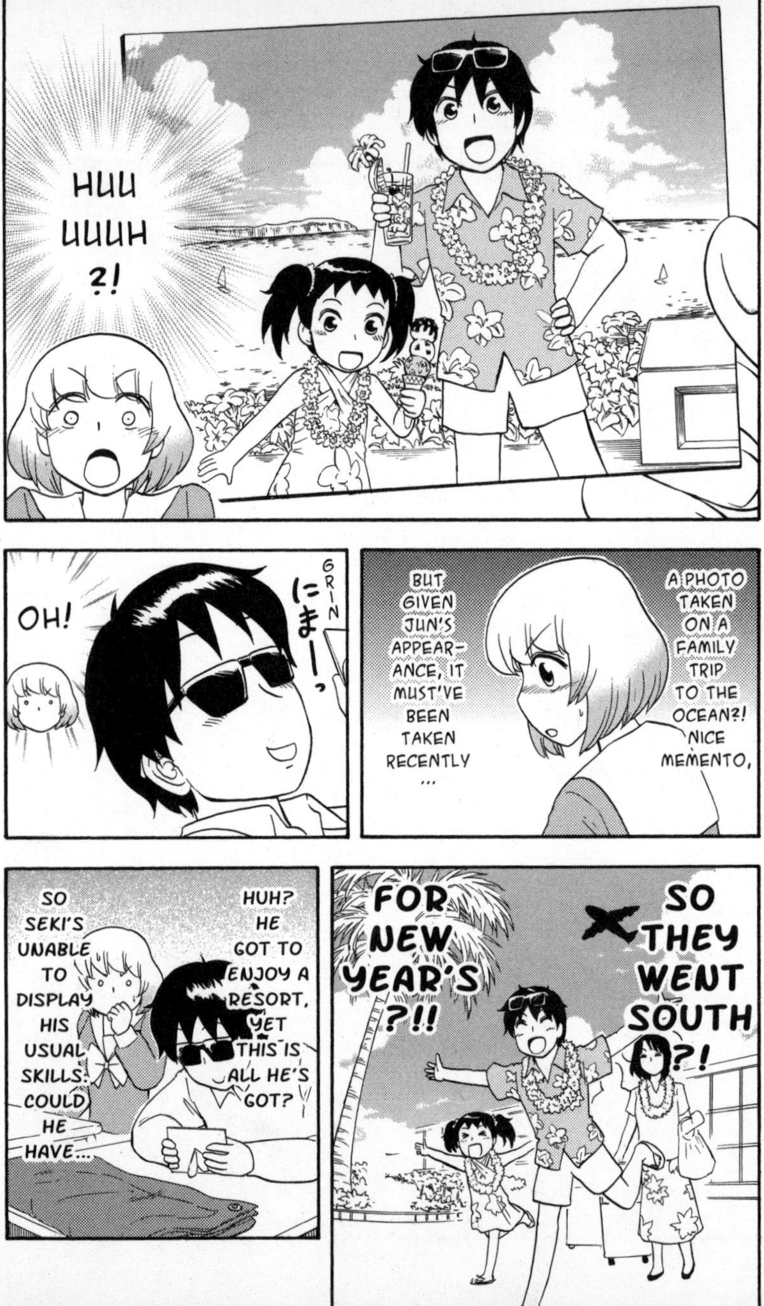
HUU UUUH ?!
A PHOTO TAKEN ON A FAMILY TRIP TO THE OCEAN?! NICE MEMENTO,
BUT GIVEN JUN'S APPEARANCE, IT MUST'VE BEEN TAKEN RECENTLY...
GRIN
にまーっ
OH!
SO THEY WENT SOUTH ?!
FOR NEW YEAR'S ?!!
HUH? HE GOT TO ENJOY A RESORT, YET THIS IS ALL HE'S GOT?
SO SEKI'S UNABLE TO DISPLAY HIS USUAL SKILLS. COULD HE HAVE...

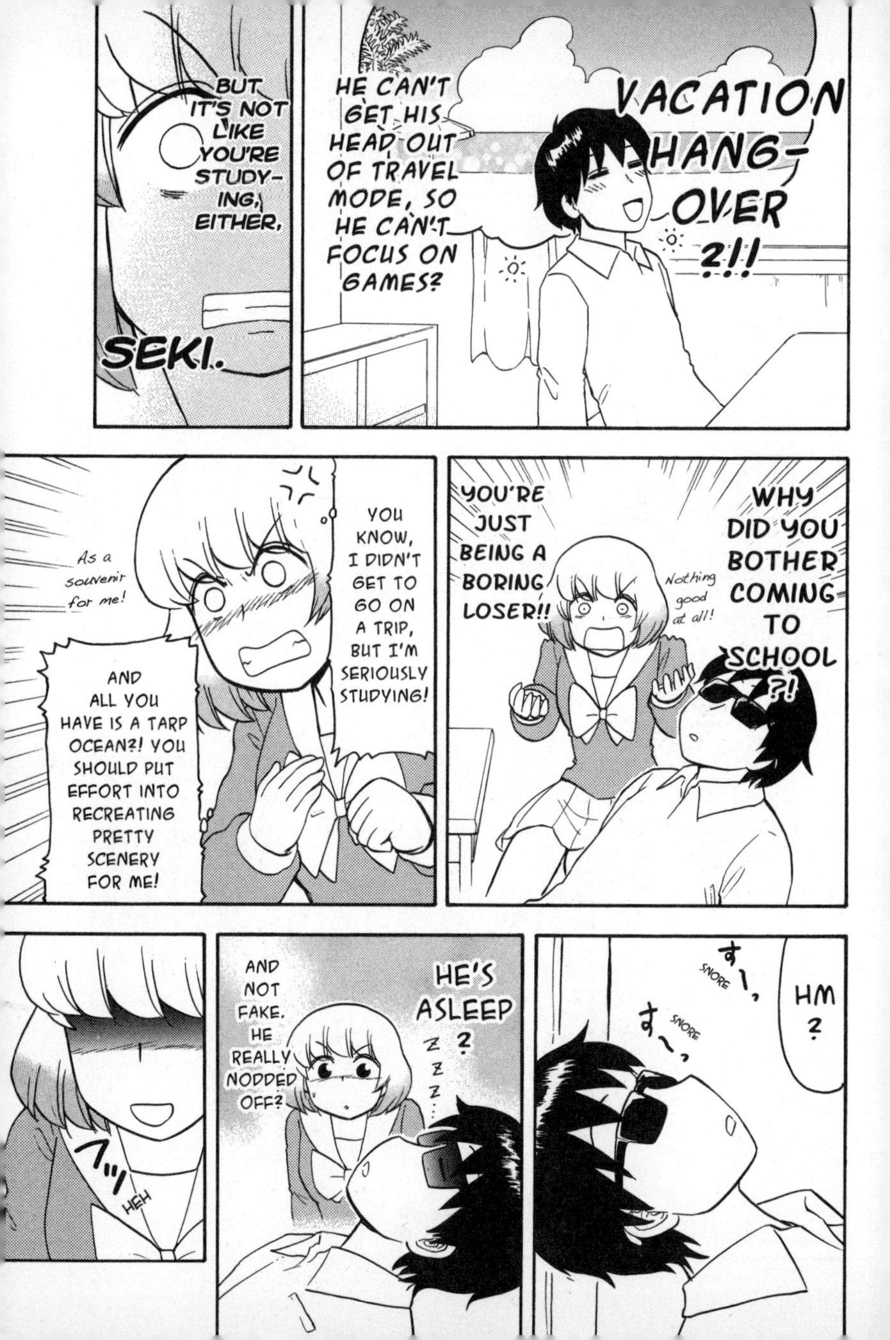
VACATION HANG-OVER ?!!
HE CAN'T GET HIS HEAD OUT OF TRAVEL MODE, SO HE CAN'T FOCUS ON GAMES?
BUT IT'S NOT LIKE YOU'RE STUDYING, EITHER,
SEKI.
WHY DID YOU BOTHER COMING TO SCHOOL ?!
Nothing good at all!
YOU'RE JUST BEING A BORING LOSER!!
YOU KNOW, I DIDN'T GET TO GO ON A TRIP, BUT I'M SERIOUSLY STUDYING!
As a souvenir for me!
AND ALL YOU HAVE IS A TARP OCEAN?! YOU SHOULD PUT EFFORT INTO RECREATING PRETTY SCENERY FOR ME!
HM ?
すー、
SNORE
すー、
SNORE
HE'S ASLEEP ?
Z Z Z...
AND NOT FAKE. HE REALLY NODDED OFF?
ヘッ
HEH

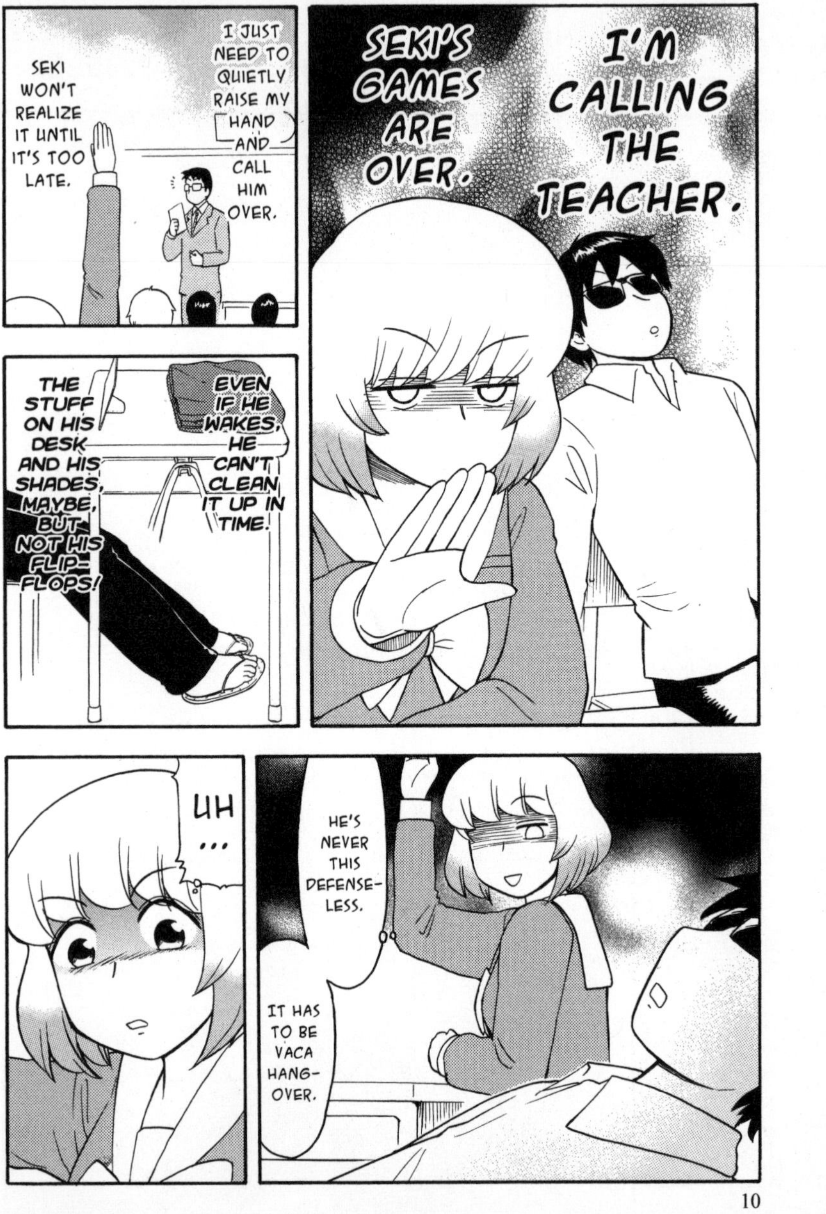
I'M CALLING THE TEACHER.
SEKI'S GAMES ARE OVER.
I JUST NEED TO QUIETLY RAISE MY HAND AND CALL HIM OVER.
SEKI WON'T REALIZE IT UNTIL IT'S TOO LATE.
EVEN IF HE WAKES, HE CAN'T CLEAN IT UP IN TIME.
THE STUFF ON HIS DESK AND HIS SHADES, MAYBE, BUT NOT HIS FLIP-FLOPS!
HE'S NEVER THIS DEFENSELESS.
IT HAS TO BE VACA HANGOVER.
UH ...

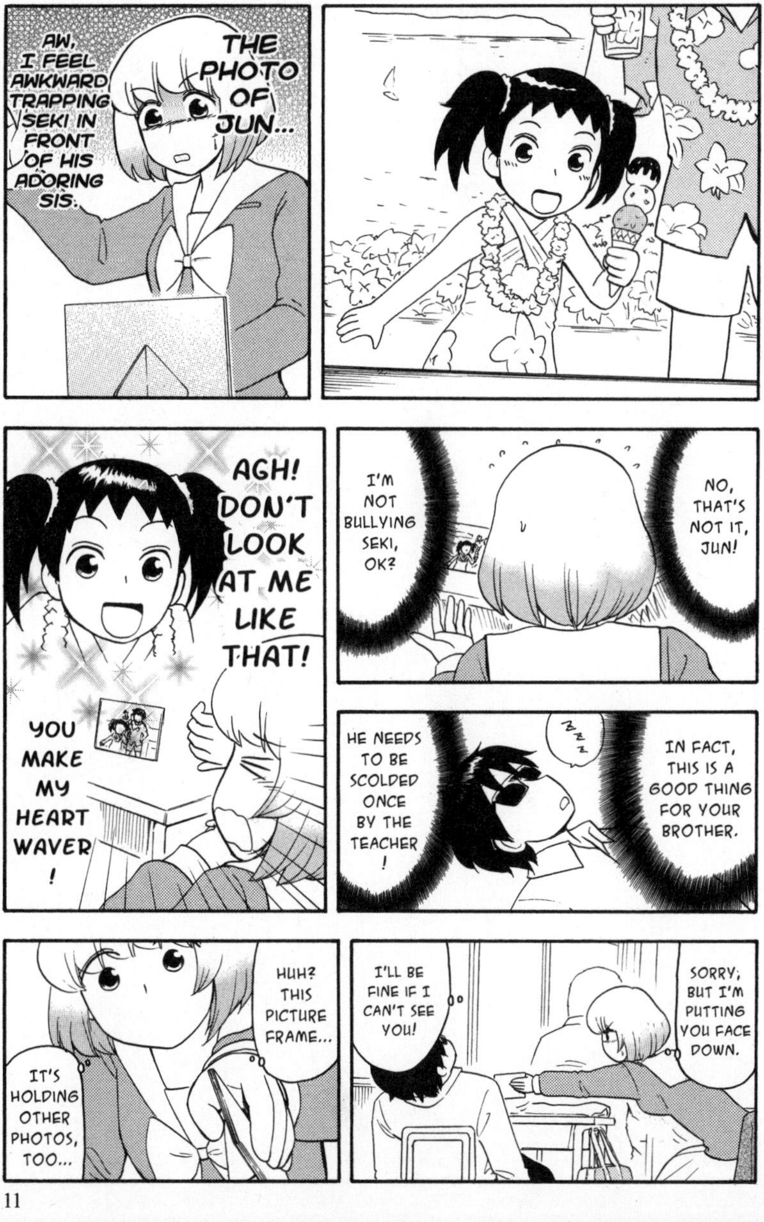
THE PHOTO OF JUN...
AW, I FEEL AWKWARD TRAPPING SEKI IN FRONT OF HIS ADORING SIS.
NO, THAT'S NOT IT, JUN!
I'M NOT BULLYING SEKI, OK?
IN FACT, THIS IS A GOOD THING FOR YOUR BROTHER.
ZZZ
HE NEEDS TO BE SCOLDED ONCE BY THE TEACHER!
AGH! DON'T LOOK AT ME LIKE THAT!
YOU MAKE MY HEART WAVER!
SORRY; BUT I'M PUTTING YOU FACE DOWN.
I'LL BE FINE IF I CAN'T SEE YOU!
HUH? THIS PICTURE FRAME...
IT'S HOLDING OTHER PHOTOS, TOO...

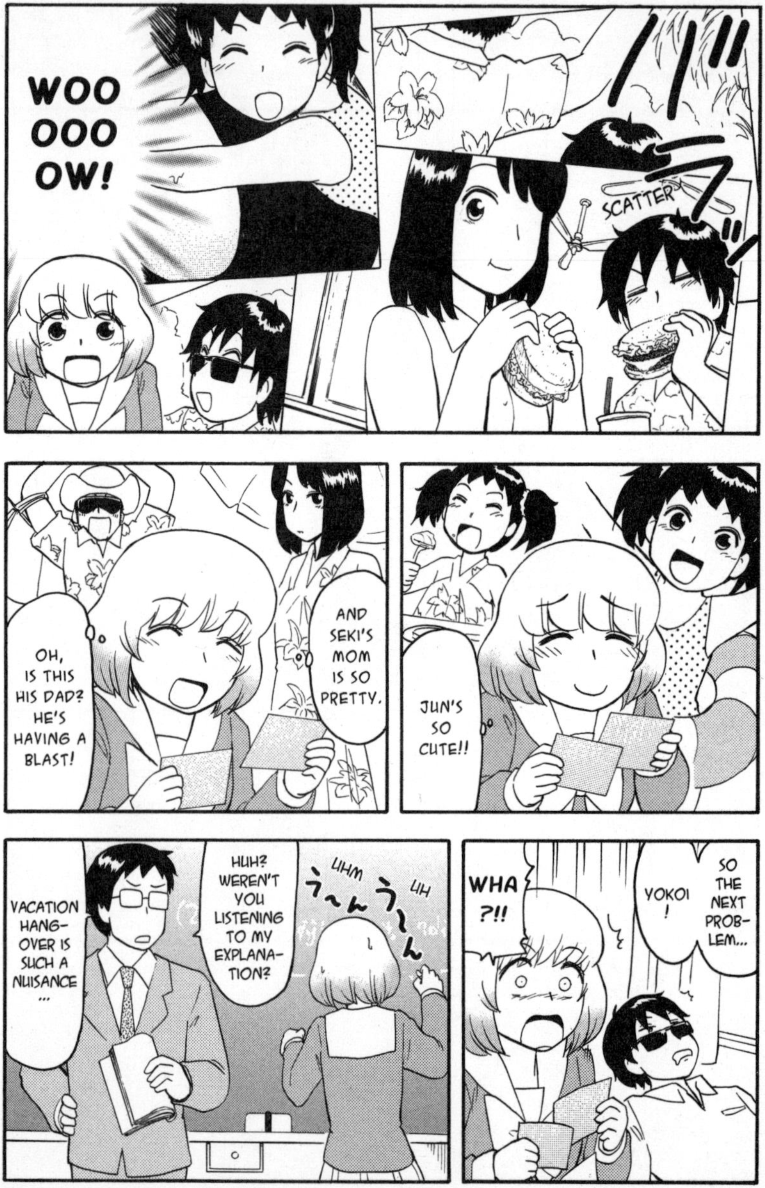
SCATTER
WOO OOO OW!
JUN'S SO CUTE!!
AND SEKI'S MOM IS SO PRETTY.
OH, IS THIS HIS DAD? HE'S HAVING A BLAST!
SO THE NEXT PROB-LEM...
YOKOI!
WHA?!!
HUH? WEREN'T YOU LISTENING TO MY EXPLANA-TION?
UHM
UH
VACATION HANG-OVER IS SUCH A NUISANCE ...

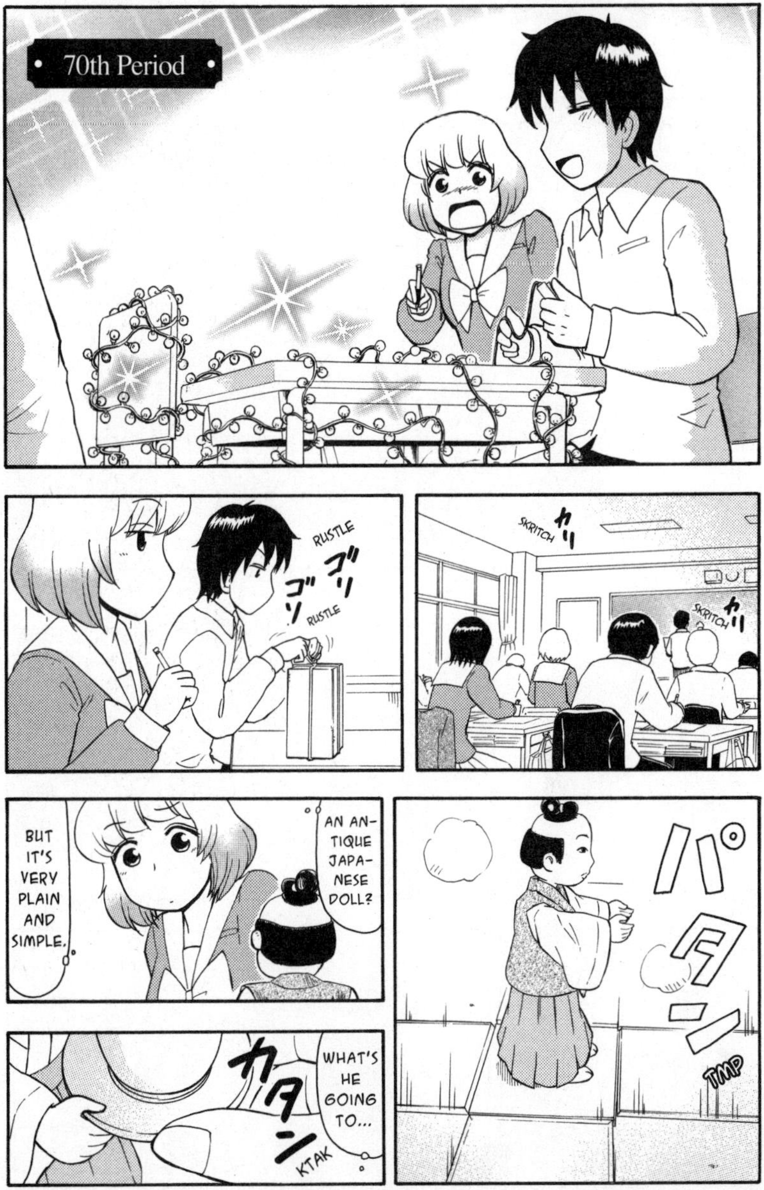
70th Period
SKRITCH カリ
SKRITCH カリ
RUSTLE ゴリ
ゴリ RUSTLE
パタン
TMP
AN ANTIQUE JAPANESE DOLL?
BUT IT'S VERY PLAIN AND SIMPLE.
WHAT'S HE GOING TO...
カタン
KTAK

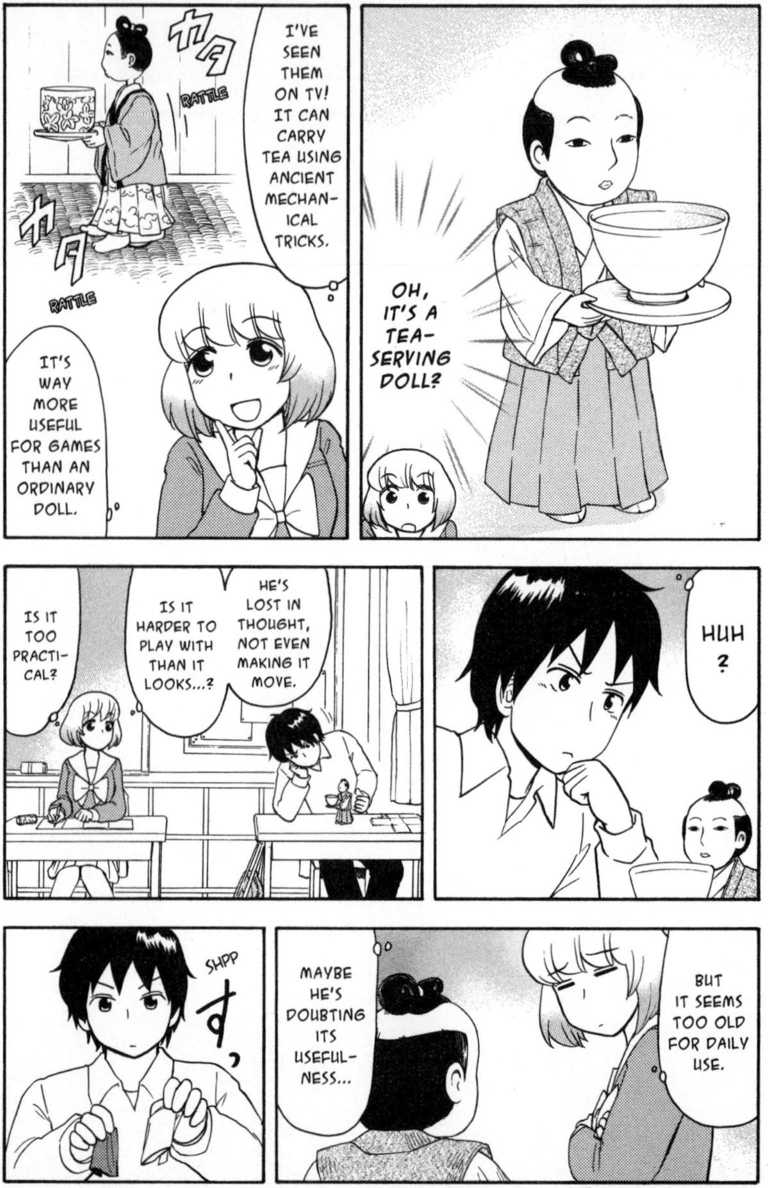
OH, IT'S A TEA-SERVING DOLL?
I'VE SEEN THEM ON TV! IT CAN CARRY TEA USING ANCIENT MECHANICAL TRICKS.
カタ
RATTLE
カタ
RATTLE
IT'S WAY MORE USEFUL FOR GAMES THAN AN ORDINARY DOLL.
HUH?
HE'S LOST IN THOUGHT, NOT EVEN MAKING IT MOVE.
IS IT HARDER TO PLAY WITH THAN IT LOOKS...?
IS IT TOO PRACTICAL?
BUT IT SEEMS TOO OLD FOR DAILY USE.
MAYBE HE'S DOUBTING ITS USEFULNESS...
SHPP
す

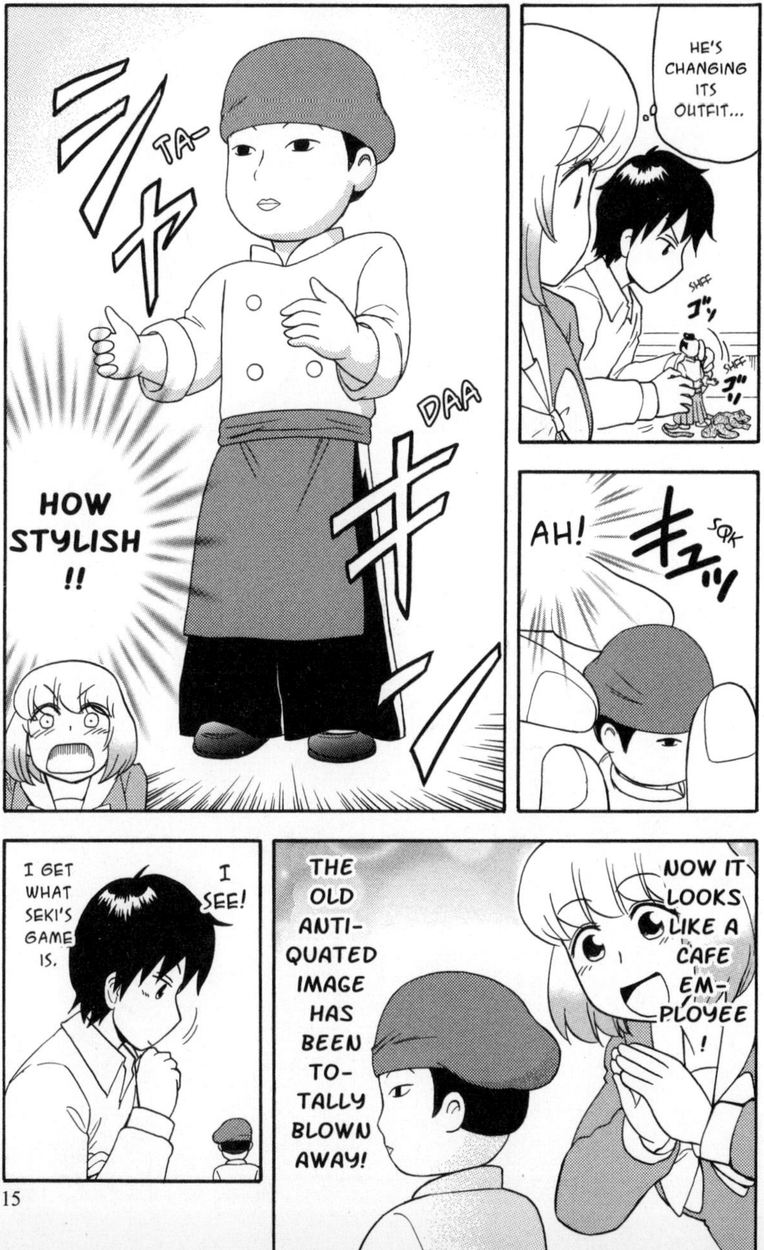
HE'S CHANGING ITS OUTFIT...
SHFF
ゴッ
SHFF
ゴッ
AH!
SQK
キュッ
TA-
DAA
HOW STYLISH !!
NOW IT LOOKS LIKE A CAFE EM-PLOYEE!
THE OLD ANTI-QUATED IMAGE HAS BEEN TO-TALLY BLOWN AWAY!
I SEE!
I GET WHAT SEKI'S GAME IS.

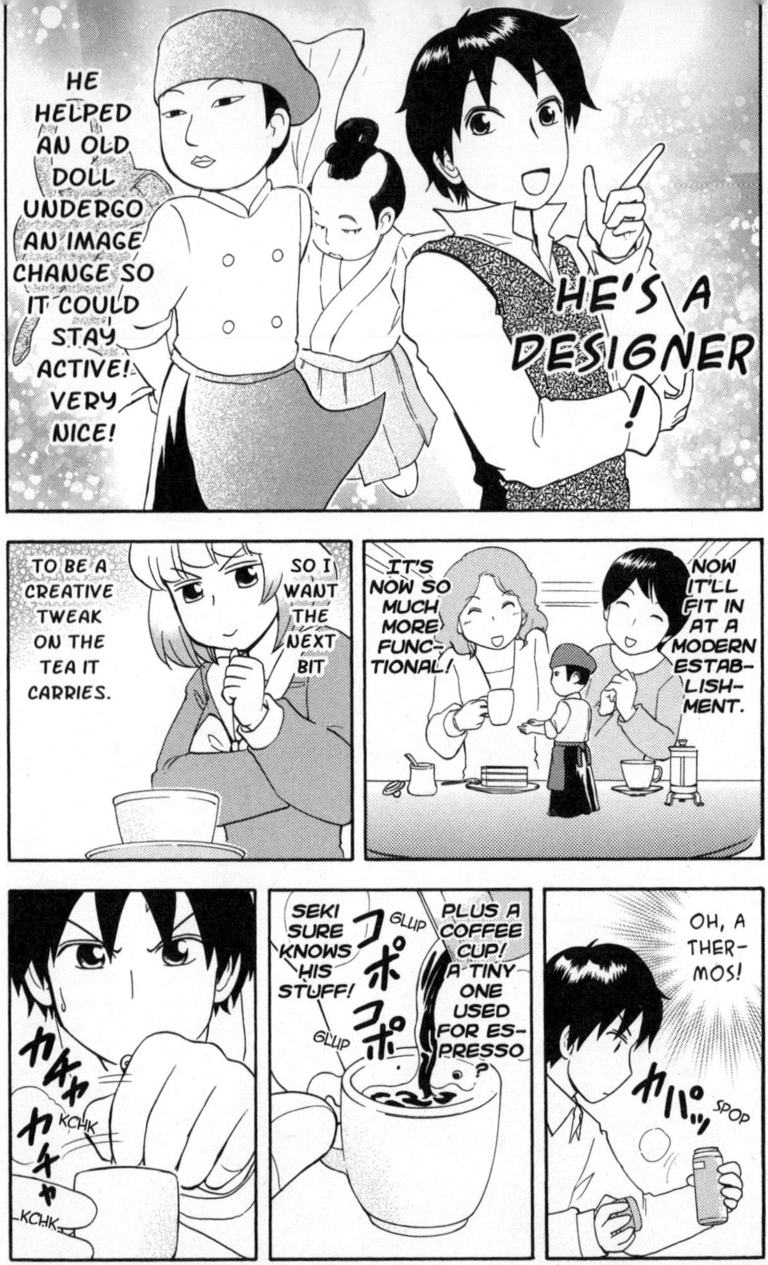
HE'S A DESIGNER!
HE HELPED AN OLD DOLL UNDERGO AN IMAGE CHANGE SO IT COULD STAY ACTIVE! VERY NICE!
NOW IT'LL FIT IN AT A MODERN ESTABLISHMENT.
IT'S NOW SO MUCH MORE FUNCTIONAL!
SO I WANT THE NEXT BIT
TO BE A CREATIVE TWEAK ON THE TEA IT CARRIES.
OH, A THERMOS!
カパッ
SPOP
PLUS A COFFEE CUP! A TINY ONE USED FOR ESPRESSO?
コポコポ
GLUP
SEKI SURE KNOWS HIS STUFF!
GLUP
カチャカチャ
KCHK
KCHK

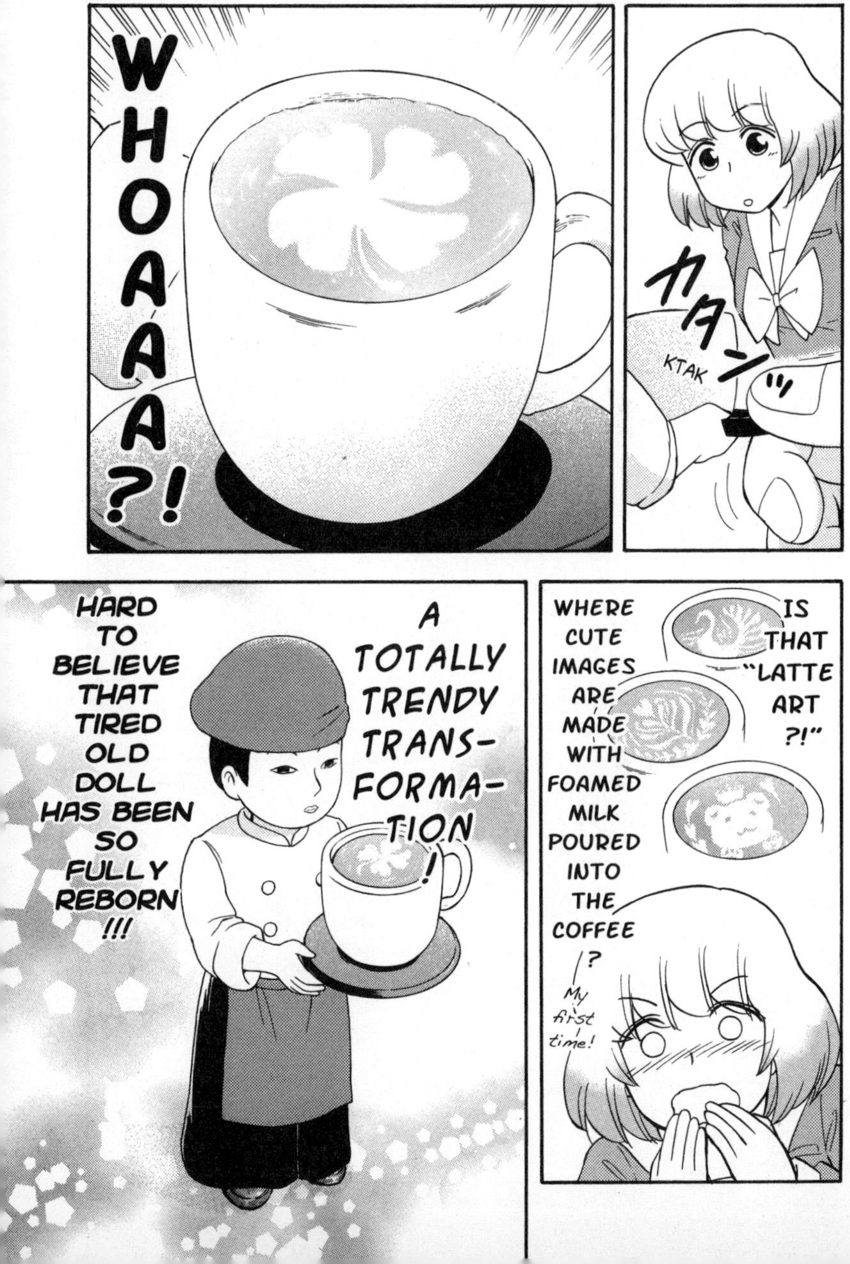
カタンッ
KTAK
WHOAAAA?!
IS THAT "LATTE ART ?!"
WHERE CUTE IMAGES ARE MADE WITH FOAMED MILK POURED INTO THE COFFEE ?
My first time!
A TOTALLY TRENDY TRANSFORMATION!
HARD TO BELIEVE THAT TIRED OLD DOLL HAS BEEN SO FULLY REBORN!!!

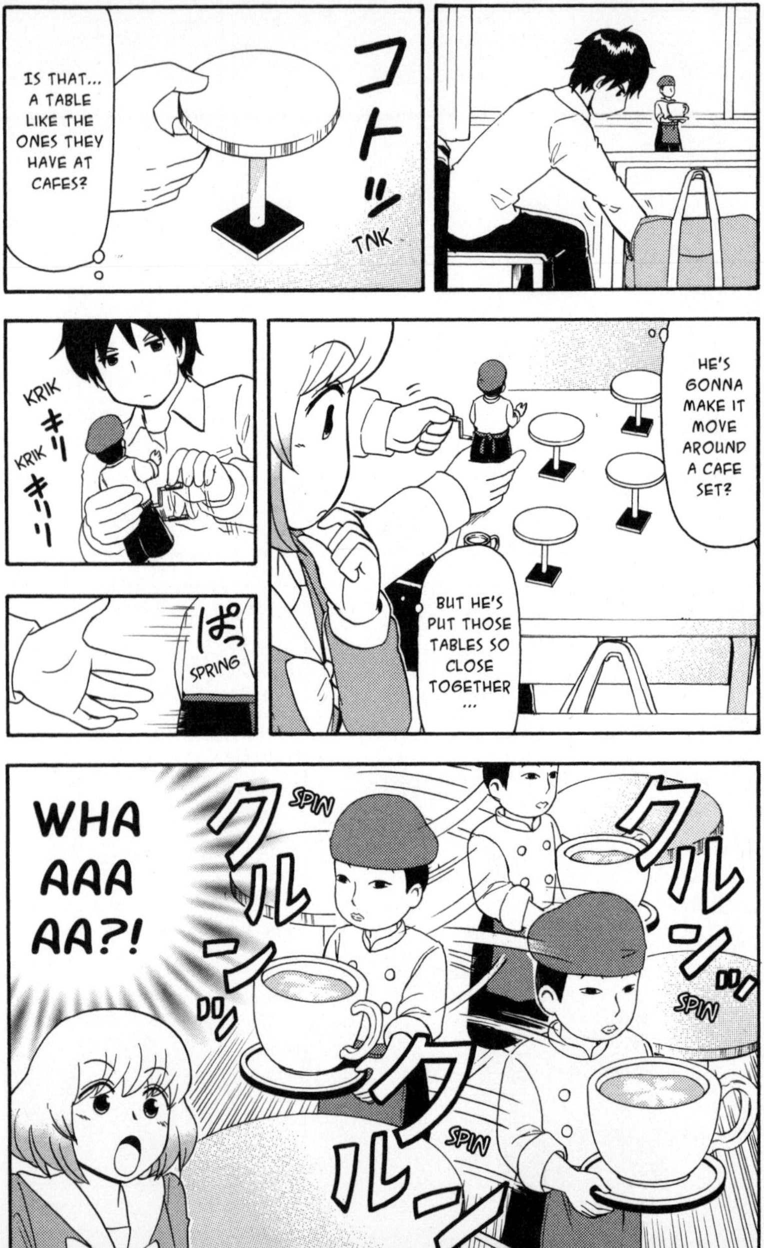
コトッ
TNK
IS THAT... A TABLE LIKE THE ONES THEY HAVE AT CAFES?
HE'S GONNA MAKE IT MOVE AROUND A CAFE SET?
BUT HE'S PUT THOSE TABLES SO CLOSE TOGETHER ...
キリ
KRIK
キリリ
KRIK
ぱっ
SPRING
クルーン
SPIN
クルーン
SPIN
WHA AAA AA?!
クルーン
SPIN

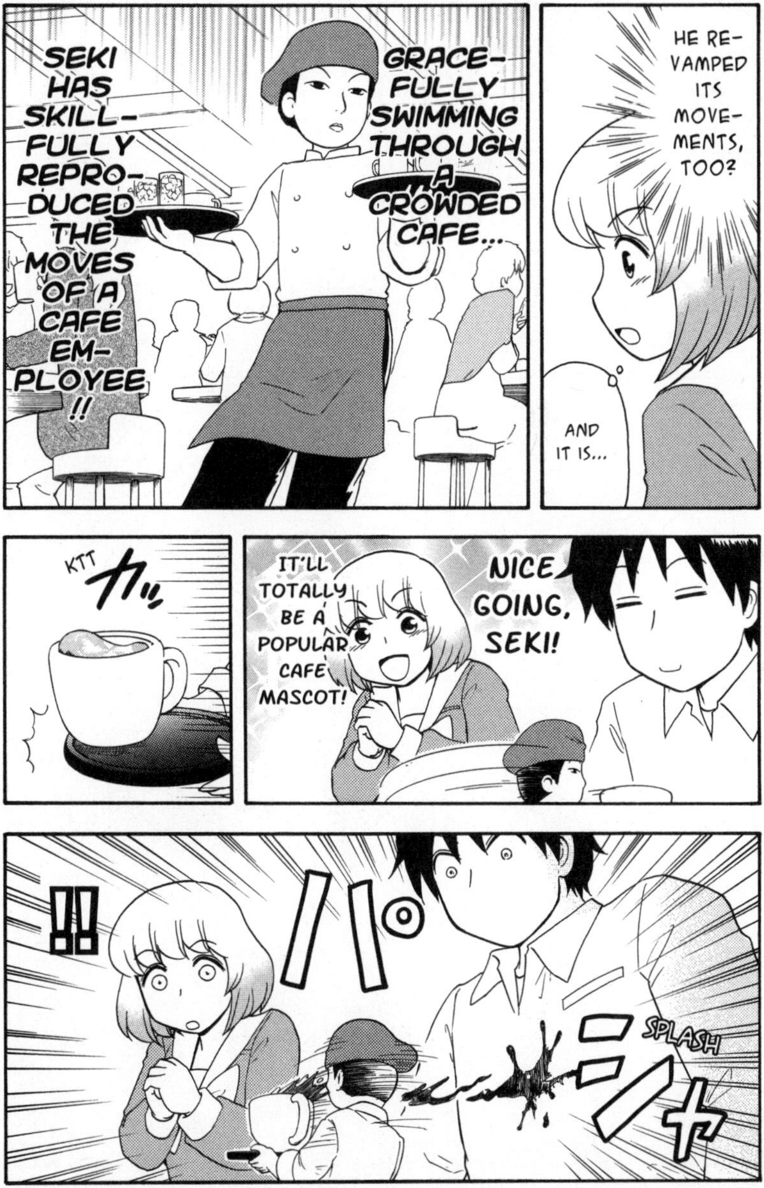

HE RE-VAMPED ITS MOVE-MENTS, TOO?
AND IT IS...
GRACE-FULLY SWIMMING THROUGH A CROWDED CAFE...
SEKI HAS SKILL-FULLY REPRO-DUCED THE MOVES OF A CAFE EM-PLOYEE !!
NICE GOING, SEKI!
IT'LL TOTALLY BE A POPULAR CAFE MASCOT!
KTT
カッ
!!
パ
SPLASH
シャ

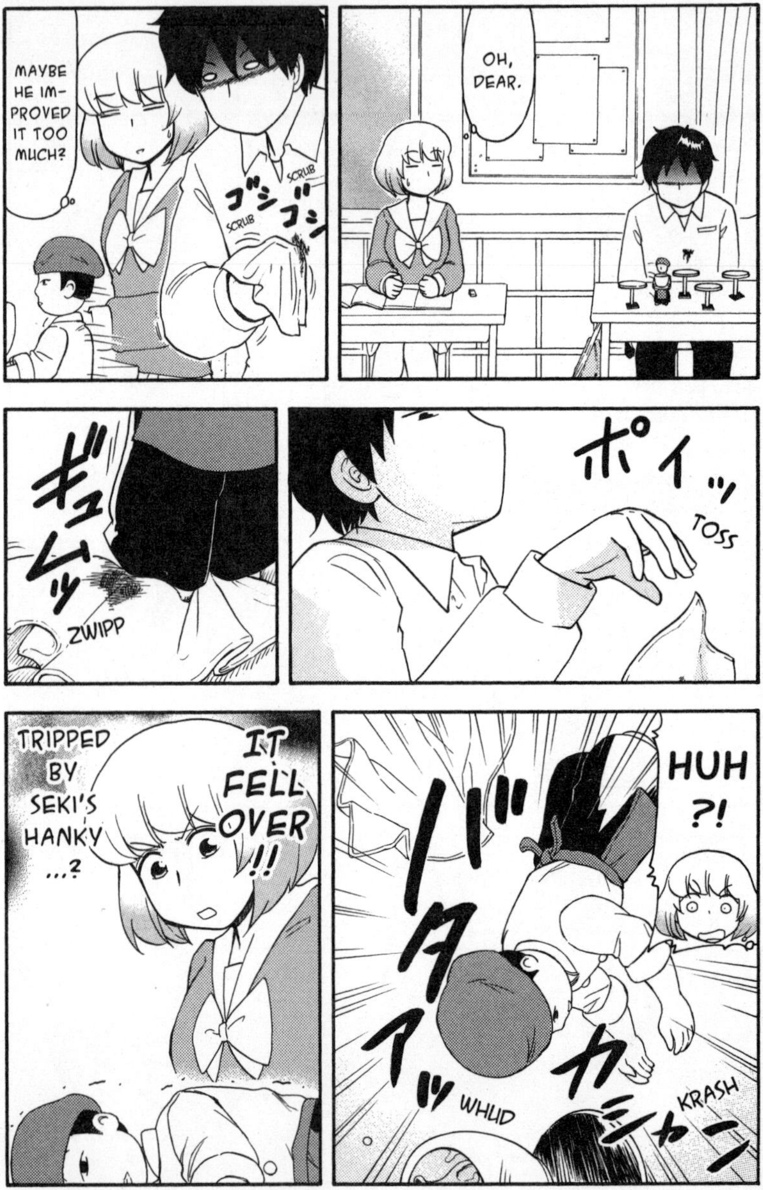
OH, DEAR.
MAYBE HE IM-PROVED IT TOO MUCH?
ゴシゴシ
SCRUB SCRUB
ポイッ
TOSS
ギュムッ
ZWIPP
HUH ?!
バタァッ
WHUD
カシャーン
KRASH
IT FELL OVER!!
TRIPPED BY SEKI'S HANKY ...?

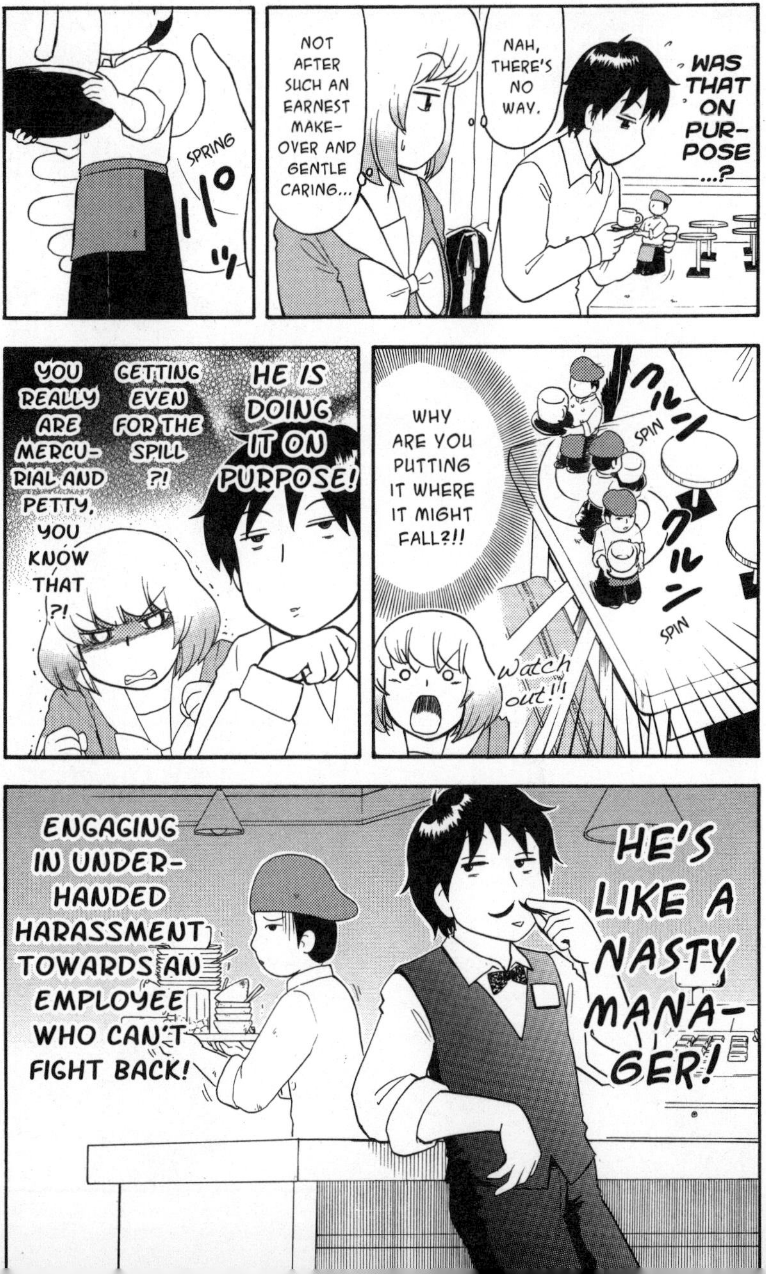
WAS THAT ON PURPOSE...?
NAH, THERE'S NO WAY.
NOT AFTER SUCH AN EARNEST MAKE-OVER AND GENTLE CARING...
SPRING
SPIN
WHY ARE YOU PUTTING IT WHERE IT MIGHT FALL?!!
SPIN
Watch out!!
HE IS DOING IT ON PURPOSE!
GETTING EVEN FOR THE SPILL?!
YOU REALLY ARE MERCURIAL AND PETTY, YOU KNOW THAT?!
HE'S LIKE A NASTY MANAGER!
ENGAGING IN UNDERHANDED HARASSMENT TOWARDS AN EMPLOYEE WHO CAN'T FIGHT BACK!

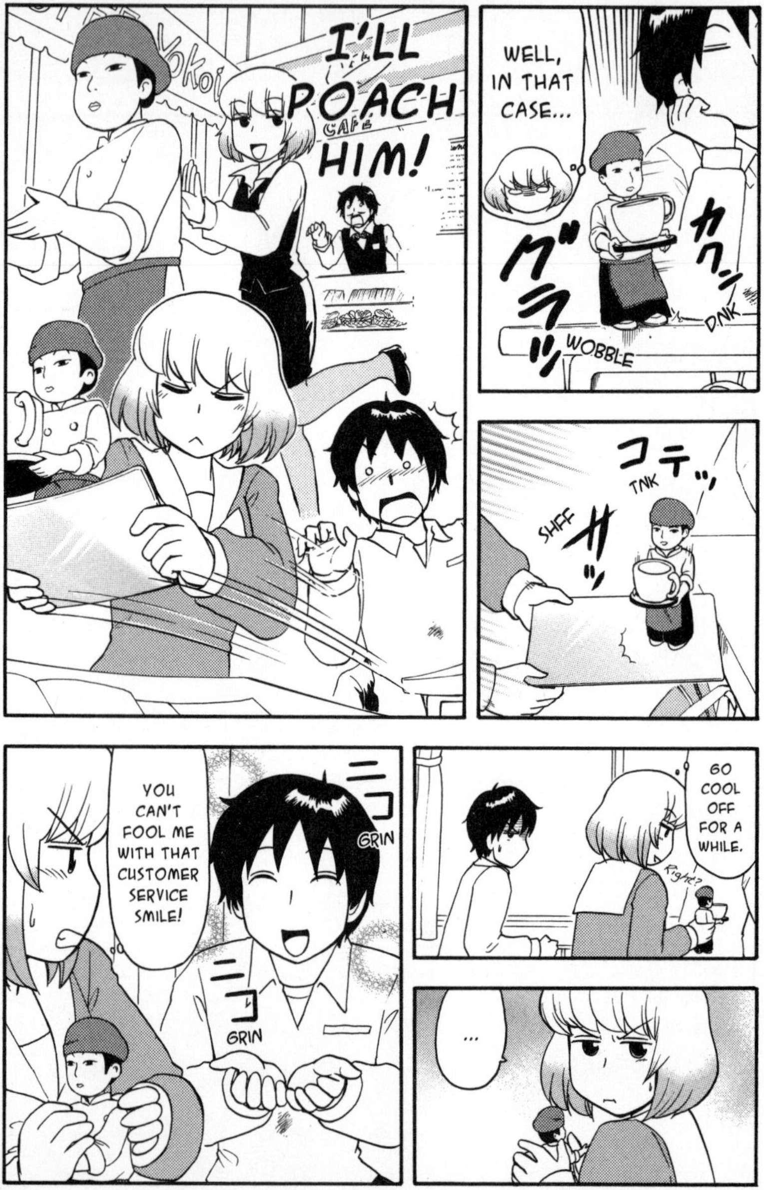
WELL, IN THAT CASE...
グラッ
WOBBLE
カクン
DNK
コテッ
TNK
サッ
SHFF
I'LL POACH HIM!
CAFE
GO COOL OFF FOR A WHILE.
Right?
...
YOU CAN'T FOOL ME WITH THAT CUSTOMER SERVICE SMILE!
ニコ
GRIN
ニコ
GRIN

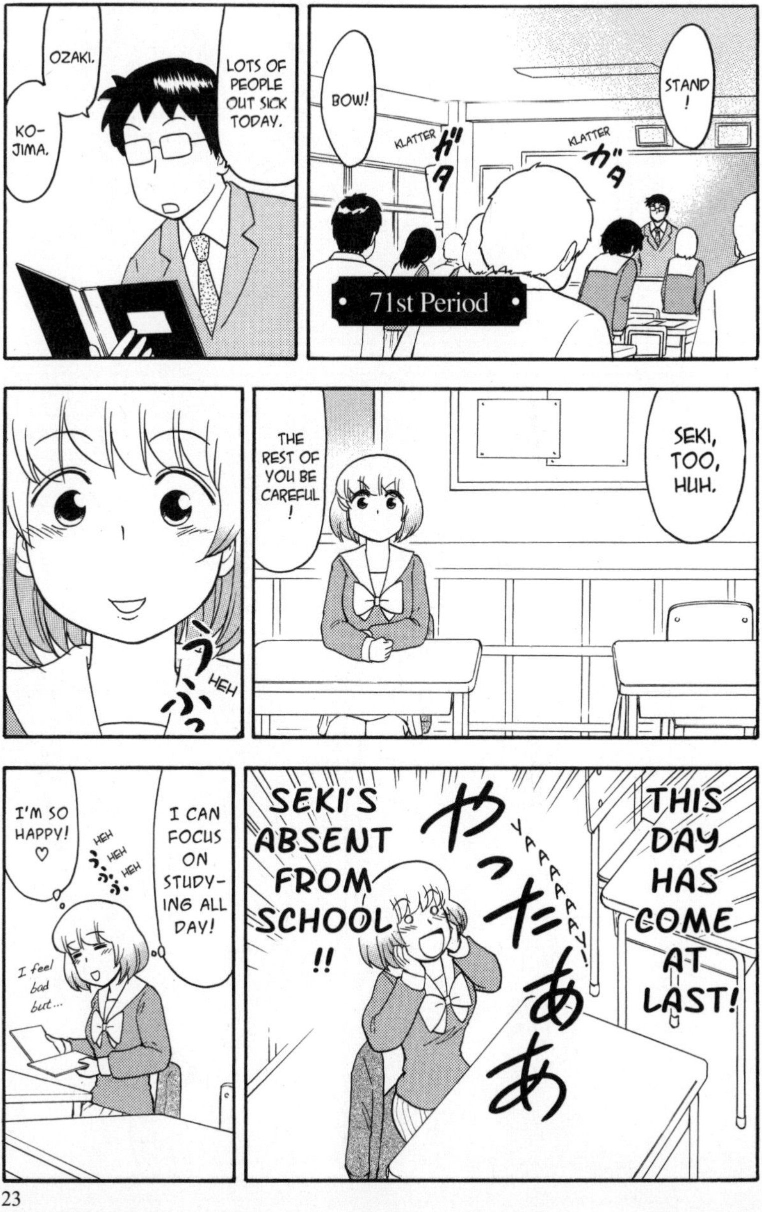
STAND!
BOW!
KLATTER ガタ
KLATTER ガタ
71st Period
LOTS OF PEOPLE OUT SICK TODAY.
OZAKI.
KO-JIMA.
SEKI, TOO, HUH.
THE REST OF YOU BE CAREFUL!
うふっ HEH
THIS DAY HAS COME AT LAST!
やったあぁ
YAAAAAAAY!
SEKI'S ABSENT FROM SCHOOL!!
I CAN FOCUS ON STUDY-ING ALL DAY!
I'M SO HAPPY! ♡
うふふ HEH HEH HEH
I feel bad but...

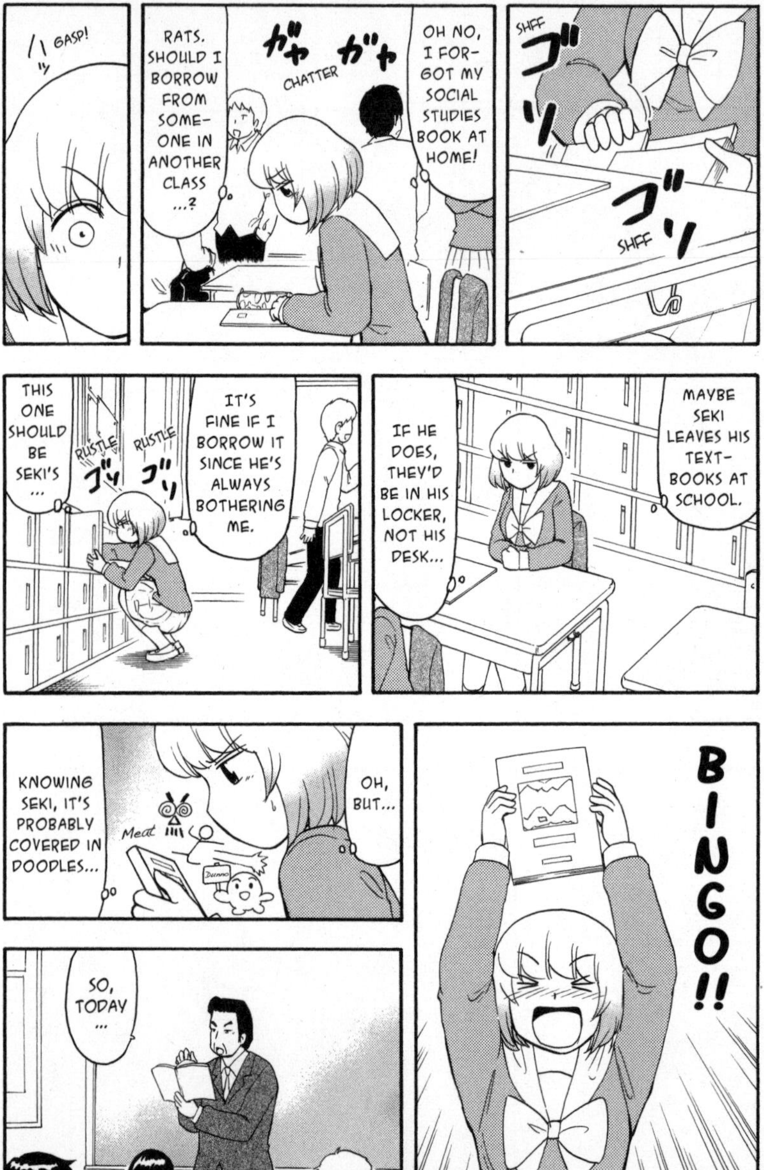
SHFF
ゴソ
ゴソ
SHFF
OH NO, I FORGOT MY SOCIAL STUDIES BOOK AT HOME!
ガヤガヤ
CHATTER
RATS. SHOULD I BORROW FROM SOMEONE IN ANOTHER CLASS ...?
ハッ
GASP!
MAYBE SEKI LEAVES HIS TEXTBOOKS AT SCHOOL.
IF HE DOES, THEY'D BE IN HIS LOCKER, NOT HIS DESK...
IT'S FINE IF I BORROW IT SINCE HE'S ALWAYS BOTHERING ME.
RUSTLE
ゴソ
RUSTLE
ゴソ
THIS ONE SHOULD BE SEKI'S ...
BINGO!!
OH, BUT...
KNOWING SEKI, IT'S PROBABLY COVERED IN DOODLES...
Meat
Dunno
SO, TODAY ...

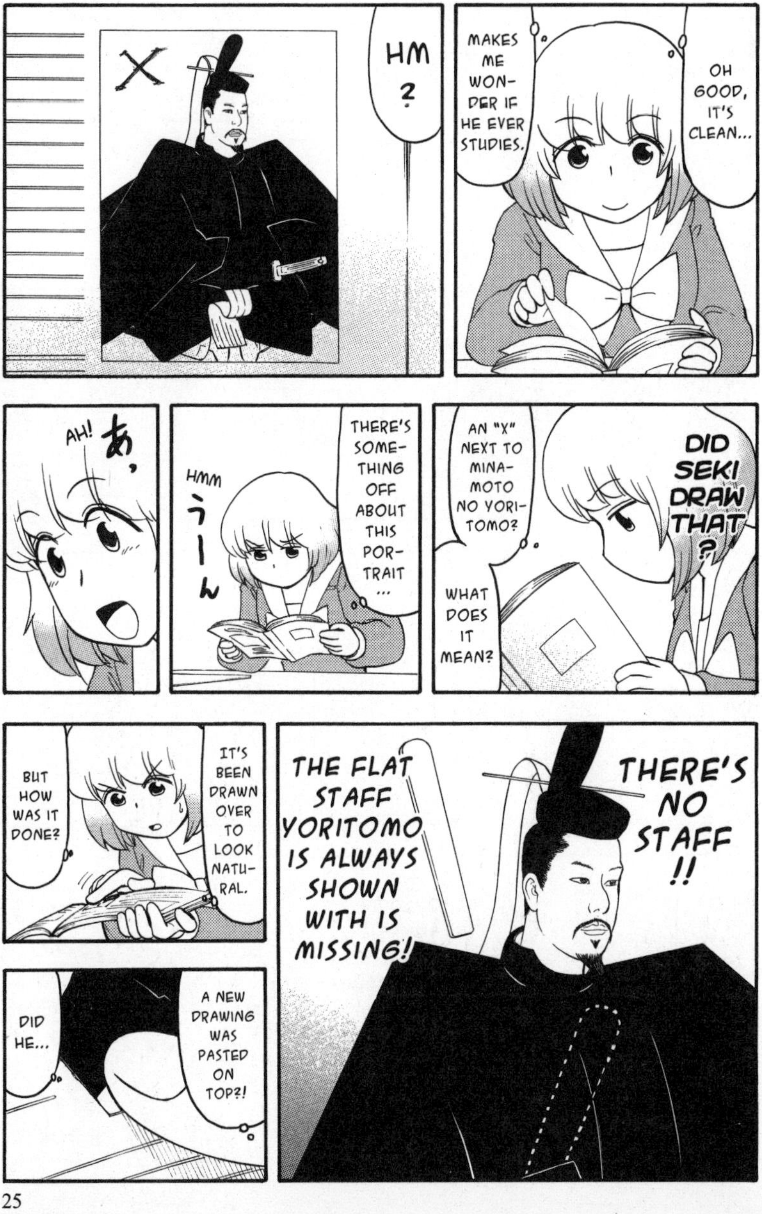
OH GOOD, IT'S CLEAN...
MAKES ME WONDER IF HE EVER STUDIES.
HM?
DID SEKI DRAW THAT?
AN "X" NEXT TO MINAMOTO NO YORITOMO?
WHAT DOES IT MEAN?
THERE'S SOMETHING OFF ABOUT THIS PORTRAIT...
HMM
うーん
AH!
あ、
THERE'S NO STAFF!!
THE FLAT STAFF YORITOMO IS ALWAYS SHOWN WITH IS MISSING!
IT'S BEEN DRAWN OVER TO LOOK NATURAL.
BUT HOW WAS IT DONE?
A NEW DRAWING WAS PASTED ON TOP?!
DID HE...

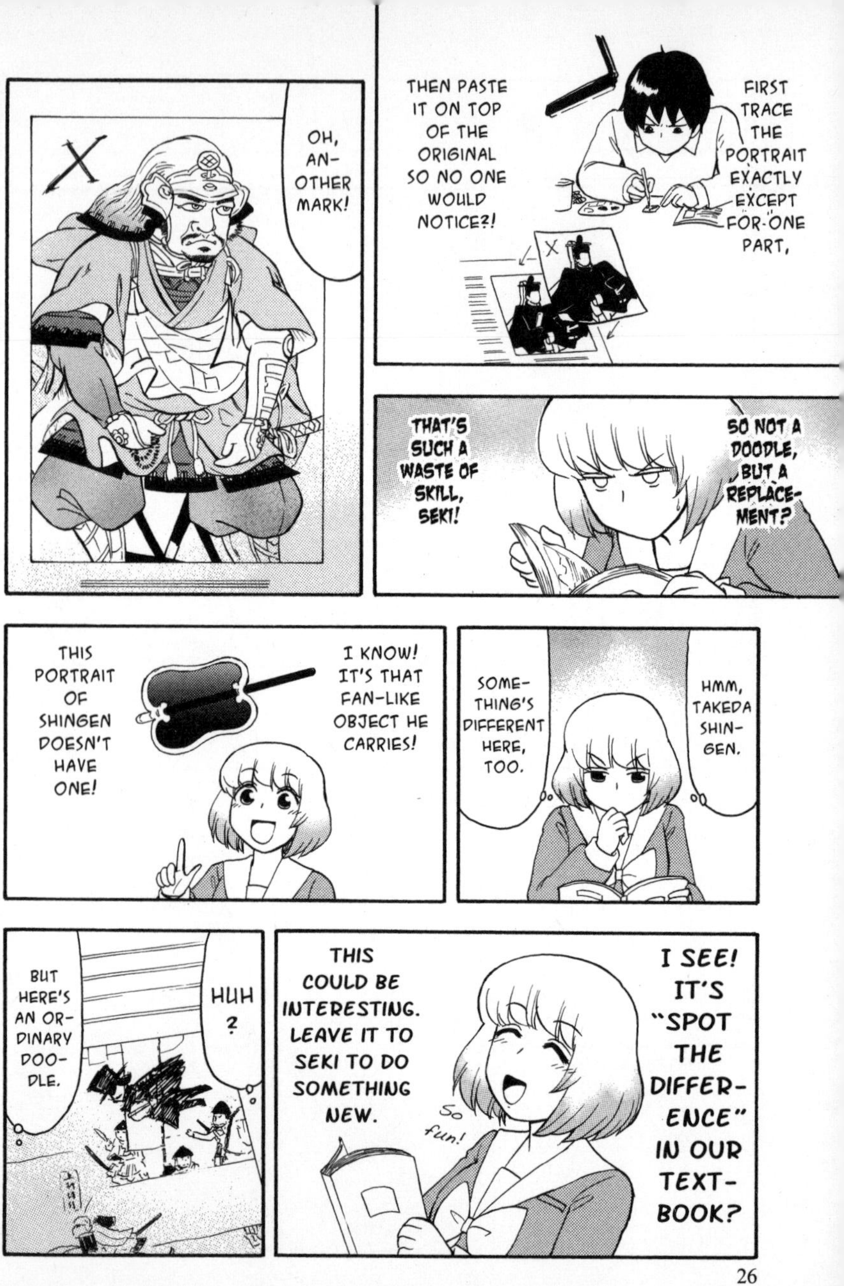
FIRST TRACE THE PORTRAIT EXACTLY EXCEPT FOR ONE PART,
THEN PASTE IT ON TOP OF THE ORIGINAL SO NO ONE WOULD NOTICE?!
SO NOT A DOODLE, BUT A REPLACEMENT?
THAT'S SUCH A WASTE OF SKILL, SEKI!
OH, ANOTHER MARK!
HMM, TAKEDA SHINGEN.
SOMETHING'S DIFFERENT HERE, TOO.
I KNOW! IT'S THAT FAN-LIKE OBJECT HE CARRIES!
THIS PORTRAIT OF SHINGEN DOESN'T HAVE ONE!
I SEE! IT'S "SPOT THE DIFFERENCE" IN OUR TEXTBOOK?
So fun!
THIS COULD BE INTERESTING. LEAVE IT TO SEKI TO DO SOMETHING NEW.
HUH?
BUT HERE'S AN ORDINARY DOODLE.

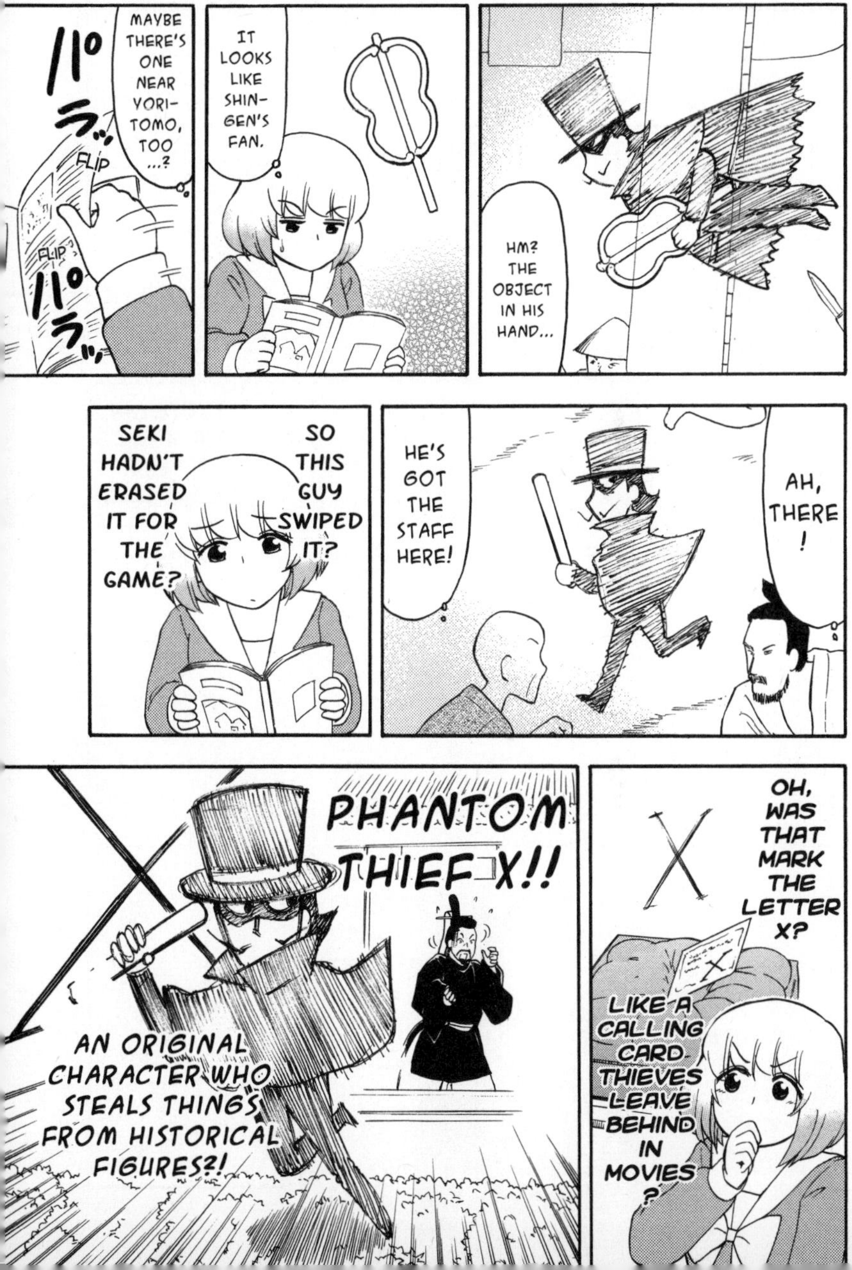
HM? THE OBJECT IN HIS HAND...
IT LOOKS LIKE SHIN-GEN'S FAN.
MAYBE THERE'S ONE NEAR YORI-TOMO, TOO ...?
パラッ
FLIP
パラッ
FLIP
AH, THERE!
HE'S GOT THE STAFF HERE!
SO THIS GUY SWIPED IT?
SEKI HADN'T ERASED IT FOR THE GAME?
OH, WAS THAT MARK THE LETTER X?
LIKE A CALLING CARD THIEVES LEAVE BEHIND IN MOVIES?
PHANTOM THIEF X!!
AN ORIGINAL CHARACTER WHO STEALS THINGS FROM HISTORICAL FIGURES?!

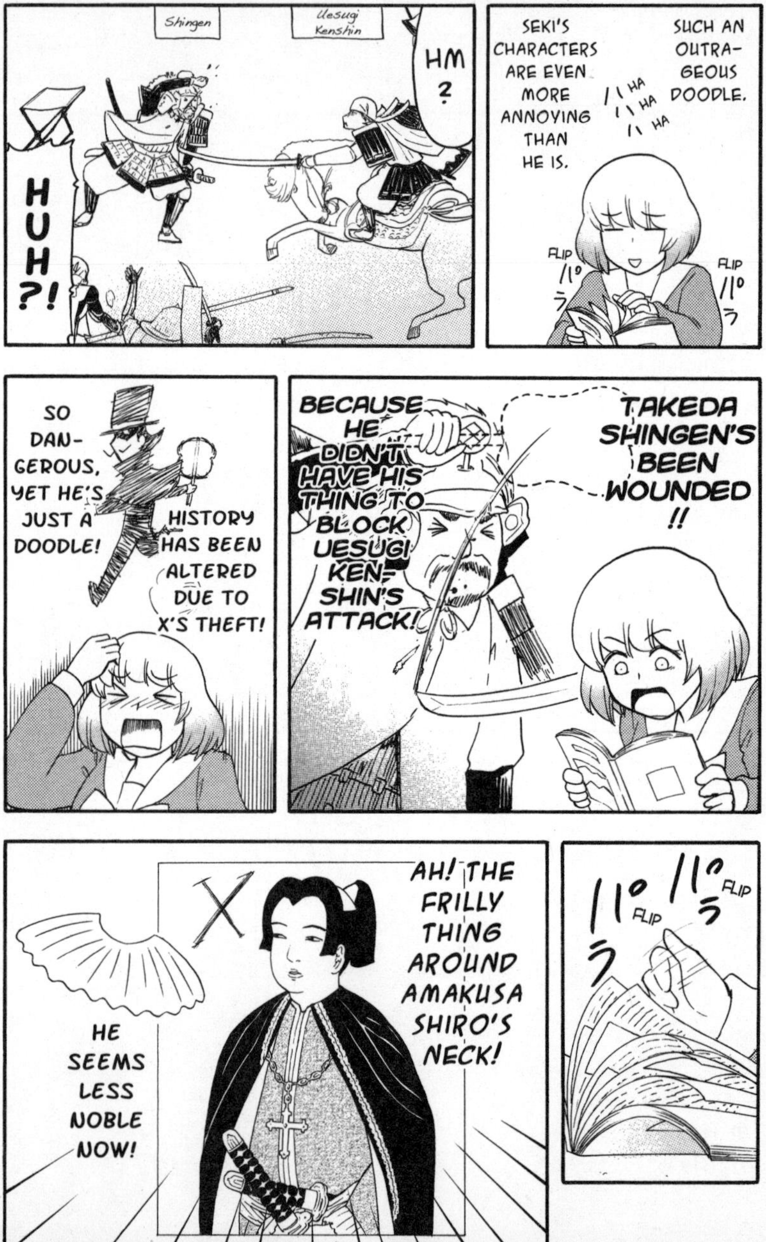
SUCH AN OUTRAGEOUS DOODLE.
HA HA HA
SEKI'S CHARACTERS ARE EVEN MORE ANNOYING THAN HE IS.
FLIP
FLIP
Uesugi Kenshin
Shingen
HM?
HUH?!
TAKEDA SHINGEN'S BEEN WOUNDED!!
BECAUSE HE DIDN'T HAVE HIS THING TO BLOCK UESUGI KENSHIN'S ATTACK!
HISTORY HAS BEEN ALTERED DUE TO X'S THEFT!
SO DANGEROUS, YET HE'S JUST A DOODLE!
FLIP
FLIP
AH! THE FRILLY THING AROUND AMAKUSA SHIRO'S NECK!
HE SEEMS LESS NOBLE NOW!

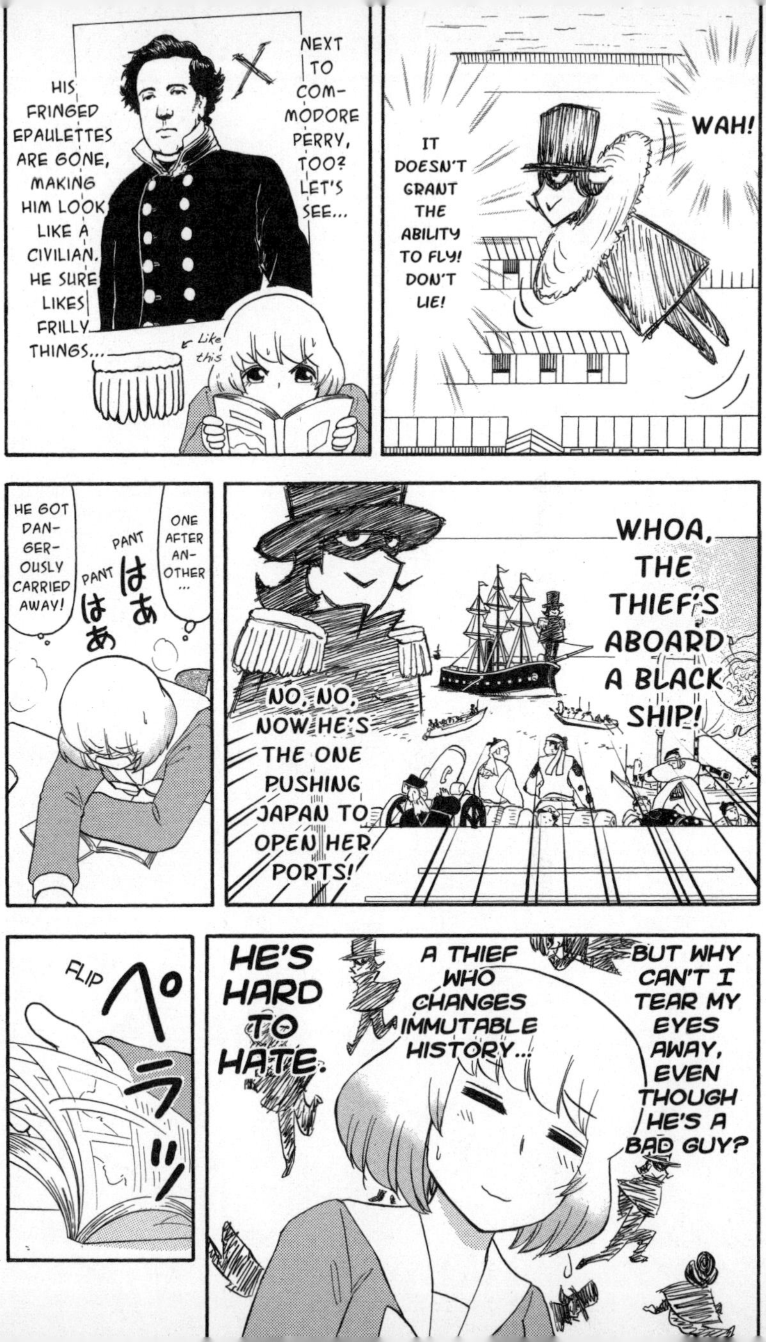
WAH!
IT DOESN'T GRANT THE ABILITY TO FLY! DON'T LIE!
NEXT TO COM-MODORE PERRY, TOO? LET'S SEE...
HIS FRINGED EPAULETTES ARE GONE, MAKING HIM LOOK LIKE A CIVILIAN. HE SURE LIKES FRILLY THINGS...
Like this
WHOA, THE THIEF'S ABOARD A BLACK SHIP!
NO, NO, NOW HE'S THE ONE PUSHING JAPAN TO OPEN HER PORTS!
ONE AFTER AN-OTHER...
はあ PANT
はあ PANT
HE GOT DAN-GER-OUSLY CARRIED AWAY!
BUT WHY CAN'T I TEAR MY EYES AWAY, EVEN THOUGH HE'S A BAD GUY?
A THIEF WHO CHANGES IMMUTABLE HISTORY...
HE'S HARD TO HATE.
ペラッ FLIP

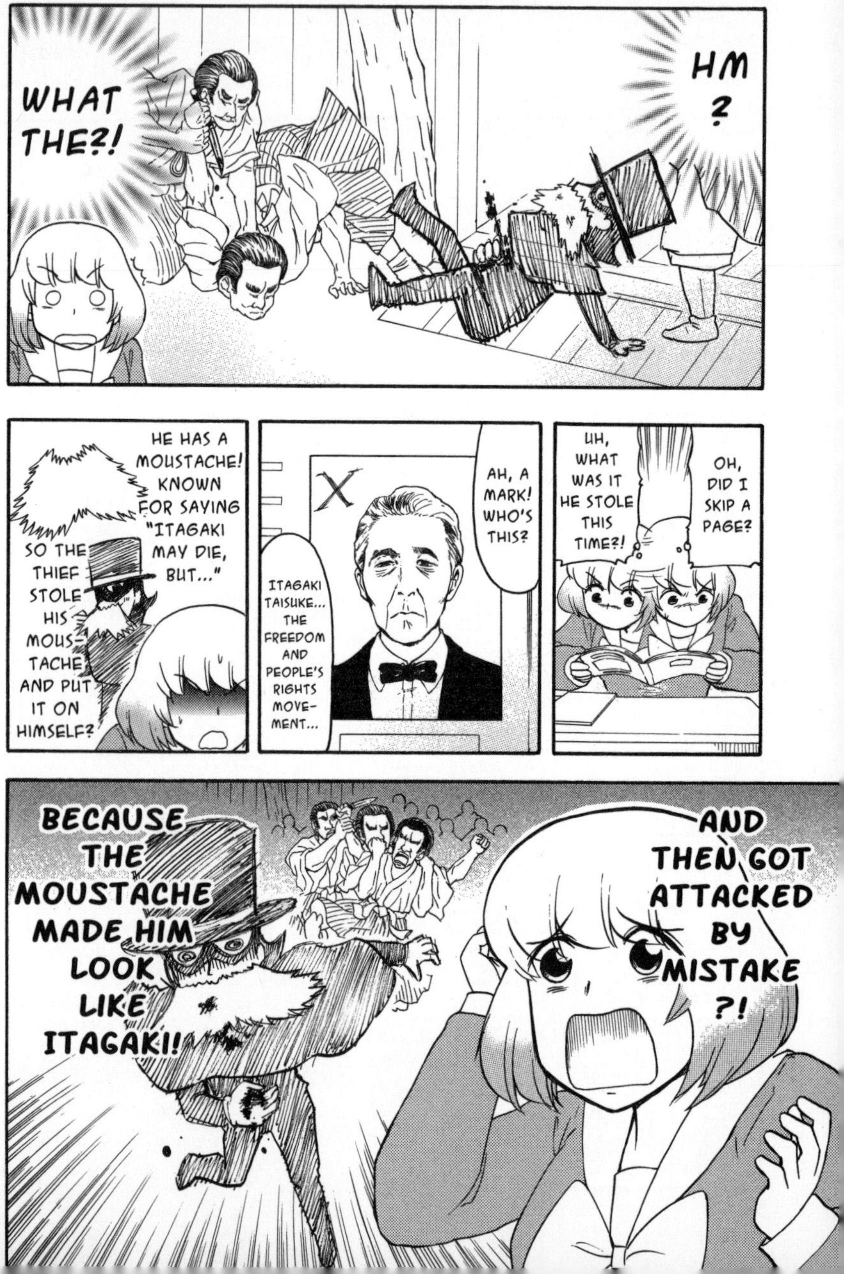
HM ?
WHAT THE?!
OH, DID I SKIP A PAGE?
UH, WHAT WAS IT HE STOLE THIS TIME?!
AH, A MARK! WHO'S THIS?
ITAGAKI TAISUKE... THE FREEDOM AND PEOPLE'S RIGHTS MOVEMENT...
HE HAS A MOUSTACHE! KNOWN FOR SAYING "ITAGAKI MAY DIE, BUT..."
SO THE THIEF STOLE HIS MOUSTACHE AND PUT IT ON HIMSELF?
AND THEN GOT ATTACKED BY MISTAKE ?!
BECAUSE THE MOUSTACHE MADE HIM LOOK LIKE ITAGAKI!

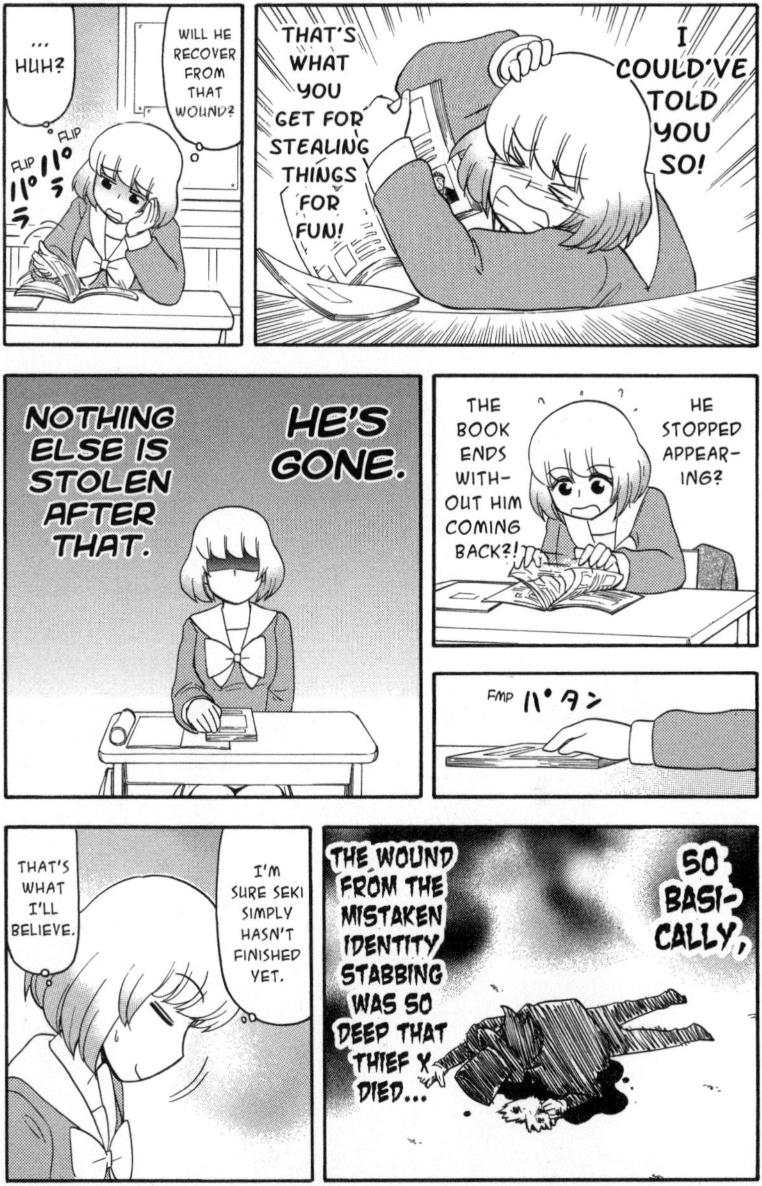
I COULD'VE TOLD YOU SO!
THAT'S WHAT YOU GET FOR STEALING THINGS FOR FUN!
WILL HE RECOVER FROM THAT WOUND?
... HUH?
FLIP パラ
FLIP パラ
HE STOPPED APPEAR- ING?
THE BOOK ENDS WITH- OUT HIM COMING BACK?!
FMP パタン
HE'S GONE.
NOTHING ELSE IS STOLEN AFTER THAT.
SO BASI- CALLY,
THE WOUND FROM THE MISTAKEN IDENTITY STABBING WAS SO DEEP THAT THIEF X DIED...
I'M SURE SEKI SIMPLY HASN'T FINISHED YET.
THAT'S WHAT I'LL BELIEVE.

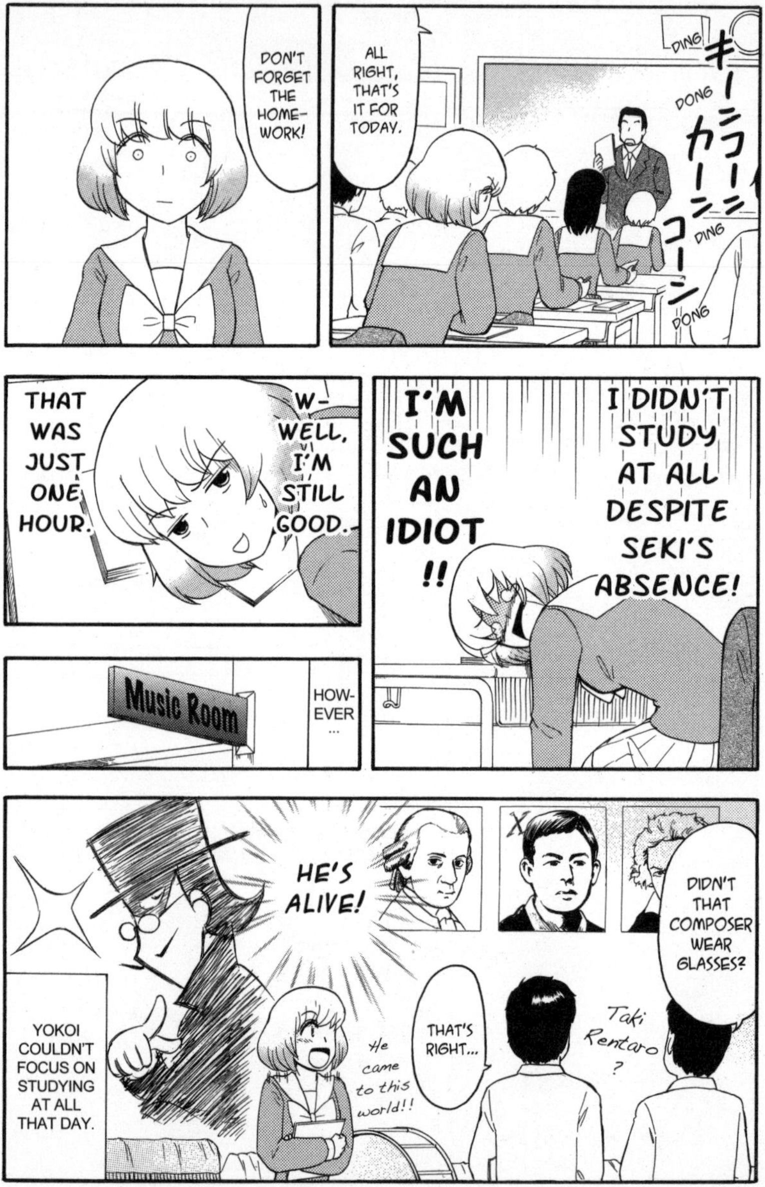
DING
DONG
DING
DONG
キーンコーンカーンコーン
ALL RIGHT, THAT'S IT FOR TODAY.
DON'T FORGET THE HOME-WORK!
I DIDN'T STUDY AT ALL DESPITE SEKI'S ABSENCE!
I'M SUCH AN IDIOT!!
W-WELL, I'M STILL GOOD.
THAT WAS JUST ONE HOUR.
HOW-EVER...
Music Room
DIDN'T THAT COMPOSER WEAR GLASSES?
Taki Rentaro?
THAT'S RIGHT...
He came to this world!!
HE'S ALIVE!
YOKOI COULDN'T FOCUS ON STUDYING AT ALL THAT DAY.

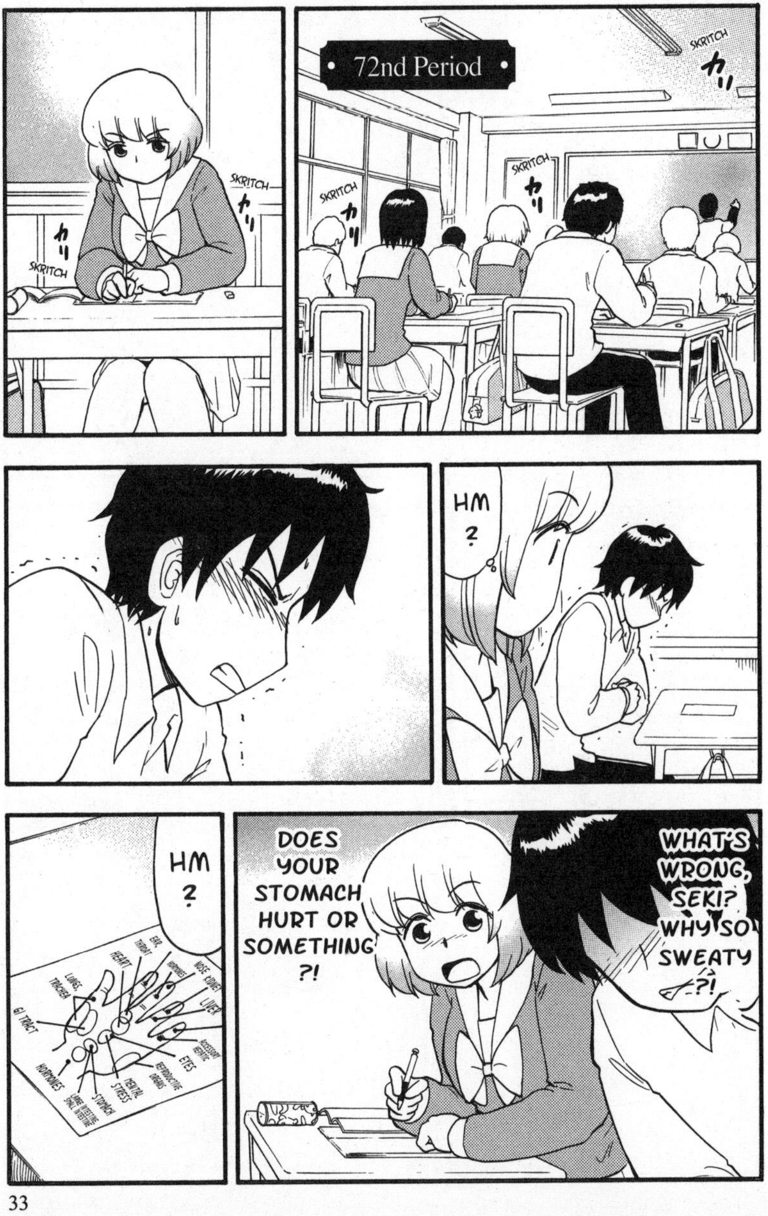
• 72nd Period •
SKRITCH
カリ
SKRITCH
カリ
SKRITCH
カリ
SKRITCH
カリ
SKRITCH
カリ
HM ?
WHAT'S WRONG, SEKI? WHY SO SWEATY ?!
DOES YOUR STOMACH HURT OR SOMETHING ?!
HM ?
EAR, THROAT
HEART
HORMONES
NOSE
KIDNEY
LUNGS, TRACHEA
LIVER
GI TRACT
ACCESSORY HEPATIC
EYES
REPRODUCTIVE ORGANS
MENTAL STRESS
STOMACH
LARGE INTESTINE SMALL INTESTINE
HORMONES

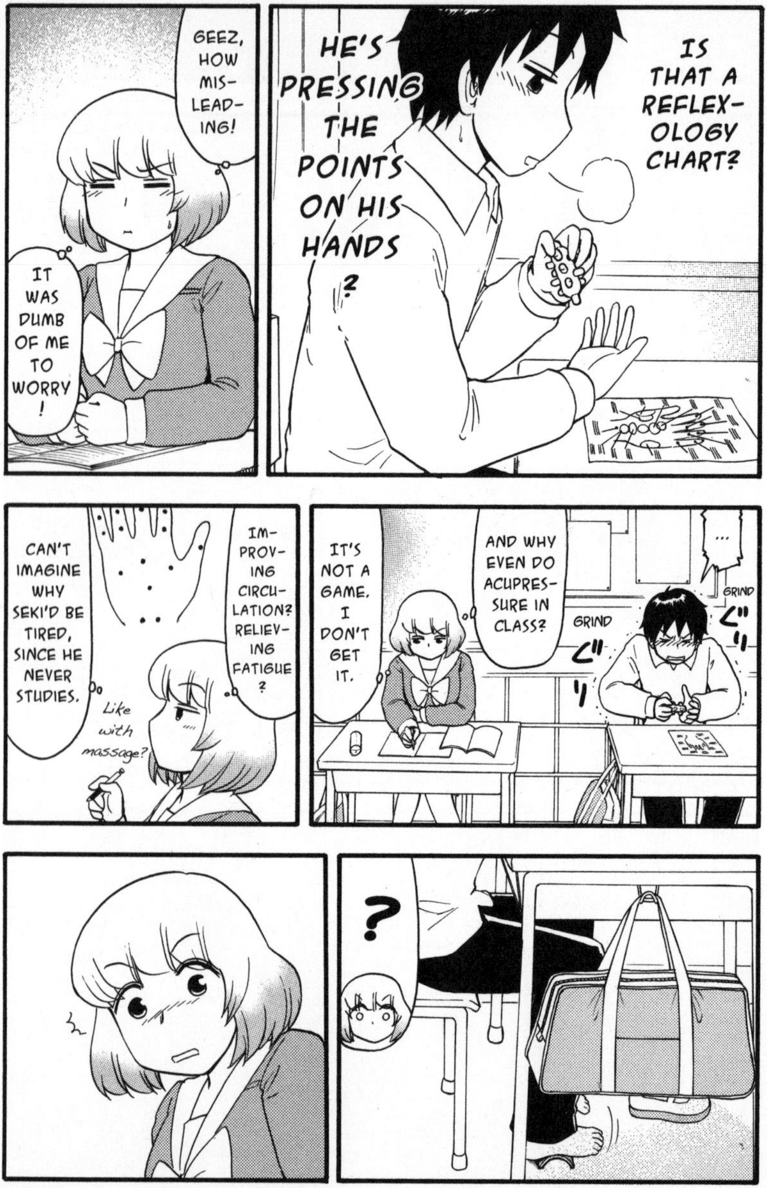
IS THAT A REFLEXOLOGY CHART?
HE'S PRESSING THE POINTS ON HIS HANDS?
GEEZ, HOW MISLEADING!
IT WAS DUMB OF ME TO WORRY!
...
GRIND
GRIND
AND WHY EVEN DO ACUPRESSURE IN CLASS?
IT'S NOT A GAME. I DON'T GET IT.
IMPROVING CIRCULATION? RELIEVING FATIGUE?
Like with massage?
CAN'T IMAGINE WHY SEKI'D BE TIRED, SINCE HE NEVER STUDIES.
?

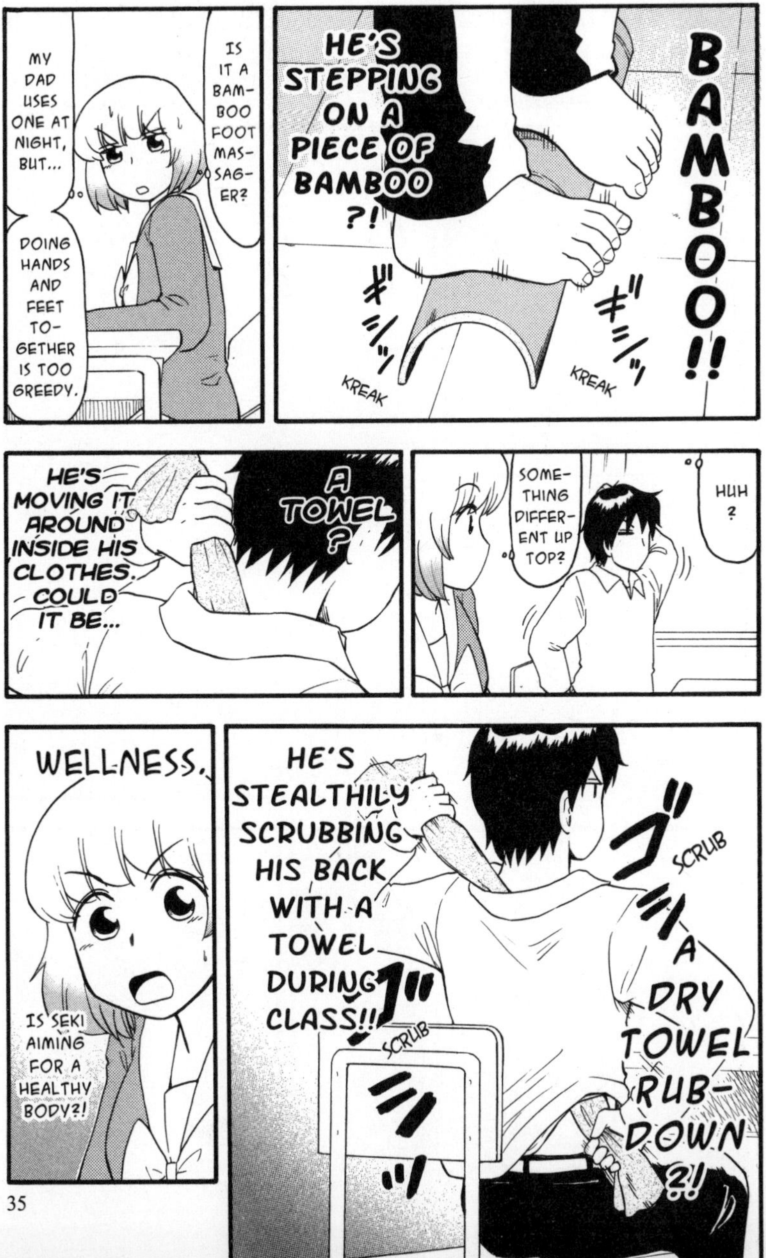

BAMBOO!!
HE'S STEPPING ON A PIECE OF BAMBOO?!
ギシッ
KREAK
ギシッ
KREAK
IS IT A BAMBOO FOOT MASSAGER?
MY DAD USES ONE AT NIGHT, BUT...
DOING HANDS AND FEET TOGETHER IS TOO GREEDY.
HUH?
SOMETHING DIFFERENT UP TOP?
A TOWEL?
HE'S MOVING IT AROUND INSIDE HIS CLOTHES. COULD IT BE...
A DRY TOWEL RUB-DOWN?!
SCRUB
HE'S STEALTHILY SCRUBBING HIS BACK WITH A TOWEL DURING CLASS!!
SCRUB
WELLNESS.
IS SEKI AIMING FOR A HEALTHY BODY?!

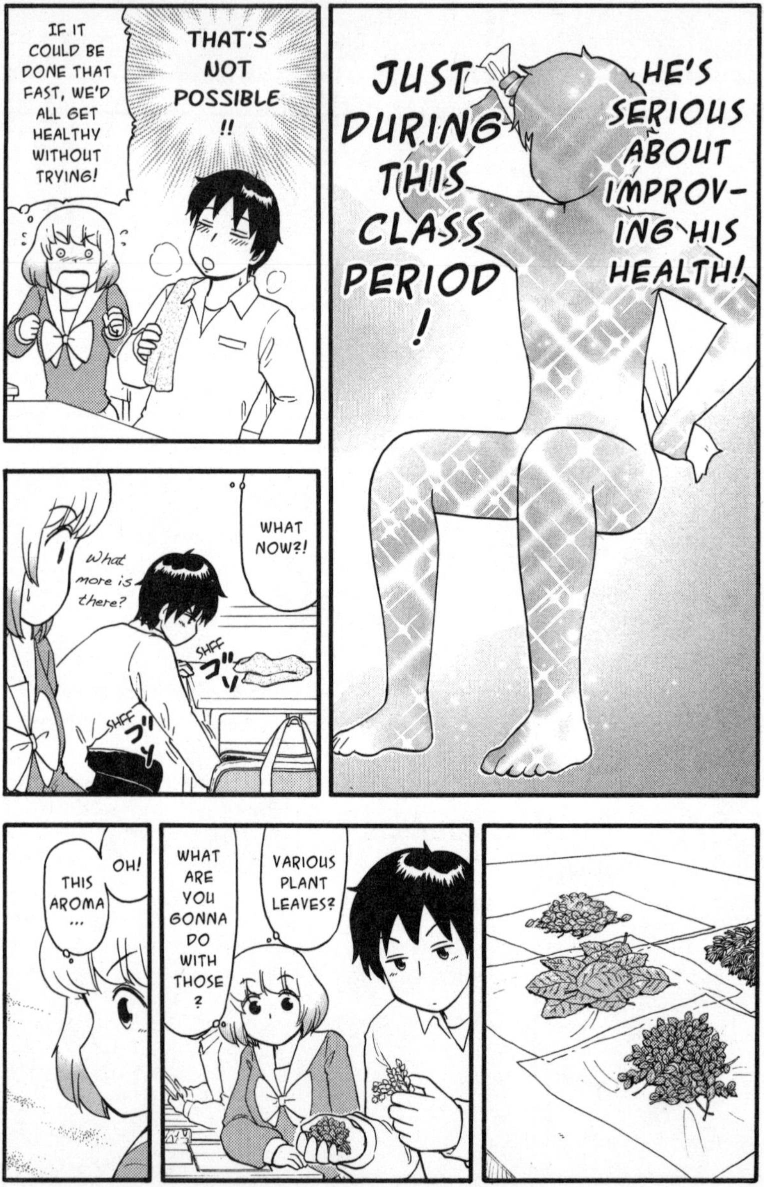
HE'S SERIOUS ABOUT IMPROVING HIS HEALTH!
JUST DURING THIS CLASS PERIOD!
THAT'S NOT POSSIBLE!!
IF IT COULD BE DONE THAT FAST, WE'D ALL GET HEALTHY WITHOUT TRYING!
WHAT NOW?!
What more is there?
SHFF
SHFF
VARIOUS PLANT LEAVES?
WHAT ARE YOU GONNA DO WITH THOSE?
OH!
THIS AROMA...

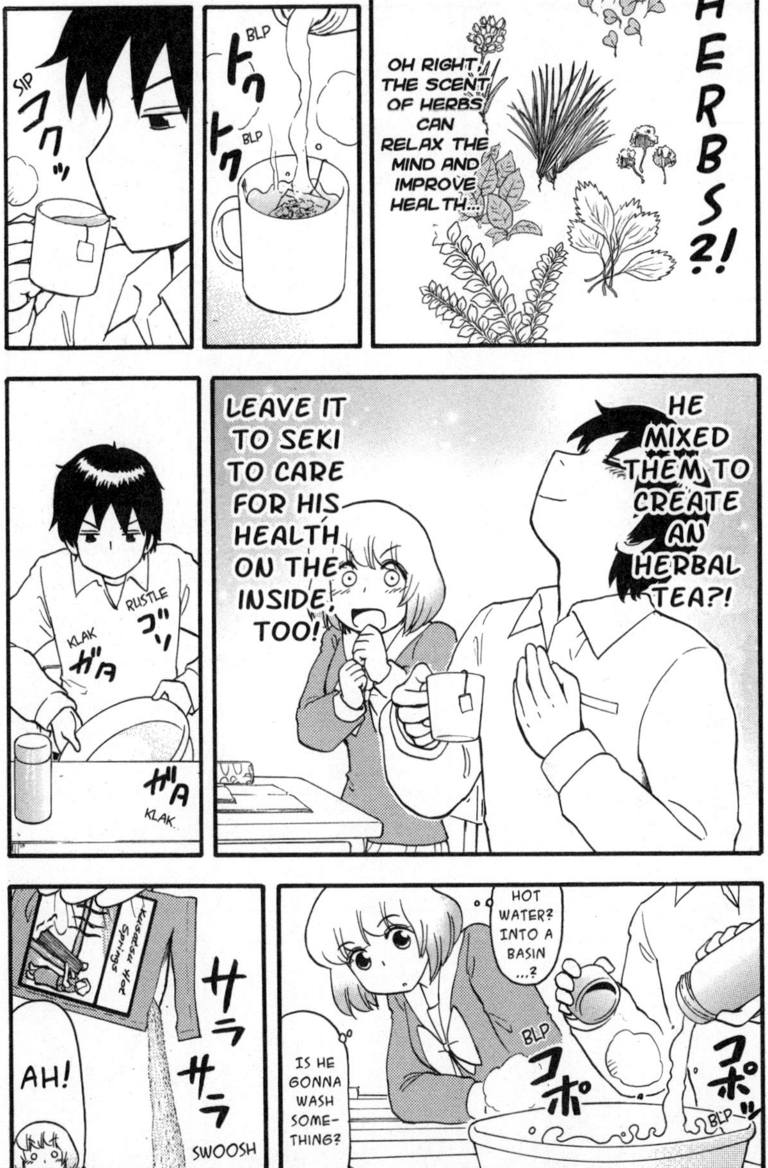
HERBS?!
OH RIGHT, THE SCENT OF HERBS CAN RELAX THE MIND AND IMPROVE HEALTH...
BLP
トク
BLP
トク
SIP
コクッ
HE MIXED THEM TO CREATE AN HERBAL TEA?!
LEAVE IT TO SEKI TO CARE FOR HIS HEALTH ON THE INSIDE, TOO!
RUSTLE
ゴソ
KLAK
ガタ
ガタ
KLAK
HOT WATER? INTO A BASIN ...?
コポッ
BLP
BLP
コポ
IS HE GONNA WASH SOME-THING?
Kusatsu Hot Springs
サラ
サラ
SWOOSH
AH!

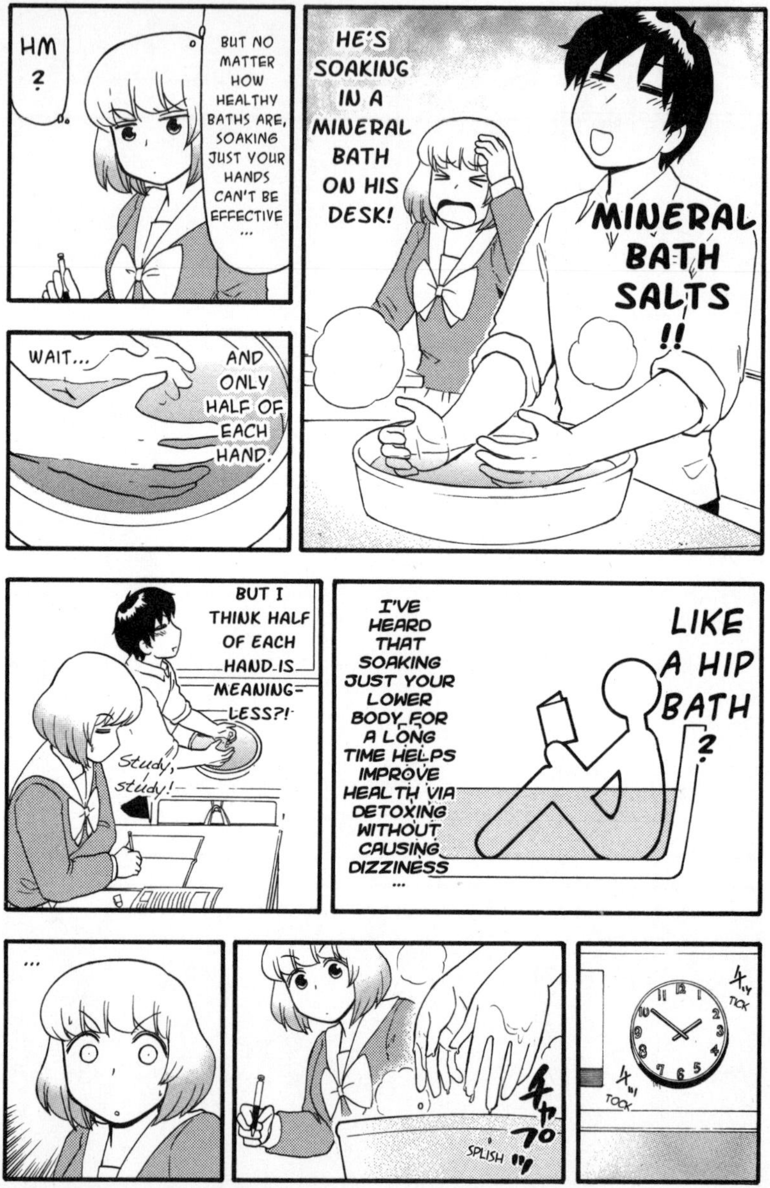
HE'S SOAKING IN A MINERAL BATH ON HIS DESK!
MINERAL BATH SALTS !!
HM ?
BUT NO MATTER HOW HEALTHY BATHS ARE, SOAKING JUST YOUR HANDS CAN'T BE EFFECTIVE ...
WAIT...
AND ONLY HALF OF EACH HAND.
LIKE A HIP BATH ?
I'VE HEARD THAT SOAKING JUST YOUR LOWER BODY FOR A LONG TIME HELPS IMPROVE HEALTH VIA DETOXING WITHOUT CAUSING DIZZINESS ...
BUT I THINK HALF OF EACH HAND IS MEANING-LESS?!
Study, study!
TICK
TOCK
SPLISH
...

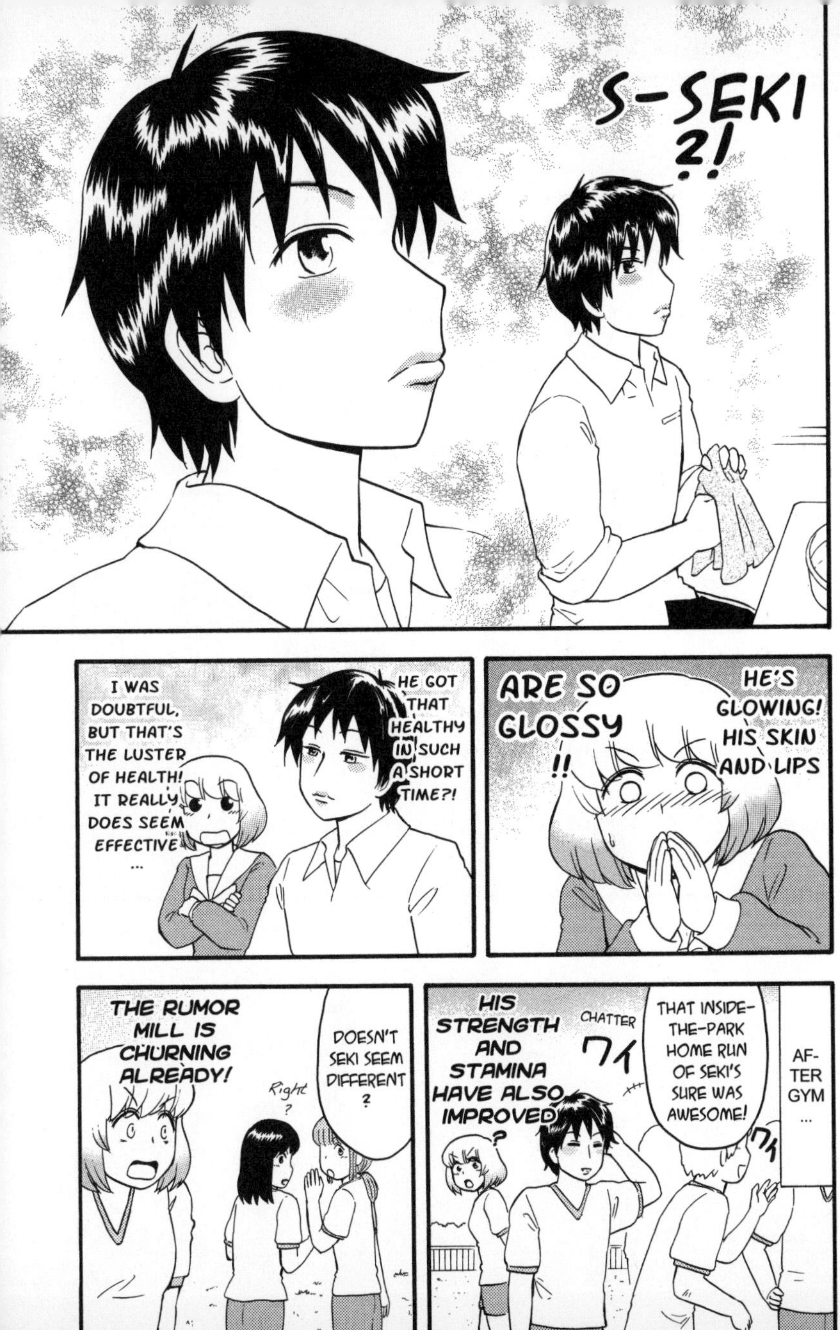

S-SEKI ?!
HE'S GLOWING! HIS SKIN AND LIPS ARE SO GLOSSY !!
HE GOT THAT HEALTHY IN SUCH A SHORT TIME?!
I WAS DOUBTFUL, BUT THAT'S THE LUSTER OF HEALTH! IT REALLY DOES SEEM EFFECTIVE ...
AF-TER GYM ...
THAT INSIDE-THE-PARK HOME RUN OF SEKI'S SURE WAS AWESOME!
CHATTER
ワイ
HIS STRENGTH AND STAMINA HAVE ALSO IMPROVED ?
DOESN'T SEKI SEEM DIFFERENT ?
Right ?
THE RUMOR MILL IS CHURNING ALREADY!

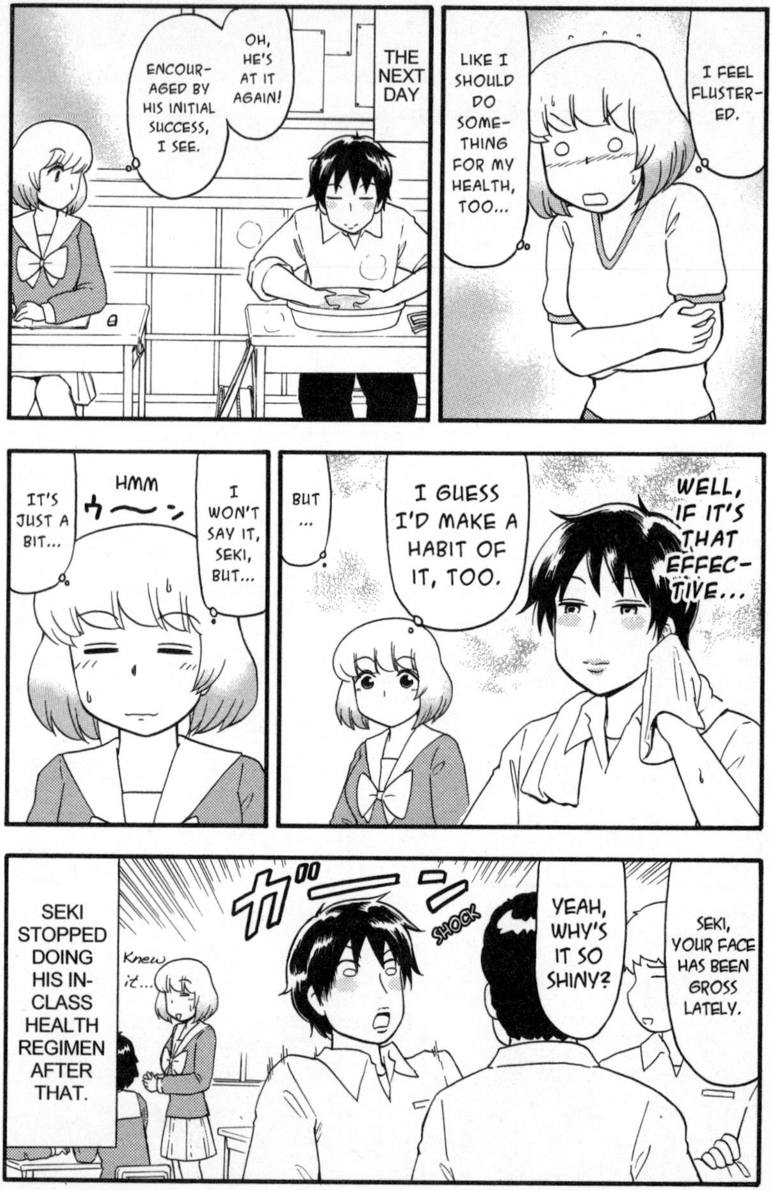
I FEEL FLUSTERED.
LIKE I SHOULD DO SOMETHING FOR MY HEALTH, TOO...
THE NEXT DAY
OH, HE'S AT IT AGAIN!
ENCOURAGED BY HIS INITIAL SUCCESS, I SEE.
WELL, IF IT'S THAT EFFECTIVE...
I GUESS I'D MAKE A HABIT OF IT, TOO.
BUT ...
I WON'T SAY IT, SEKI, BUT...
HMM ウ〜ン
IT'S JUST A BIT...
SEKI, YOUR FACE HAS BEEN GROSS LATELY.
YEAH, WHY'S IT SO SHINY?
ガーン SHOCK
Knew it...
SEKI STOPPED DOING HIS IN-CLASS HEALTH REGIMEN AFTER THAT.

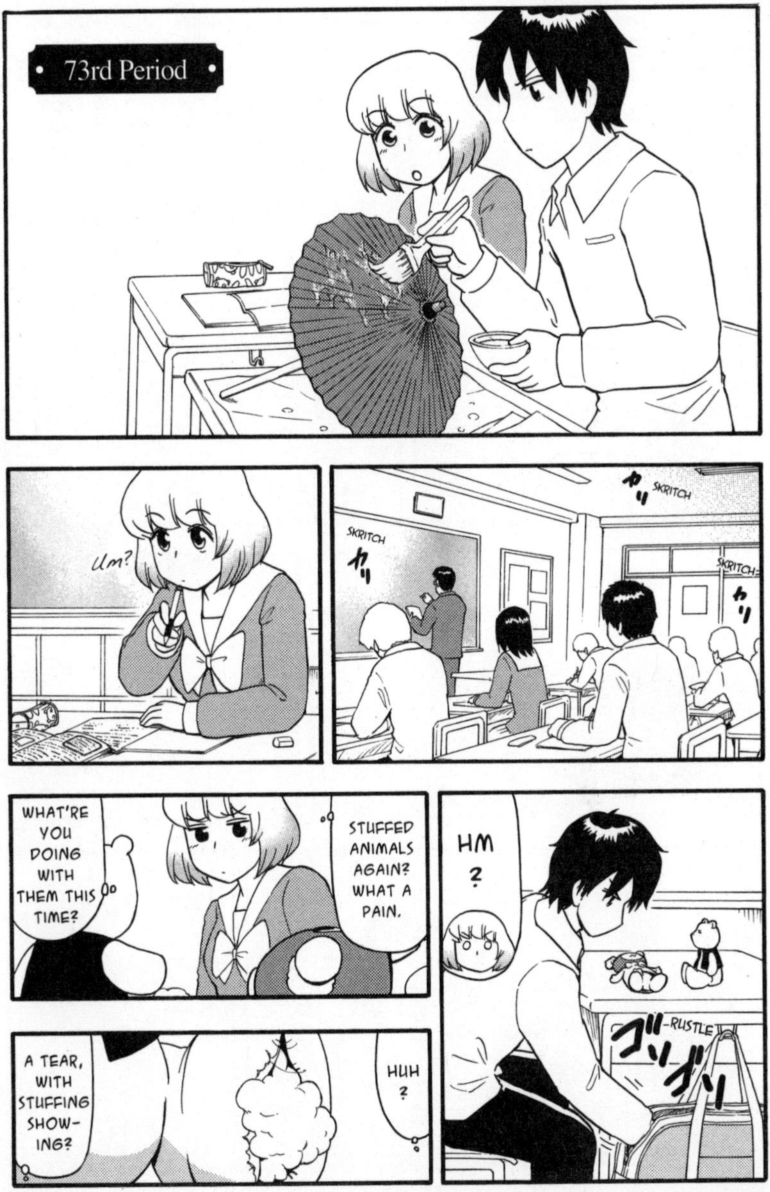
73rd Period
SKRITCH
SKRITCH
SKRITCH
Um?
HM ?
RUSTLE
STUFFED ANIMALS AGAIN? WHAT A PAIN.
WHAT'RE YOU DOING WITH THEM THIS TIME?
HUH ?
A TEAR, WITH STUFFING SHOW-ING?

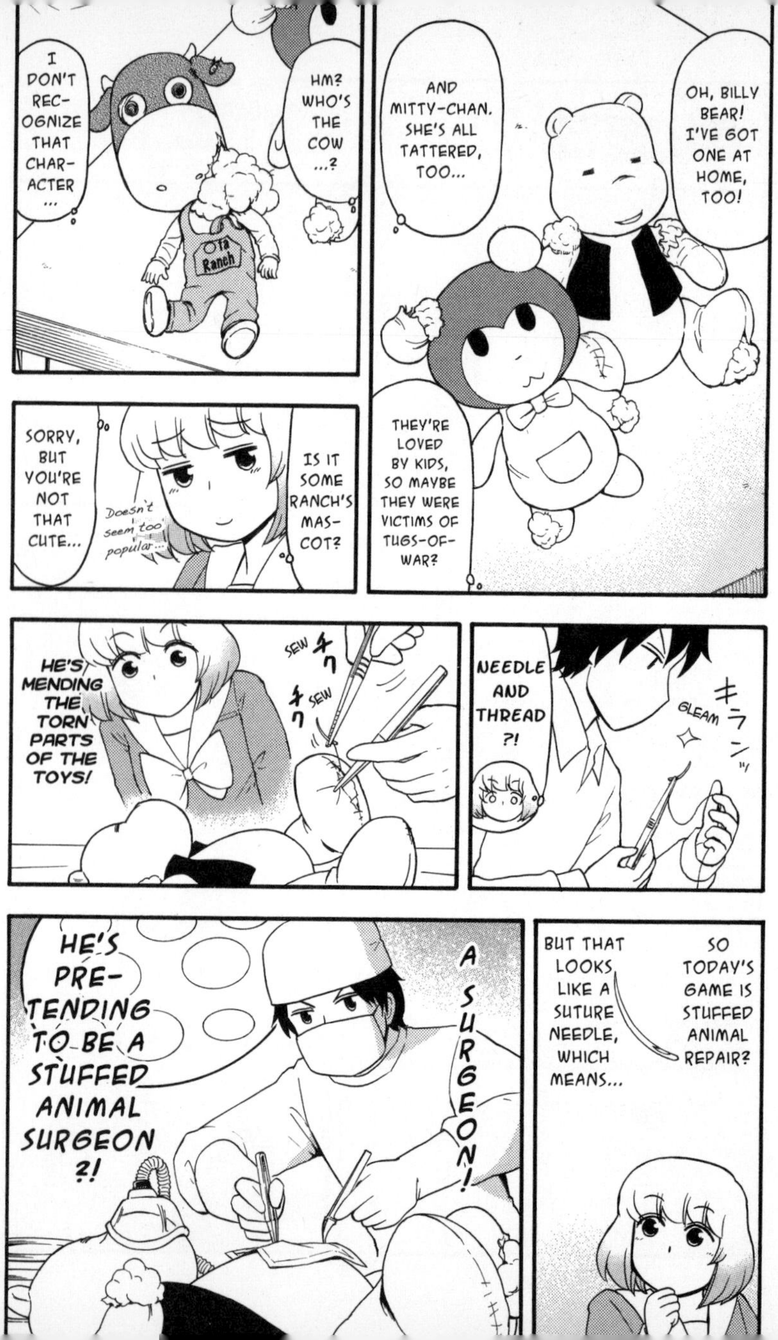
OH, BILLY BEAR! I'VE GOT ONE AT HOME, TOO!
AND MITTY-CHAN. SHE'S ALL TATTERED, TOO...
THEY'RE LOVED BY KIDS, SO MAYBE THEY WERE VICTIMS OF TUGS-OF-WAR?
HM? WHO'S THE COW ...?
I DON'T REC-OGNIZE THAT CHAR-ACTER ...
IS IT SOME RANCH'S MAS-COT?
Doesn't seem too popular...
SORRY, BUT YOU'RE NOT THAT CUTE...
NEEDLE AND THREAD ?!
キラーン
GLEAM
チク
SEW
チク
SEW
HE'S MENDING THE TORN PARTS OF THE TOYS!
SO TODAY'S GAME IS STUFFED ANIMAL REPAIR?
BUT THAT LOOKS LIKE A SUTURE NEEDLE, WHICH MEANS...
A SURGEON!
HE'S PRE-TENDING TO BE A STUFFED ANIMAL SURGEON ?!

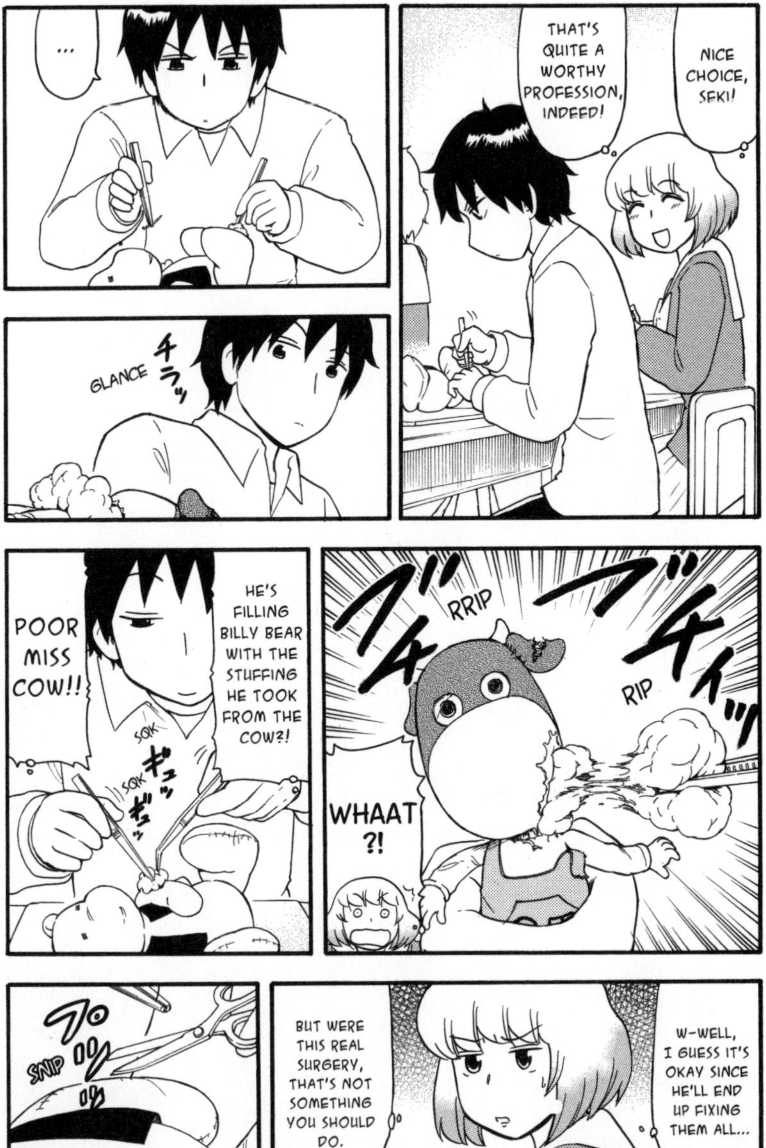
NICE CHOICE, SEKI!
THAT'S QUITE A WORTHY PROFESSION, INDEED!
...
GLANCE
チラッ
RIP
RRIP
WHAAT?!
HE'S FILLING BILLY BEAR WITH THE STUFFING HE TOOK FROM THE COW?!
POOR MISS COW!!
SQK
SQK
W-WELL, I GUESS IT'S OKAY SINCE HE'LL END UP FIXING THEM ALL...
BUT WERE THIS REAL SURGERY, THAT'S NOT SOMETHING YOU SHOULD DO.
SNIP

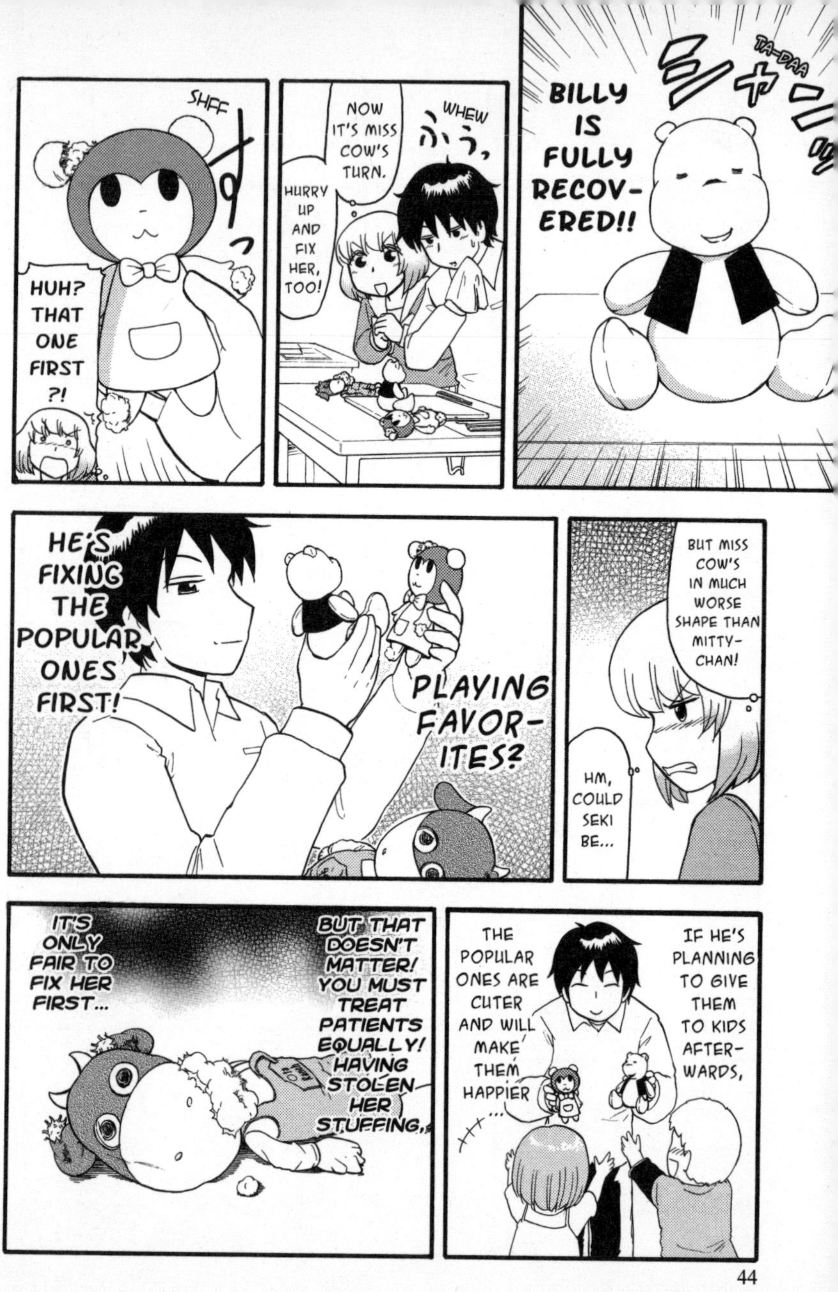
TA-DAA
シャロン
BILLY IS FULLY RECOV-ERED!!
WHEW
ふう、
NOW IT'S MISS COW'S TURN.
HURRY UP AND FIX HER, TOO!
SHFF
HUH? THAT ONE FIRST ?!
BUT MISS COW'S IN MUCH WORSE SHAPE THAN MITTY-CHAN!
HM, COULD SEKI BE...
PLAYING FAVOR-ITES?
HE'S FIXING THE POPULAR ONES FIRST!
IF HE'S PLANNING TO GIVE THEM TO KIDS AFTER-WARDS,
THE POPULAR ONES ARE CUTER AND WILL MAKE THEM HAPPIER...
BUT THAT DOESN'T MATTER! YOU MUST TREAT PATIENTS EQUALLY! HAVING STOLEN HER STUFFING,
IT'S ONLY FAIR TO FIX HER FIRST...

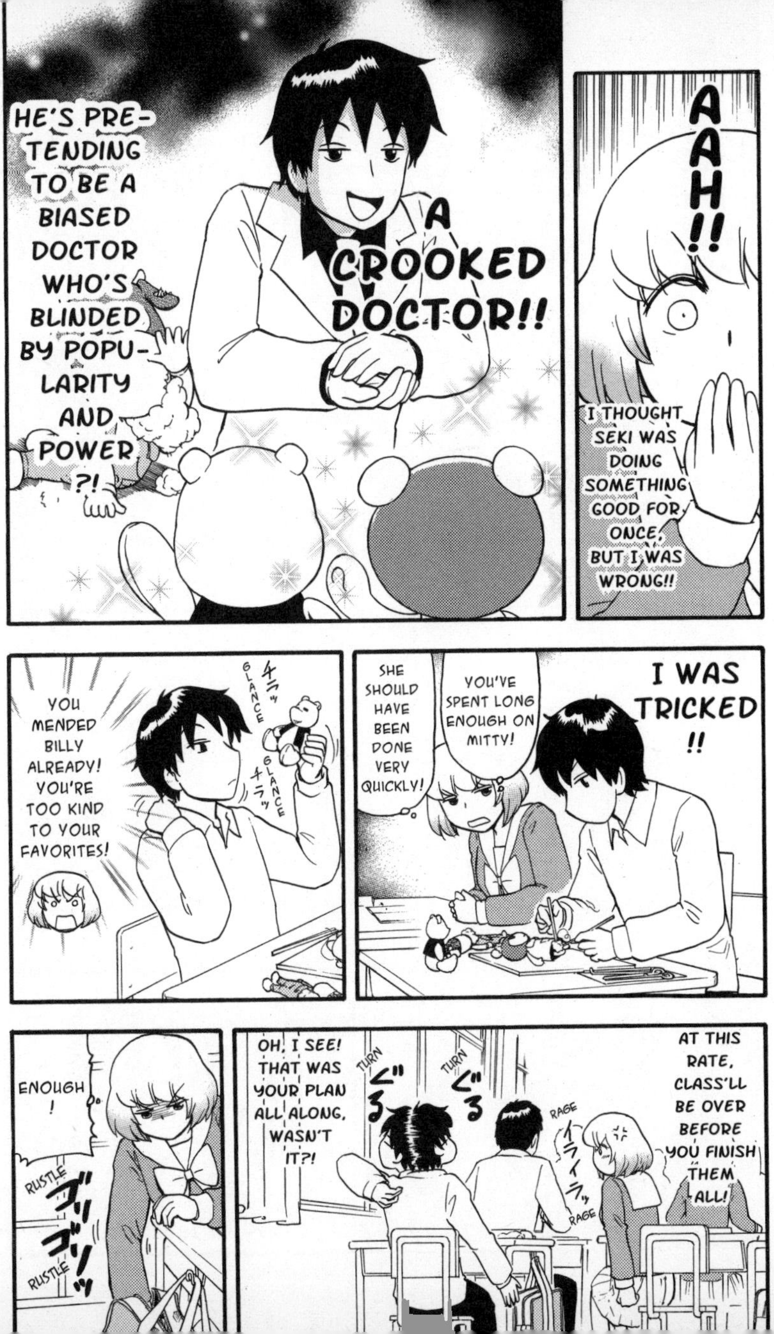

AAH!!
I THOUGHT SEKI WAS DOING SOMETHING GOOD FOR ONCE, BUT I WAS WRONG!!
A CROOKED DOCTOR!!
HE'S PRE-TENDING TO BE A BIASED DOCTOR WHO'S BLINDED BY POPU-LARITY AND POWER?!
I WAS TRICKED!!
YOU'VE SPENT LONG ENOUGH ON MITTY!
SHE SHOULD HAVE BEEN DONE VERY QUICKLY!
チラッ GLANCE
チラッ GLANCE
YOU MENDED BILLY ALREADY! YOU'RE TOO KIND TO YOUR FAVORITES!
AT THIS RATE, CLASS'LL BE OVER BEFORE YOU FINISH THEM ALL!
イライラッ RAGE RAGE
ぐる TURN
ぐる TURN
OH, I SEE! THAT WAS YOUR PLAN ALL ALONG, WASN'T IT?!
ENOUGH!
ゴソゴソッ RUSTLE RUSTLE

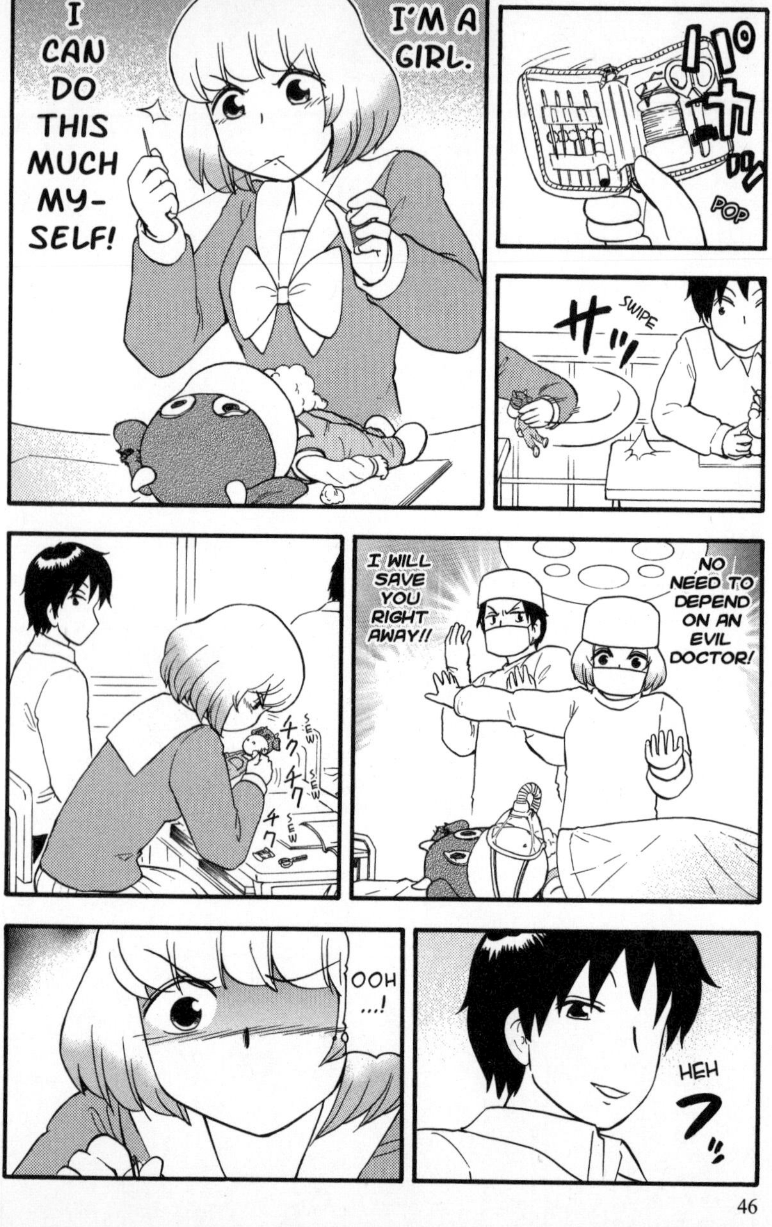
パカッ
POP
サッ
SWIPE
I'M A GIRL.
I CAN DO THIS MUCH MY-SELF!
NO NEED TO DEPEND ON AN EVIL DOCTOR!
I WILL SAVE YOU RIGHT AWAY!!
チクチクチク
SEW SEW SEW
HEH
フッ
OOH ...!

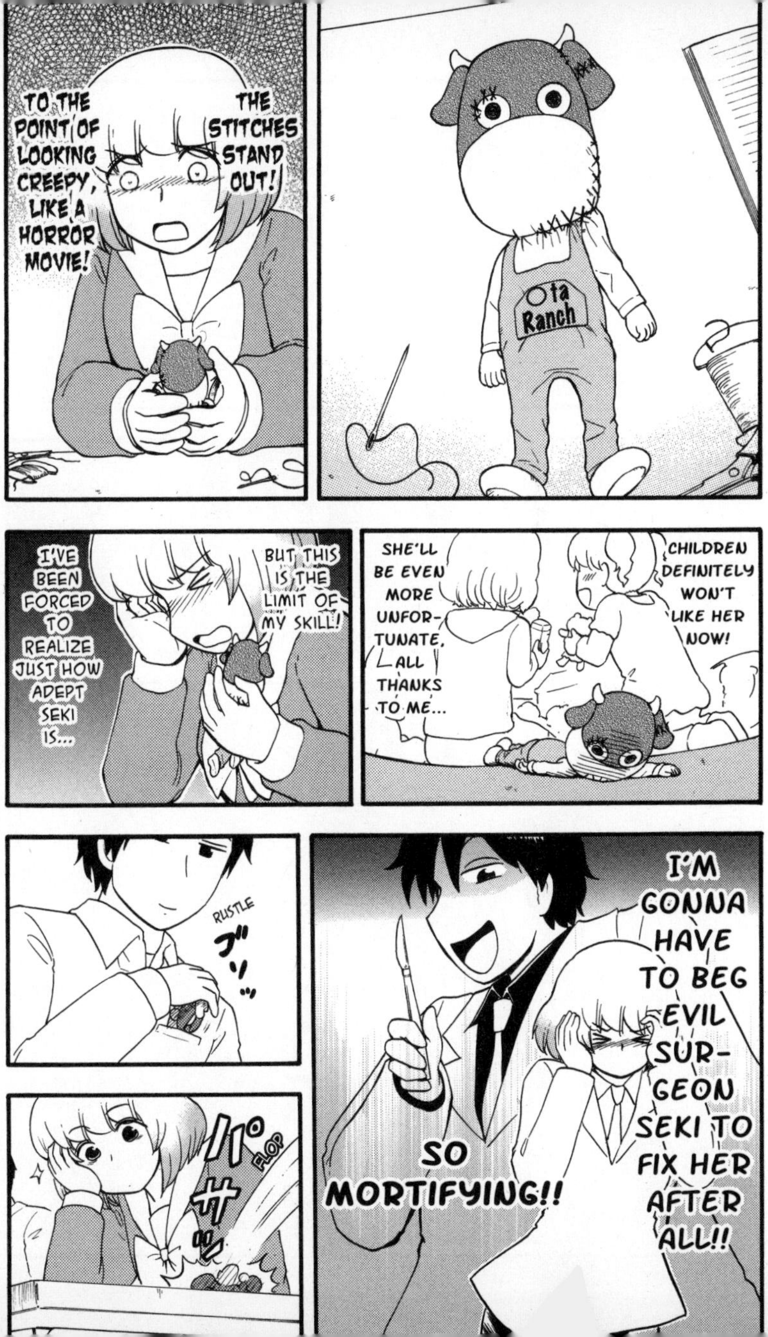
○ta Ranch
THE STITCHES STAND OUT!
TO THE POINT OF LOOKING CREEPY, LIKE A HORROR MOVIE!
CHILDREN DEFINITELY WON'T LIKE HER NOW!
SHE'LL BE EVEN MORE UNFORTUNATE, ALL THANKS TO ME...
BUT THIS IS THE LIMIT OF MY SKILL!
I'VE BEEN FORCED TO REALIZE JUST HOW ADEPT SEKI IS...
I'M GONNA HAVE TO BEG EVIL SURGEON SEKI TO FIX HER AFTER ALL!!
SO MORTIFYING!!
RUSTLE
FLOP

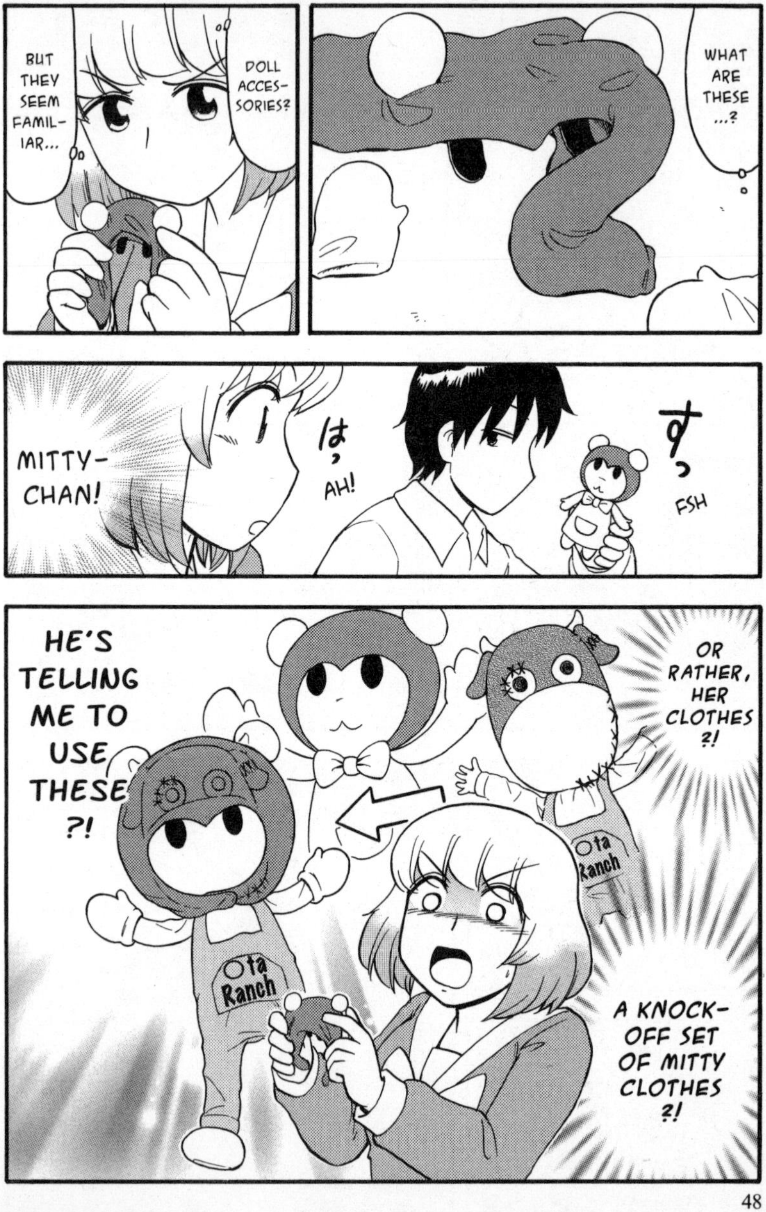
WHAT ARE THESE ...?
DOLL ACCESSORIES?
BUT THEY SEEM FAMILIAR...
すっ
FSH
は
AH!
MITTY-CHAN!
OR RATHER, HER CLOTHES?!
HE'S TELLING ME TO USE THESE?!
Ota Ranch
Ota Ranch
A KNOCK-OFF SET OF MITTY CLOTHES?!

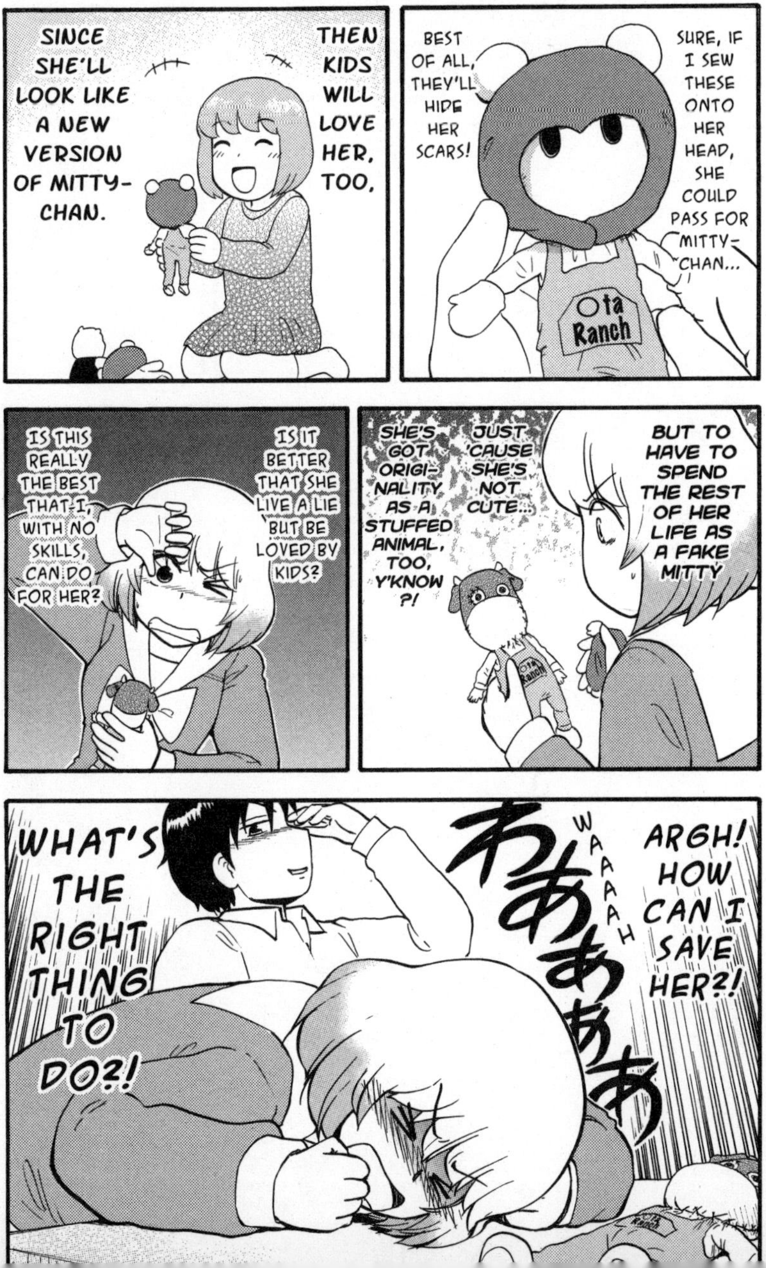
SURE, IF I SEW THESE ONTO HER HEAD, SHE COULD PASS FOR MITTY-CHAN...
BEST OF ALL, THEY'LL HIDE HER SCARS!
Ota Ranch
THEN KIDS WILL LOVE HER, TOO,
SINCE SHE'LL LOOK LIKE A NEW VERSION OF MITTY-CHAN.
BUT TO HAVE TO SPEND THE REST OF HER LIFE AS A FAKE MITTY
JUST 'CAUSE SHE'S NOT CUTE...
SHE'S GOT ORIGINALITY AS A STUFFED ANIMAL, TOO, Y'KNOW?!
IS IT BETTER THAT SHE LIVE A LIE BUT BE LOVED BY KIDS?
IS THIS REALLY THE BEST THAT I, WITH NO SKILLS, CAN DO FOR HER?
ARGH! HOW CAN I SAVE HER?!
わあああああ
WAAAAAH
WHAT'S THE RIGHT THING TO DO?!

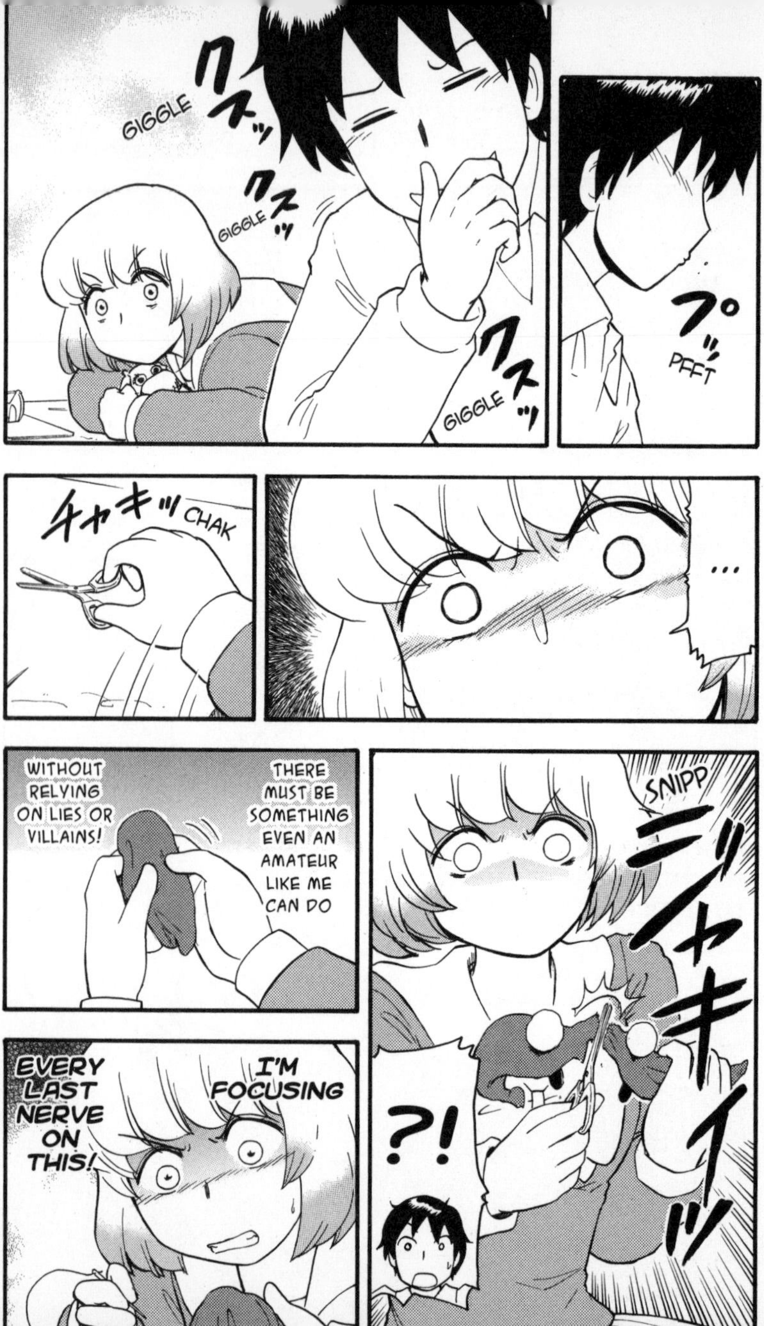

プッ
PFFT
クスッ
GIGGLE
クスッ
GIGGLE
クスッ
GIGGLE
...
チャキッ
CHAK
SNIPP
ジャキイッ
?!
THERE MUST BE SOMETHING EVEN AN AMATEUR LIKE ME CAN DO
WITHOUT RELYING ON LIES OR VILLAINS!
I'M FOCUSING
EVERY LAST NERVE ON THIS!

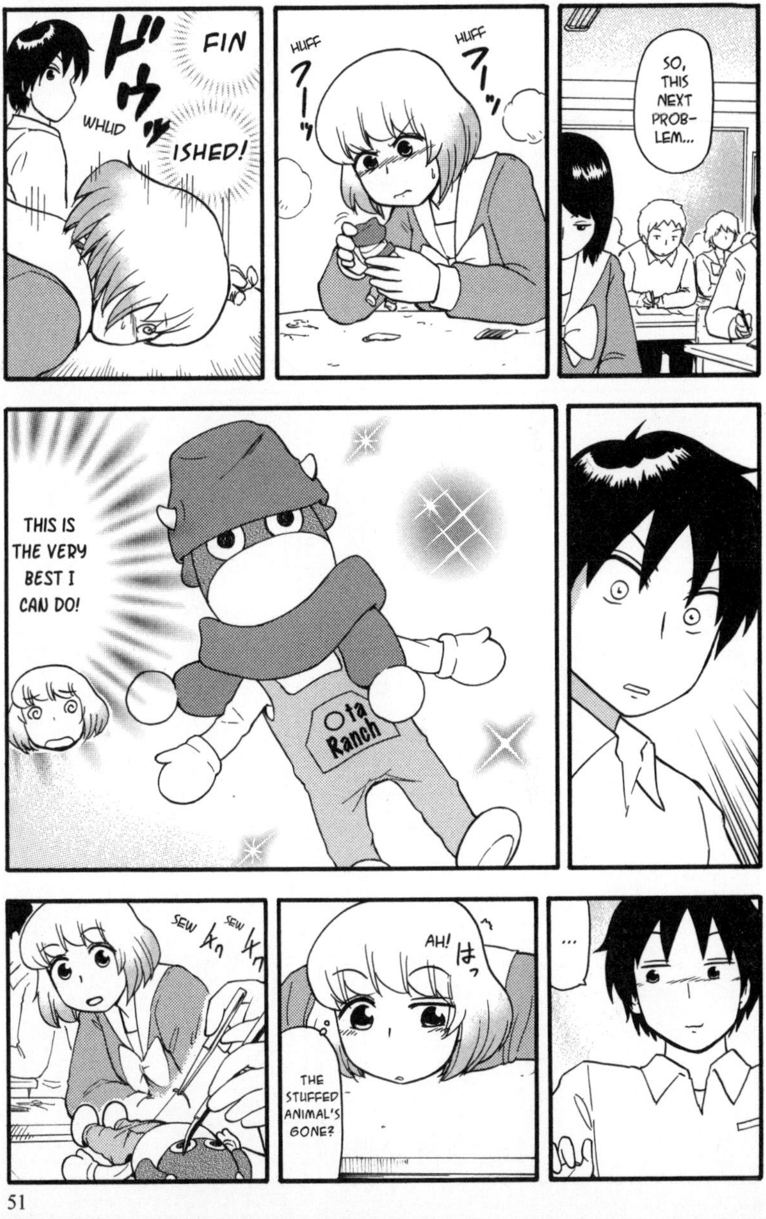

SO, THIS NEXT PROB-LEM...
HUFF
フーッ
HUFF
フーッ
FIN
ISHED!
ドゥッ
WHUD
THIS IS THE VERY BEST I CAN DO!
Ota Ranch
...
AH! はっ
THE STUFFED ANIMAL'S GONE?
SEW
SEW

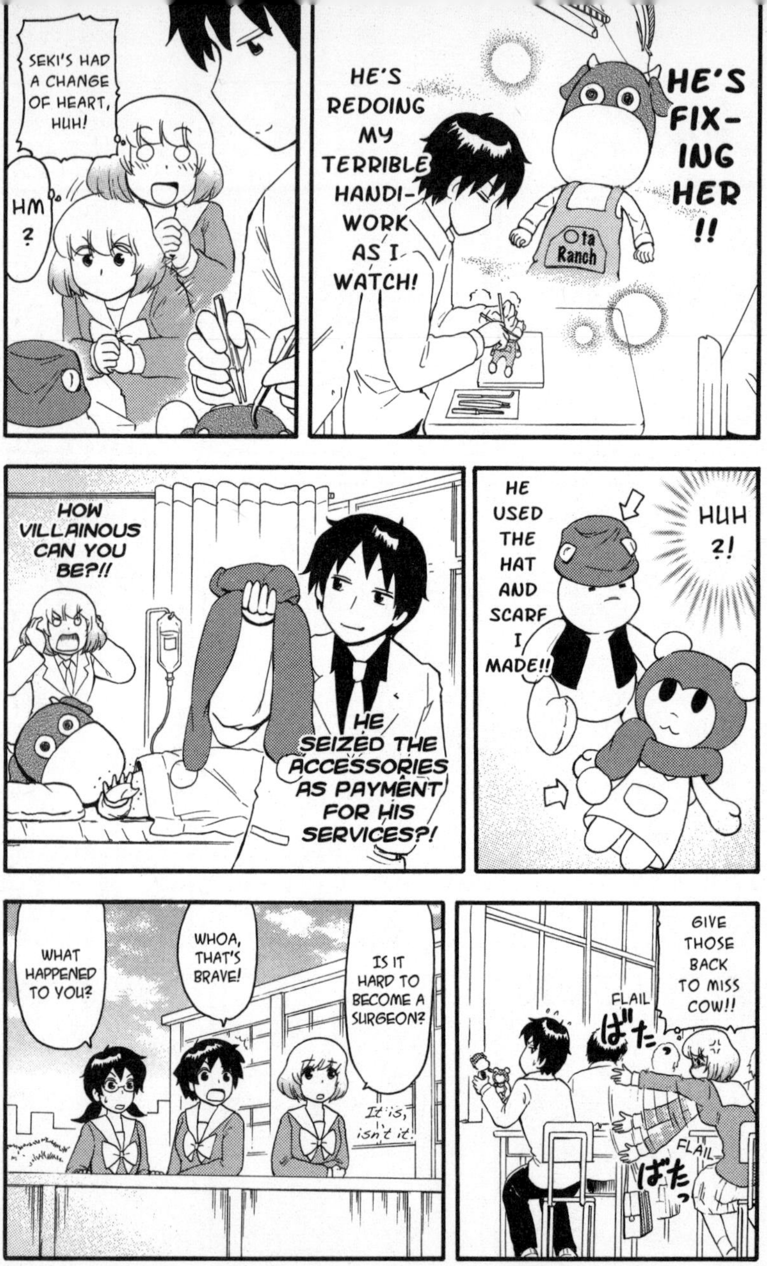
HE'S FIX-ING HER!!
HE'S REDOING MY TERRIBLE HANDI-WORK AS I WATCH!
Ota Ranch
SEKI'S HAD A CHANGE OF HEART, HUH!
HM?
HUH?!
HE USED THE HAT AND SCARF I MADE!!
HE SEIZED THE ACCESSORIES AS PAYMENT FOR HIS SERVICES?!
HOW VILLAINOUS CAN YOU BE?!!
GIVE THOSE BACK TO MISS COW!!
FLAIL
ばた
FLAIL
ばたっ
IS IT HARD TO BECOME A SURGEON?
It is, isn't it.
WHOA, THAT'S BRAVE!
WHAT HAPPENED TO YOU?

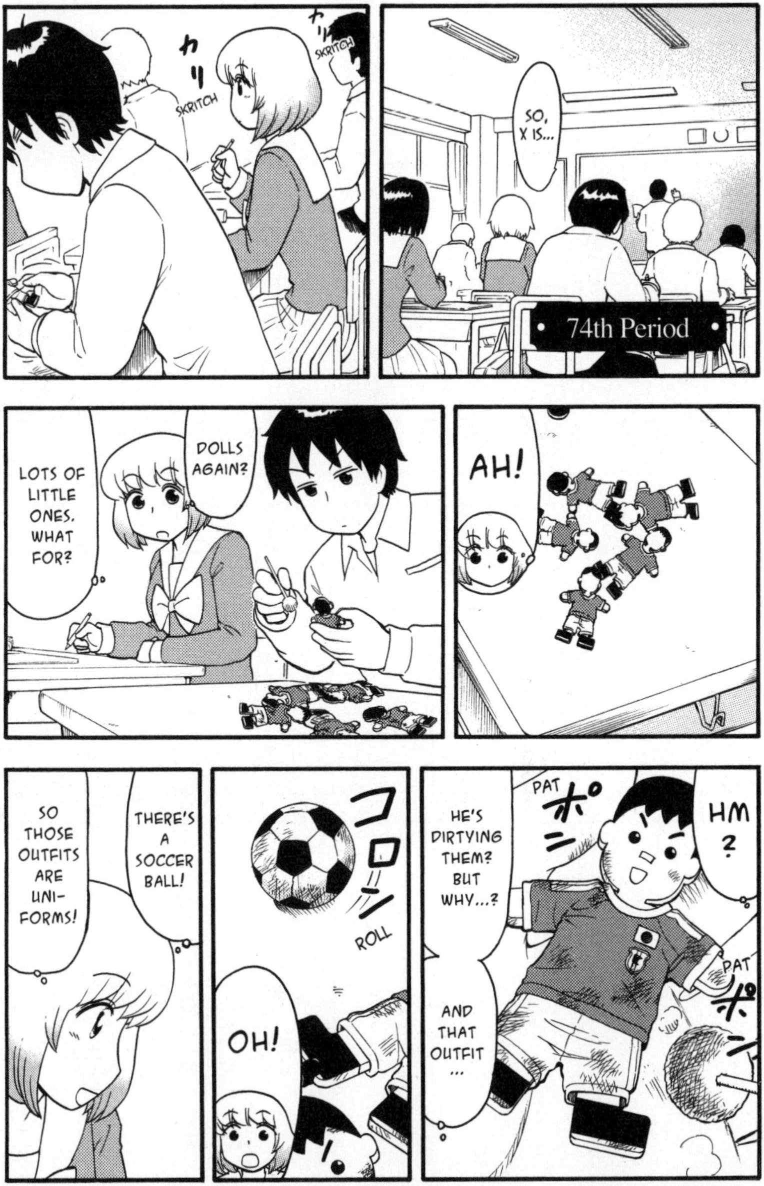
SO, X IS...
74th Period
カリ
SKRITCH
カリ
SKRITCH
AH!
DOLLS AGAIN?
LOTS OF LITTLE ONES. WHAT FOR?
HM?
PAT
ポン
HE'S DIRTYING THEM? BUT WHY...?
PAT
ポン
AND THAT OUTFIT...
コロン
ROLL
OH!
THERE'S A SOCCER BALL!
SO THOSE OUTFITS ARE UNIFORMS!

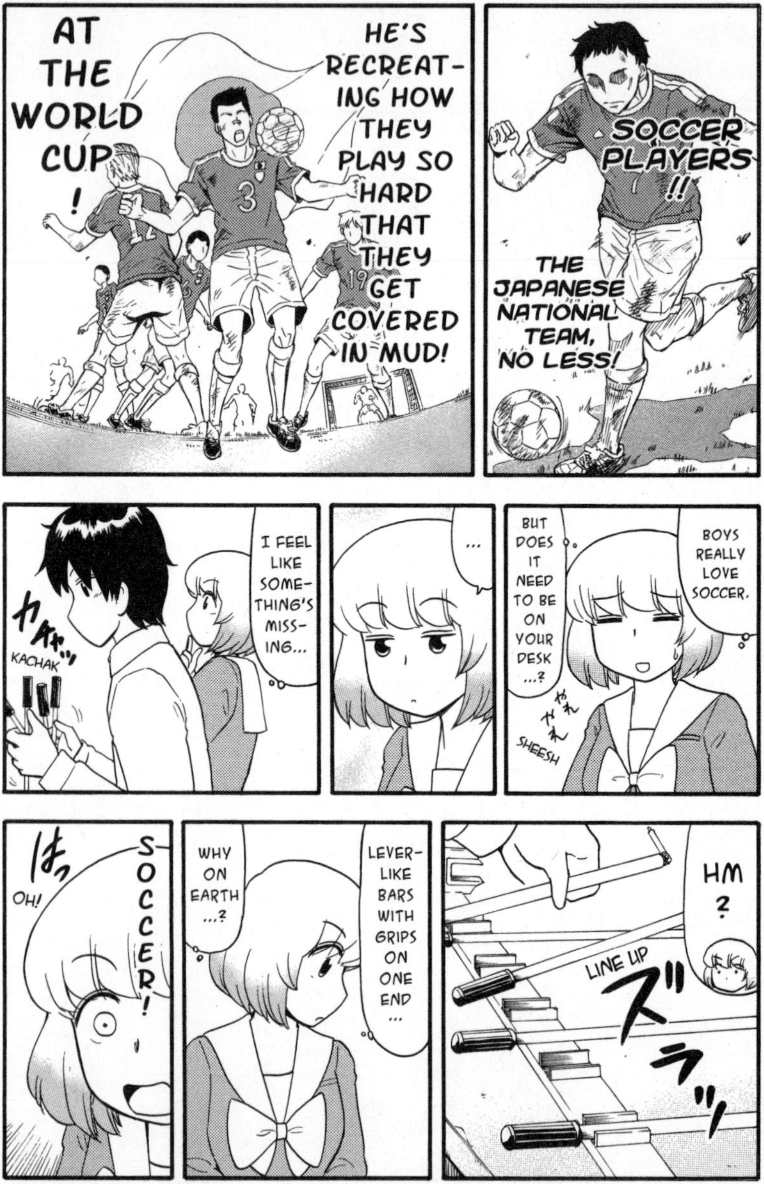
SOCCER PLAYERS!!
THE JAPANESE NATIONAL TEAM, NO LESS!
HE'S RECREATING HOW THEY PLAY SO HARD THAT THEY GET COVERED IN MUD!
AT THE WORLD CUP!
BOYS REALLY LOVE SOCCER.
BUT DOES IT NEED TO BE ON YOUR DESK...?
SHEESH
...
I FEEL LIKE SOMETHING'S MISSING...
KACHAK
HM?
LINE UP
LEVER-LIKE BARS WITH GRIPS ON ONE END...
WHY ON EARTH...?
SOCCER!
OH!

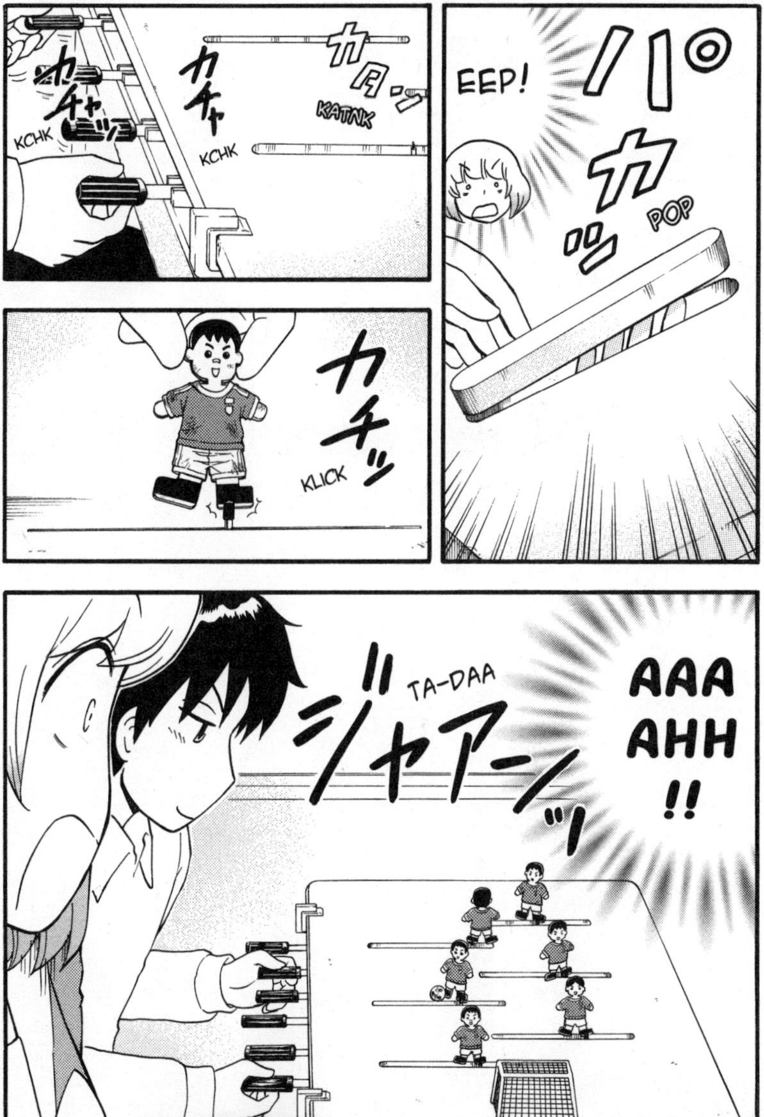

EEP!
パカッ
POP
カチャ
KCHK
カチャ
KCHK
カタン
KATNK
カチッ
KLICK
ジャーンッ
TA-DAA
AAAAHH!!

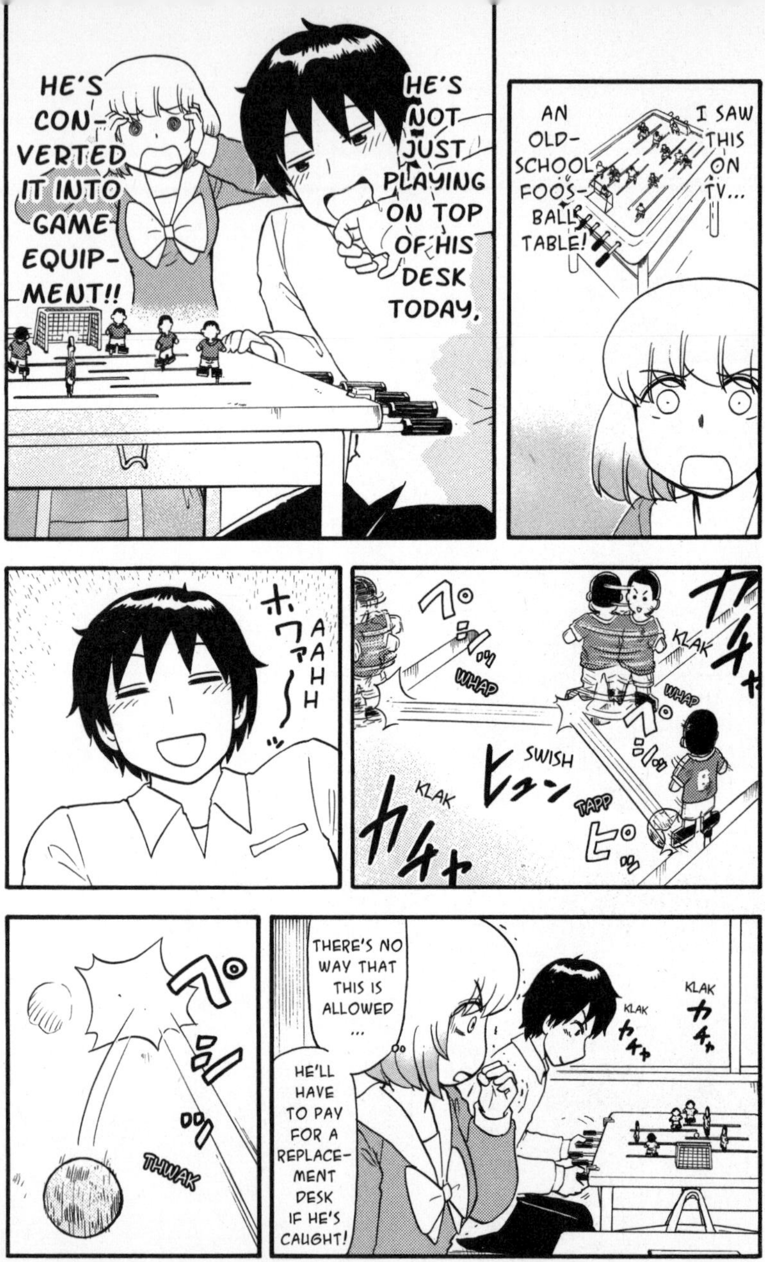
I SAW THIS ON TV...
AN OLD-SCHOOL FOOSBALL TABLE!
HE'S NOT JUST PLAYING ON TOP OF HIS DESK TODAY.
HE'S CONVERTED IT INTO GAME EQUIPMENT!!
KLAK
WHAP
WHAP
SWISH
KLAK
TAPP
AAHH
KLAK
KLAK
THERE'S NO WAY THAT THIS IS ALLOWED...
HE'LL HAVE TO PAY FOR A REPLACEMENT DESK IF HE'S CAUGHT!
THWAK

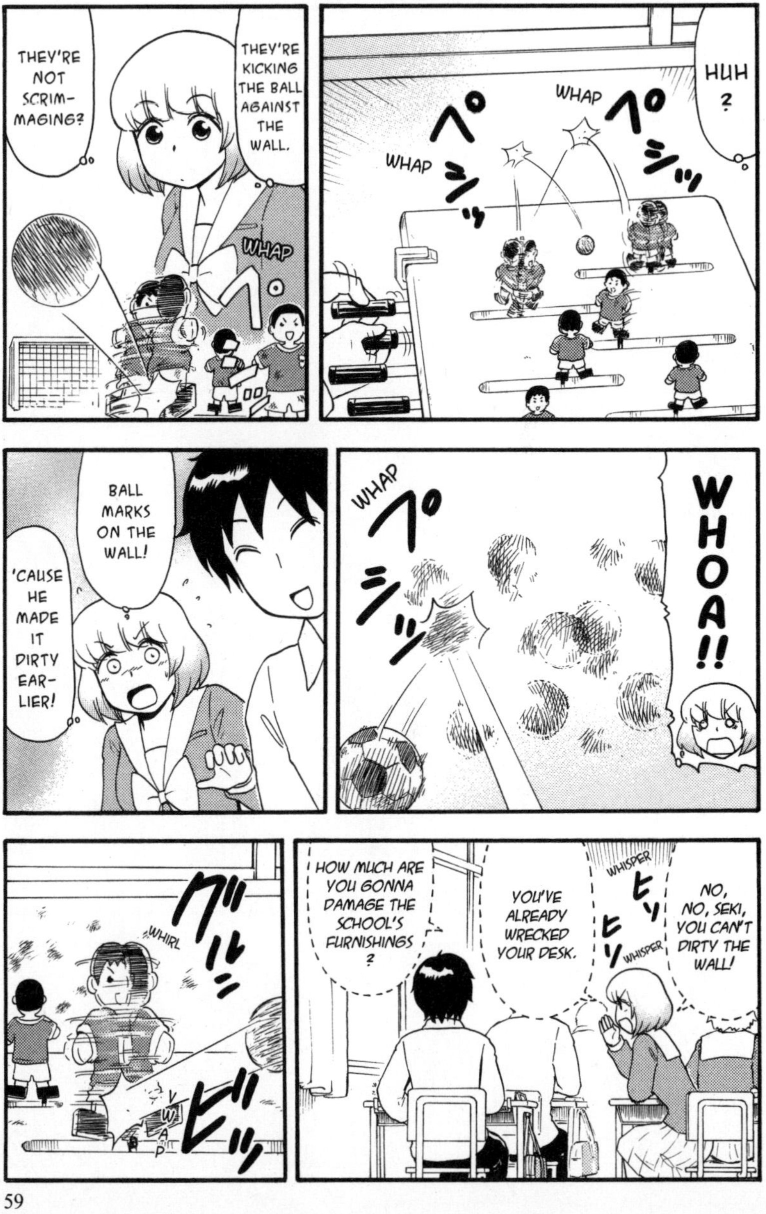
HUH?
WHAP
ペシッ
WHAP
ペシッ
THEY'RE KICKING THE BALL AGAINST THE WALL.
THEY'RE NOT SCRIM-MAGING?
WHAP
WHOA!!
WHAP
ペシッ
BALL MARKS ON THE WALL!
'CAUSE HE MADE IT DIRTY EAR-LIER!
NO, NO, SEKI, YOU CAN'T DIRTY THE WALL!
WHISPER
ヒソ
ヒソ
WHISPER
YOU'VE ALREADY WRECKED YOUR DESK.
HOW MUCH ARE YOU GONNA DAMAGE THE SCHOOL'S FURNISHINGS?
WHIRL
VWAP

WHAP
WHAP
THAT WAY?!
HE'S LEAVING BALL MARKS ON MAEDA'S CHAIR, TOO!
STOP THAT RIGHT THIS MINUTE!
OH!
WHAP
A BALL MARK ON MAEDA'S BACK!
THAT'S MEAN! HE WON'T LET YOU SHRUG THIS OFF!
THIS HAS GONE TOO FAR...
GRAB

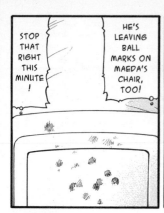

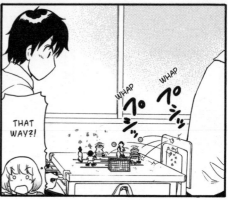

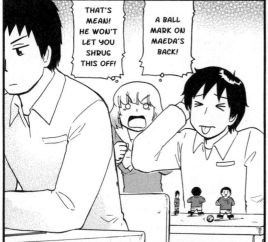

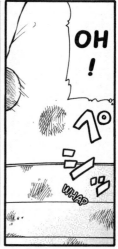

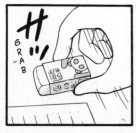

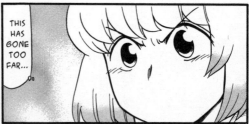

VW

AP

I'LL JUST BLAST THAT BALL OUT OF PLAY...!

!

ス

タ

ヒュッ

SWISH

WHAK

アッ

シャコン

KA-KLUNK

ポーン

PONG

ザッザッ

ZSHH-T

シュパッ

SHULPP

シュパッ

SHLUPP

シュパッ

SHULPP

SHUPP

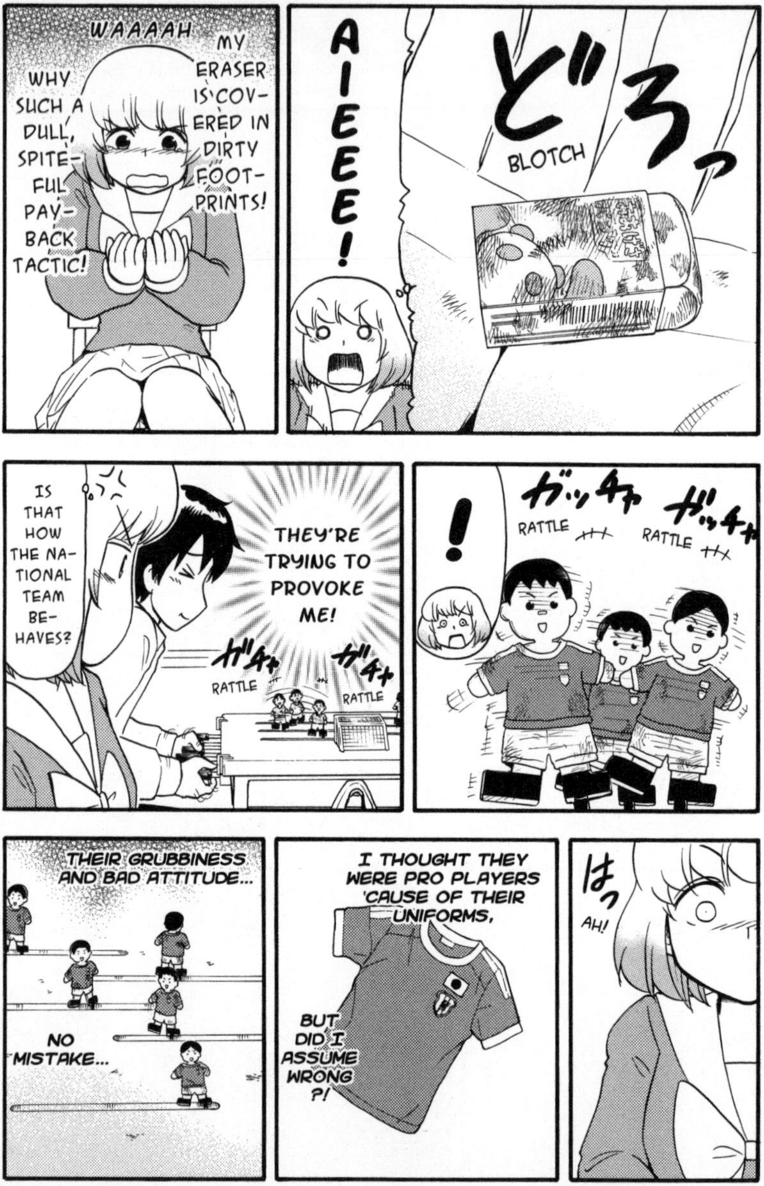
AIEEE!
どろっ
BLOTCH
WAAAAH
MY ERASER IS COVERED IN DIRTY FOOTPRINTS!
WHY SUCH A DULL, SPITEFUL PAYBACK TACTIC!
!
ガッチャ
RATTLE
ガッチャ
RATTLE
THEY'RE TRYING TO PROVOKE ME!
IS THAT HOW THE NATIONAL TEAM BEHAVES?
ガチャ
RATTLE
ガチャ
RATTLE
はっ
AH!
I THOUGHT THEY WERE PRO PLAYERS 'CAUSE OF THEIR UNIFORMS,
BUT DID I ASSUME WRONG?!
THEIR GRUBBINESS AND BAD ATTITUDE...
NO MISTAKE...

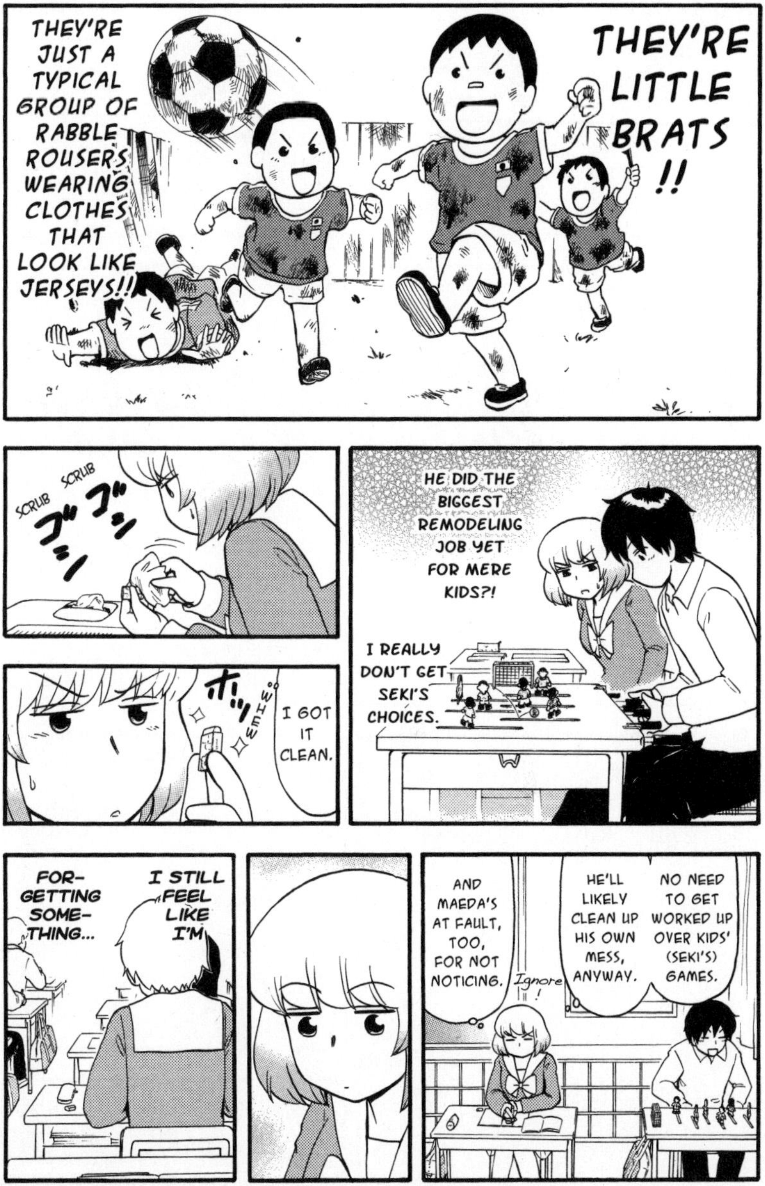
THEY'RE LITTLE BRATS!!
THEY'RE JUST A TYPICAL GROUP OF RABBLE ROUSERS WEARING CLOTHES THAT LOOK LIKE JERSEYS!!
HE DID THE BIGGEST REMODELING JOB YET FOR MERE KIDS?!
I REALLY DON'T GET SEKI'S CHOICES.
SCRUB SCRUB
ゴシゴシ
WHEW
I GOT IT CLEAN.
NO NEED TO GET WORKED UP OVER KIDS' (SEKI'S) GAMES.
HE'LL LIKELY CLEAN UP HIS OWN MESS, ANYWAY.
Ignore!
AND MAEDA'S AT FAULT, TOO, FOR NOT NOTICING.
I STILL FEEL LIKE I'M
FOR-GETTING SOME-THING...

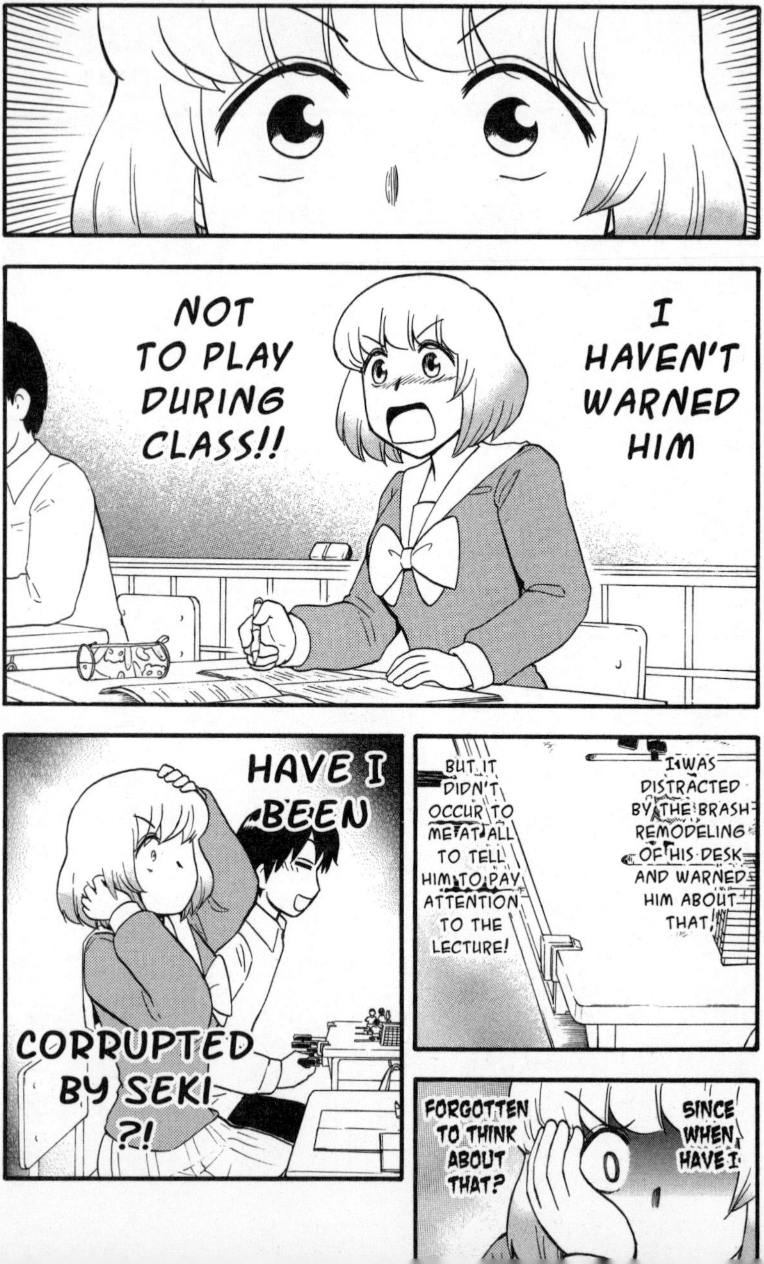
I HAVEN'T WARNED HIM
NOT TO PLAY DURING CLASS!!
I WAS DISTRACTED BY THE BRASH REMODELING OF HIS DESK AND WARNED HIM ABOUT THAT,
BUT IT DIDN'T OCCUR TO ME AT ALL TO TELL HIM TO PAY ATTENTION TO THE LECTURE!
SINCE WHEN HAVE I
FORGOTTEN TO THINK ABOUT THAT?
HAVE I BEEN
CORRUPTED BY SEKI ?!

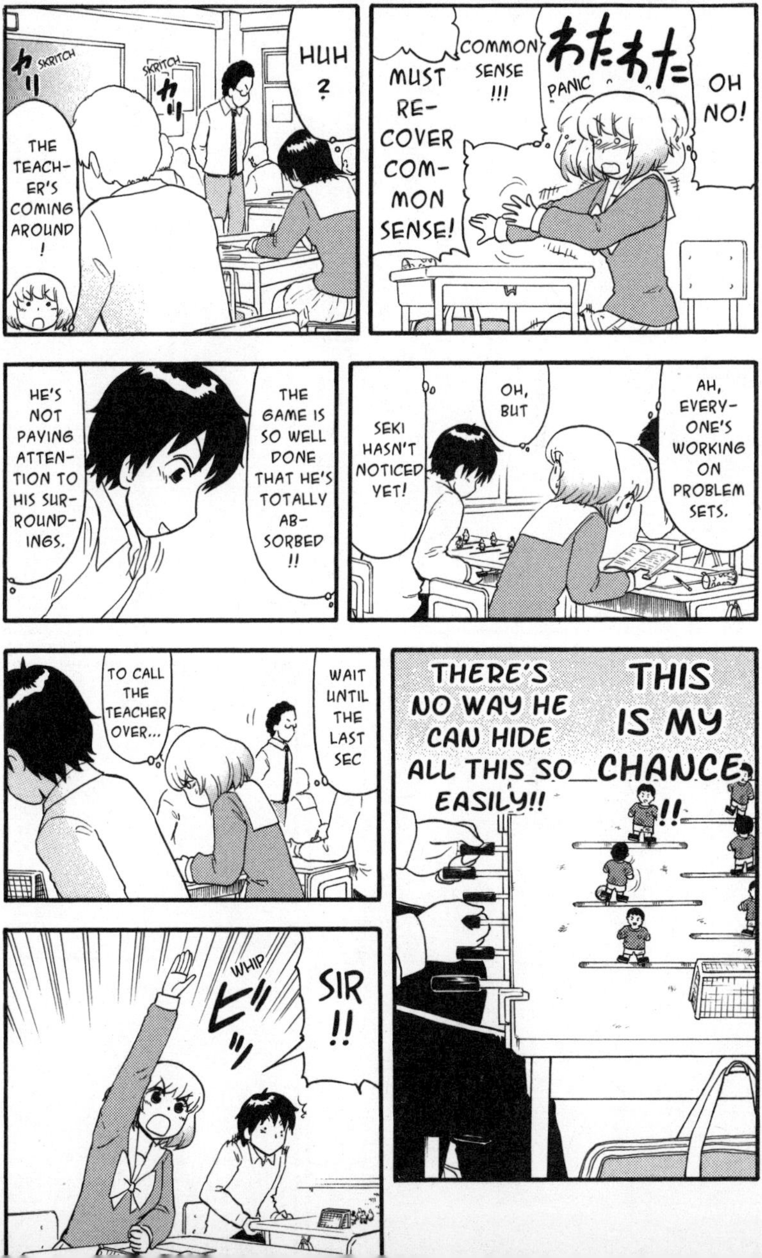
OH NO!
わたわた
PANIC
COMMON SENSE!!!
MUST RECOVER COMMON SENSE!
HUH?
カリ
SKRITCH
SKRITCH
カリ
THE TEACHER'S COMING AROUND!
AH, EVERYONE'S WORKING ON PROBLEM SETS.
OH, BUT
SEKI HASN'T NOTICED YET!
THE GAME IS SO WELL DONE THAT HE'S TOTALLY ABSORBED!!
HE'S NOT PAYING ATTENTION TO HIS SURROUNDINGS.
THIS IS MY CHANCE!!
THERE'S NO WAY HE CAN HIDE ALL THIS SO EASILY!!
WAIT UNTIL THE LAST SEC
TO CALL THE TEACHER OVER...
SIR!!
ビッ
WHIP

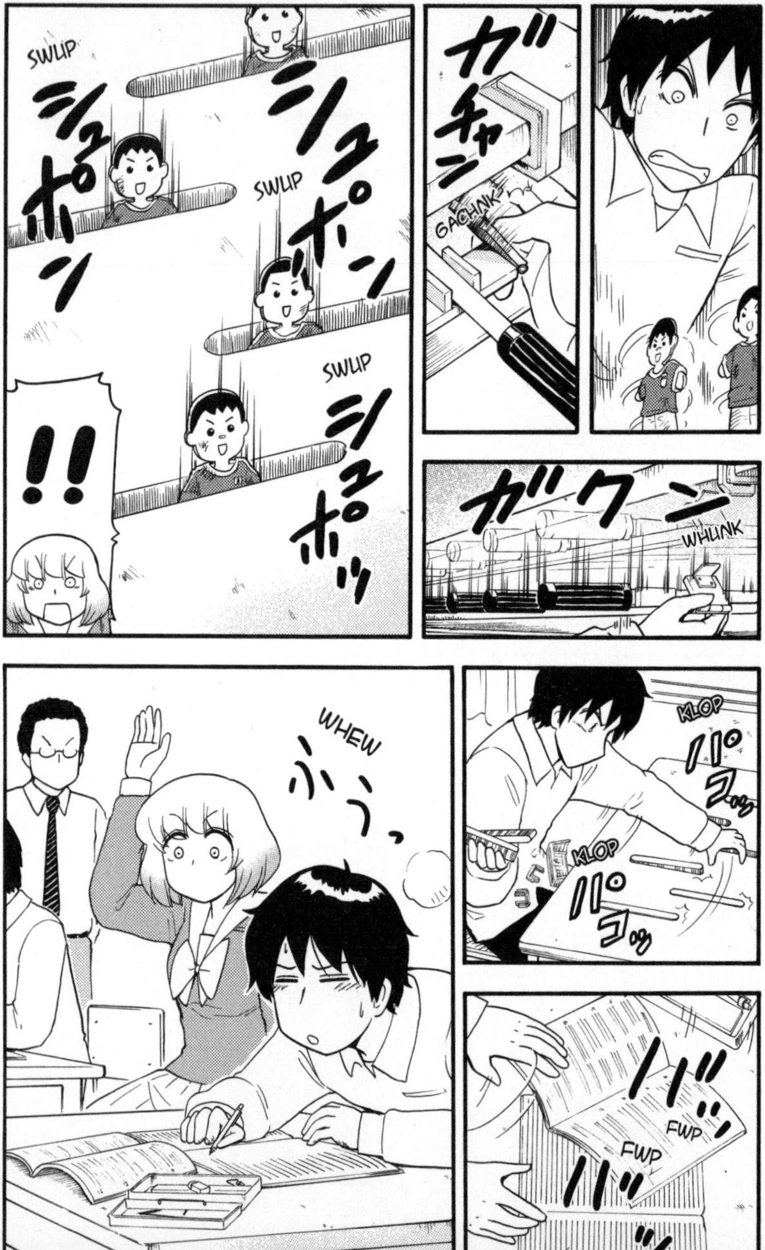

ガチャン
GACHNK
ガクン
WHUNK
SWLIP
シュポン
SWLIP
シュポン
SWLIP
シュポッ
!!
KLOP
パコッ
KLOP
パコッ
FWP
バッ
FWP
バッ
WHEW
ふぅっ

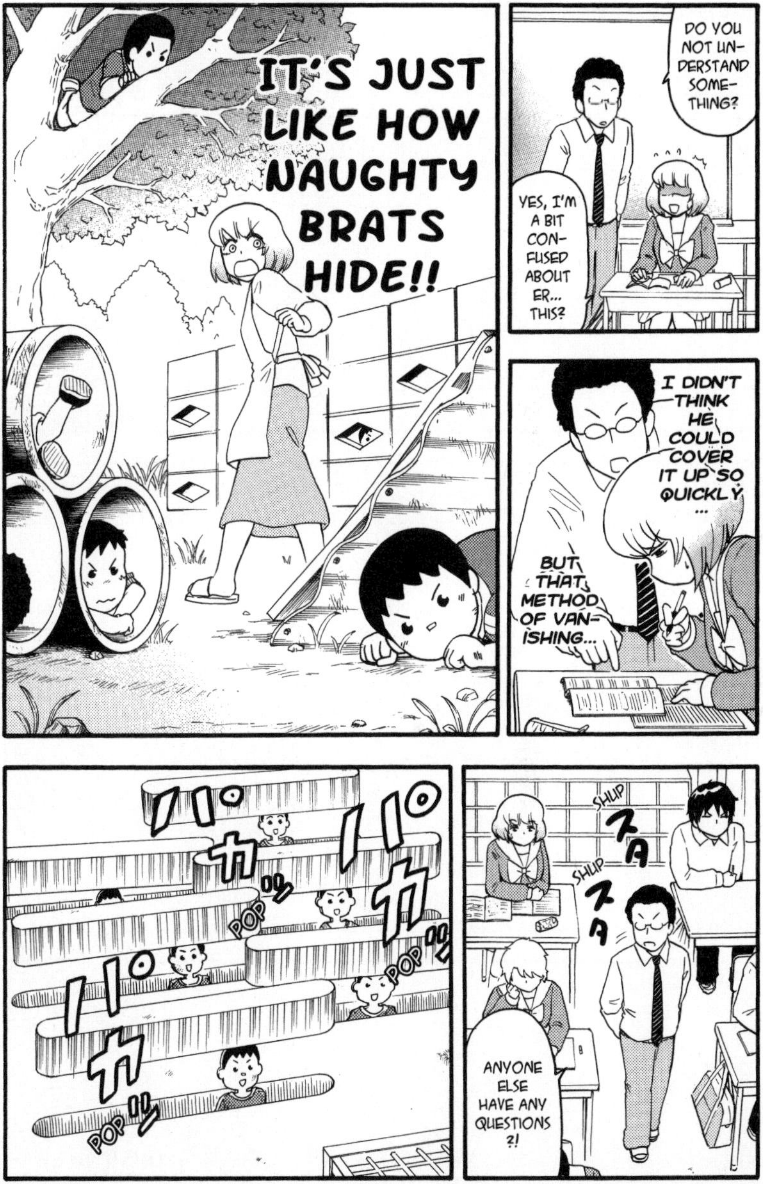
DO YOU NOT UNDERSTAND SOMETHING?
YES, I'M A BIT CONFUSED ABOUT ER... THIS?
I DIDN'T THINK HE COULD COVER IT UP SO QUICKLY...
BUT THAT METHOD OF VANISHING...
IT'S JUST LIKE HOW NAUGHTY BRATS HIDE!!
SHUP
スッ
SHUP
スッ
ANYONE ELSE HAVE ANY QUESTIONS?!
パカッ
POP
パカッ
POP
パカッ
POP

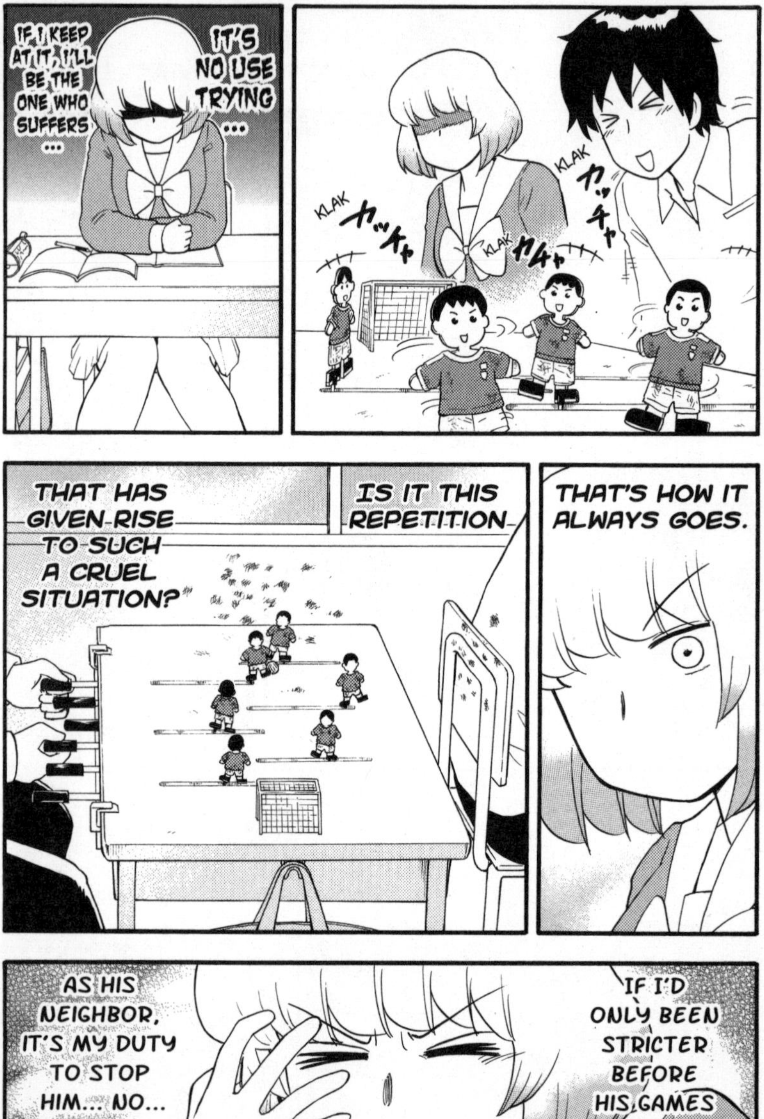
KLAK
KLAK
KLAK
IT'S NO USE TRYING...
IF I KEEP AT IT, I'LL BE THE ONE WHO SUFFERS...
THAT'S HOW IT ALWAYS GOES.
IS IT THIS REPETITION
THAT HAS GIVEN RISE TO SUCH A CRUEL SITUATION?
IF I'D ONLY BEEN STRICTER BEFORE HIS GAMES ESCALATED THIS FAR...
AS HIS NEIGHBOR, IT'S MY DUTY TO STOP HIM... NO...

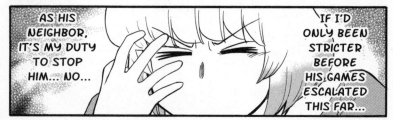

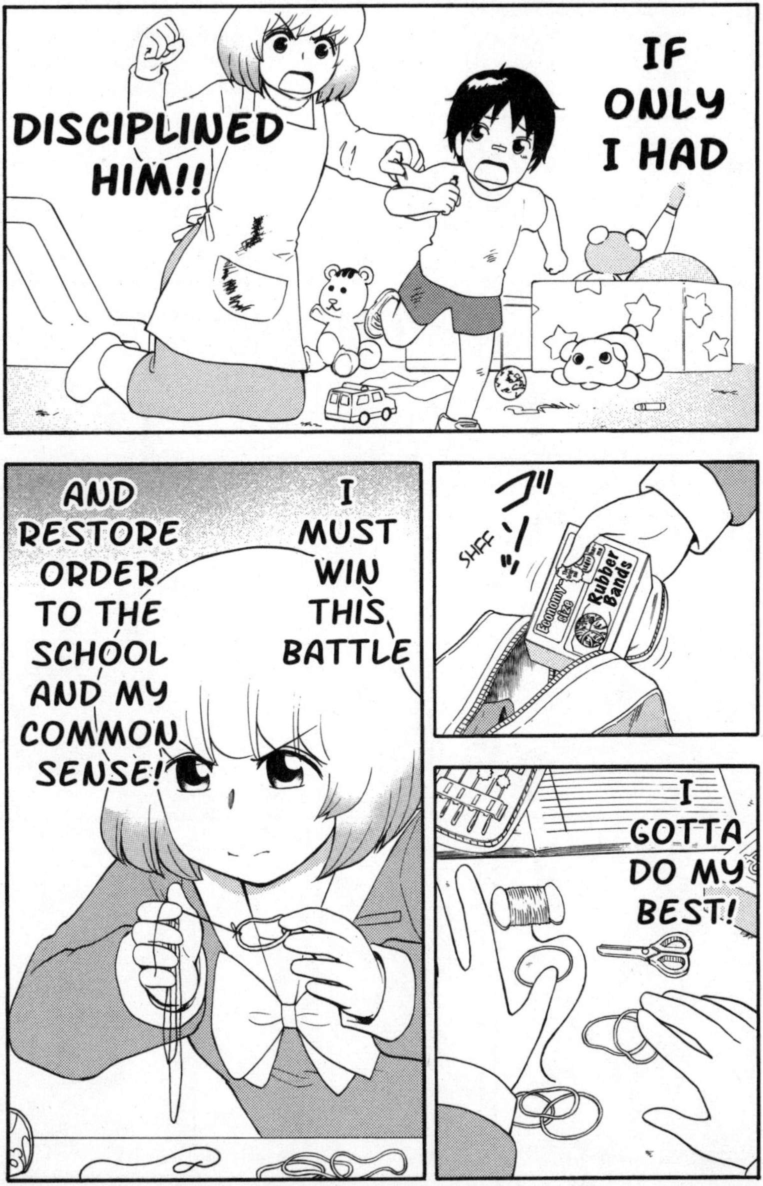
IF ONLY I HAD
DISCIPLINED HIM!!
ゴソッ
SHFF
Economy-size
Rubber Bands
I GOTTA DO MY BEST!
I MUST WIN THIS BATTLE
AND RESTORE ORDER TO THE SCHOOL AND MY COMMON SENSE!

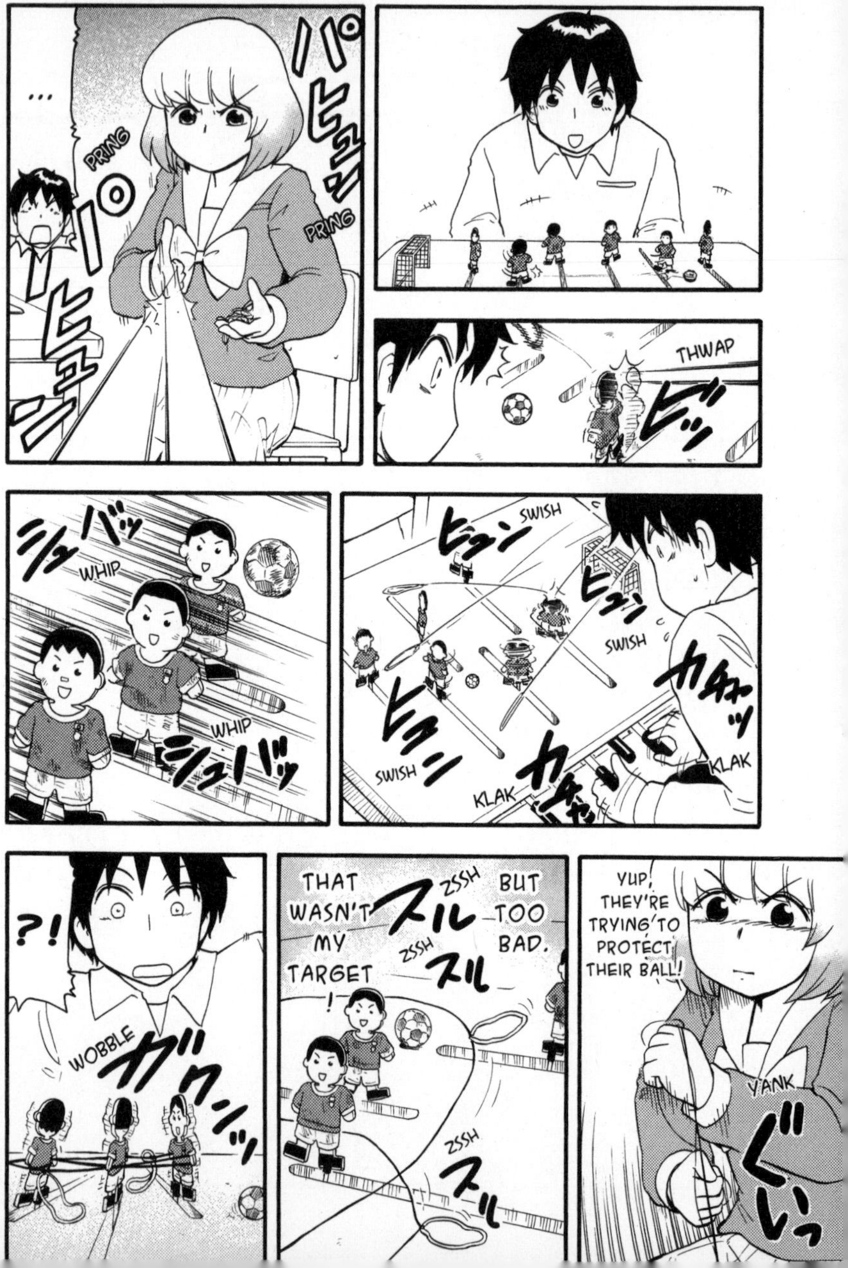

THWAP
ビッ
...
PRING
PRING
SWISH
ヒュン
SWISH
ヒュン
カチャッ
KLAK
SWISH
ヒュン
KLAK
WHIP
シュバッ
WHIP
シュバッ
YUP, THEY'RE TRYING TO PROTECT THEIR BALL!
YANK
ぐいっ
BUT TOO BAD.
ZSSH
スル
ZSSH
スル
THAT WASN'T MY TARGET!
ZSSH
スル
?!
WOBBLE
ガクンッ

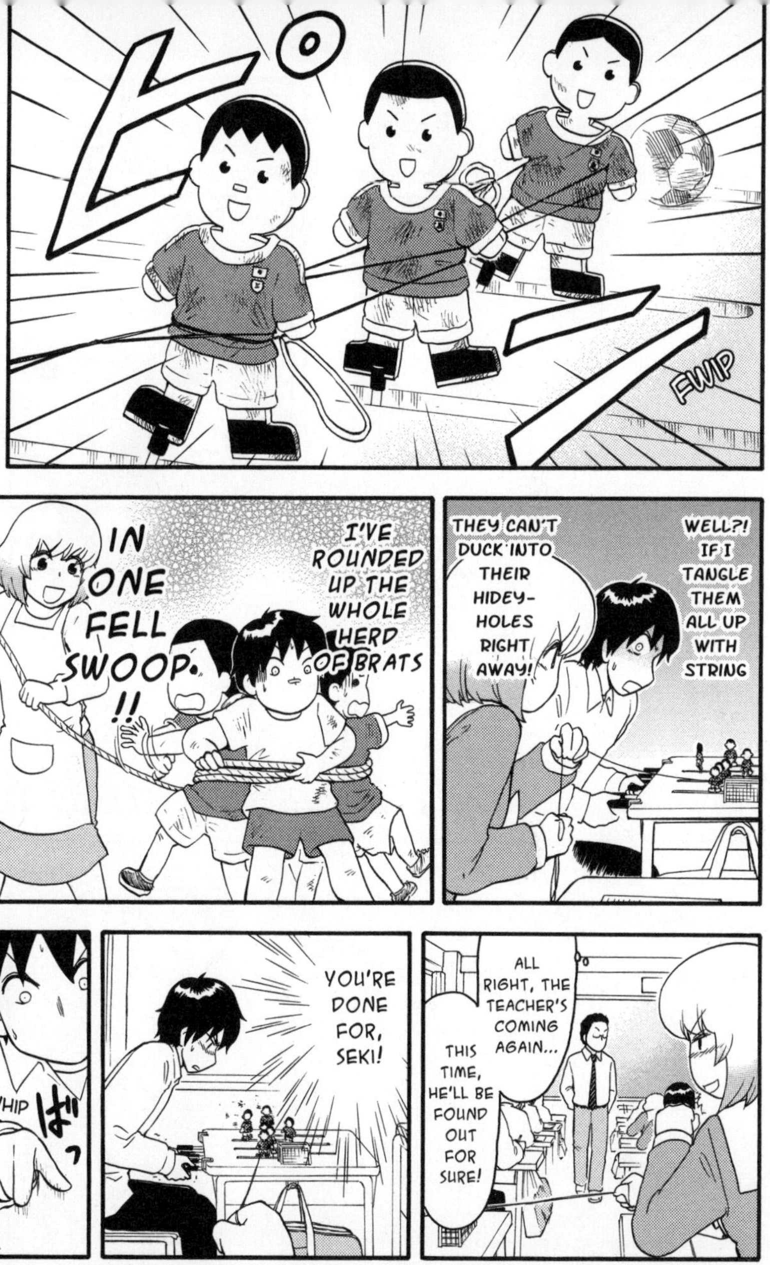
FWIP
WELL?! IF I TANGLE THEM ALL UP WITH STRING
THEY CAN'T DUCK INTO THEIR HIDEY-HOLES RIGHT AWAY!
I'VE ROUNDED UP THE WHOLE HERD OF BRATS
IN ONE FELL SWOOP!!
ALL RIGHT, THE TEACHER'S COMING AGAIN...
THIS TIME, HE'LL BE FOUND OUT FOR SURE!
YOU'RE DONE FOR, SEKI!
WHIP
ばっ

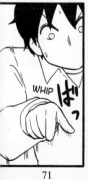

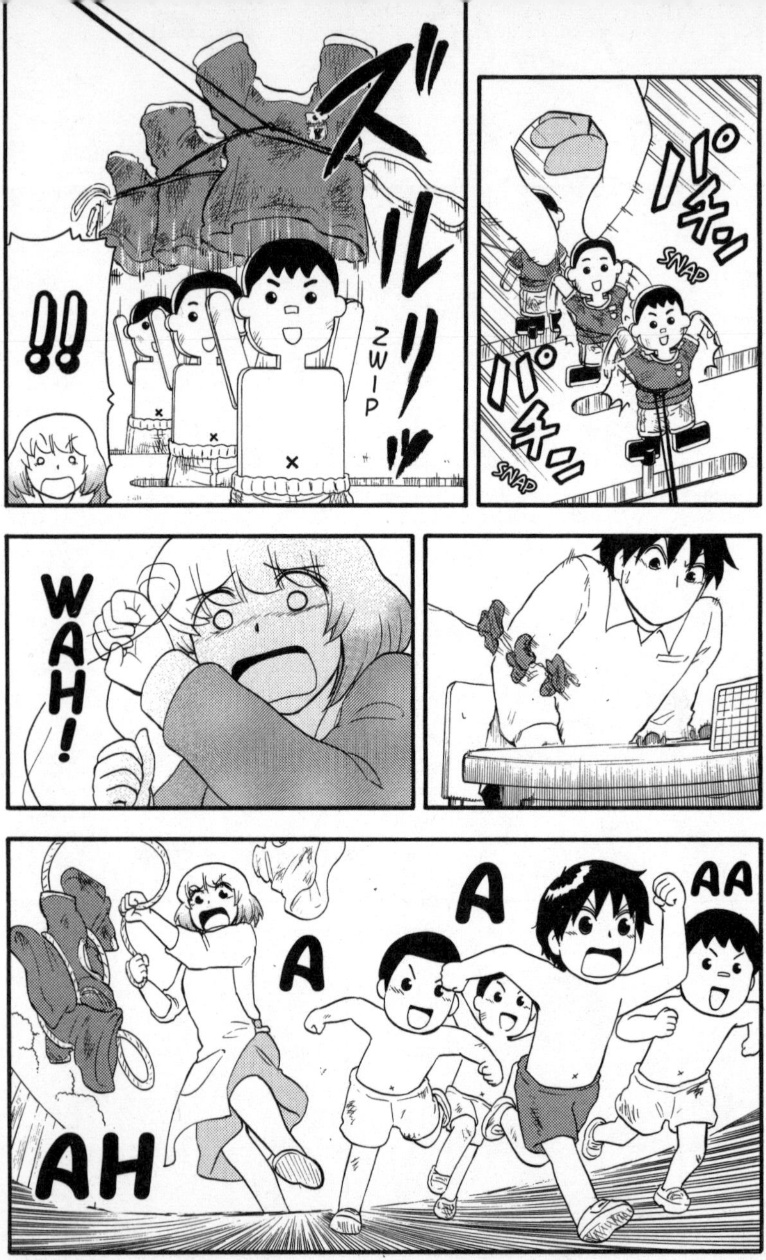

パチッ
SNAP
パチッ
SNAP
ズルリッ
ZWIP
!!
WAH!
AA
A
A
AH

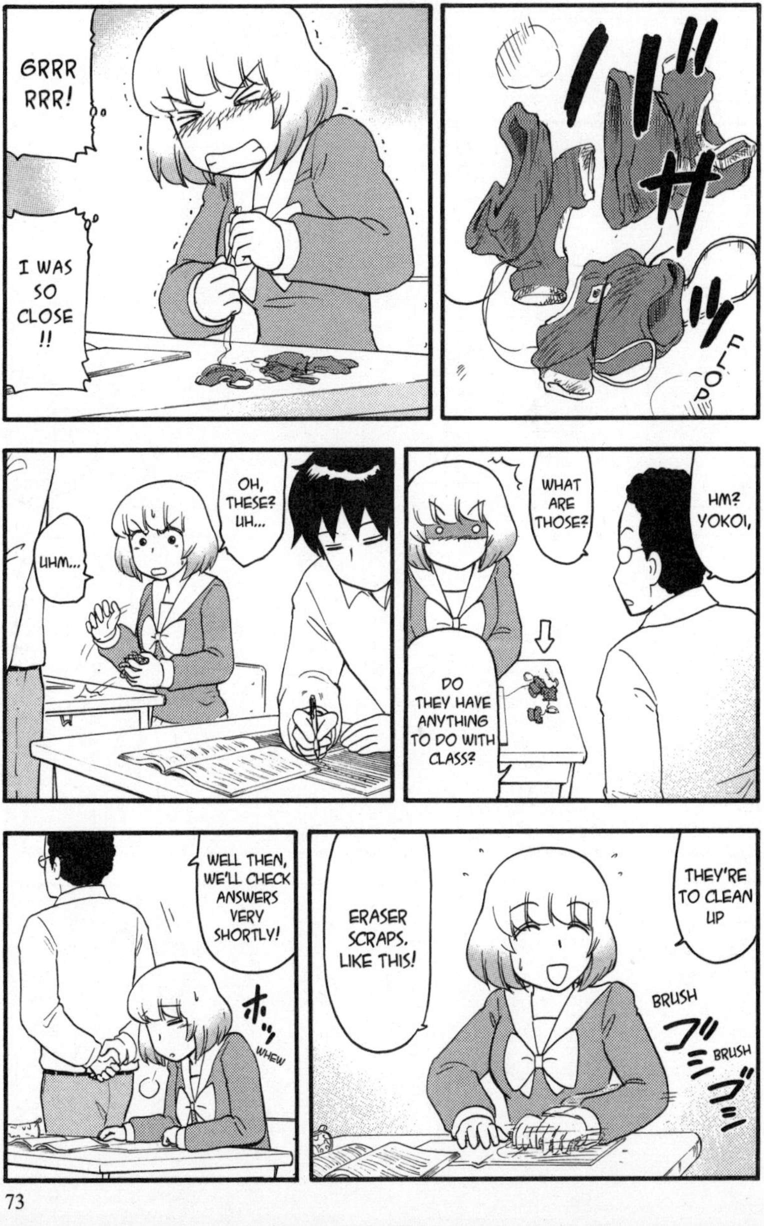
ガザッ
FLOP
GRRR RRR!
I WAS SO CLOSE !!
HM? YOKOI,
WHAT ARE THOSE?
DO THEY HAVE ANYTHING TO DO WITH CLASS?
OH, THESE? UH...
UHM...
THEY'RE TO CLEAN UP
ERASER SCRAPS, LIKE THIS!
ゴシゴシ
BRUSH
BRUSH
WELL THEN, WE'LL CHECK ANSWERS VERY SHORTLY!
ホッ
WHEW

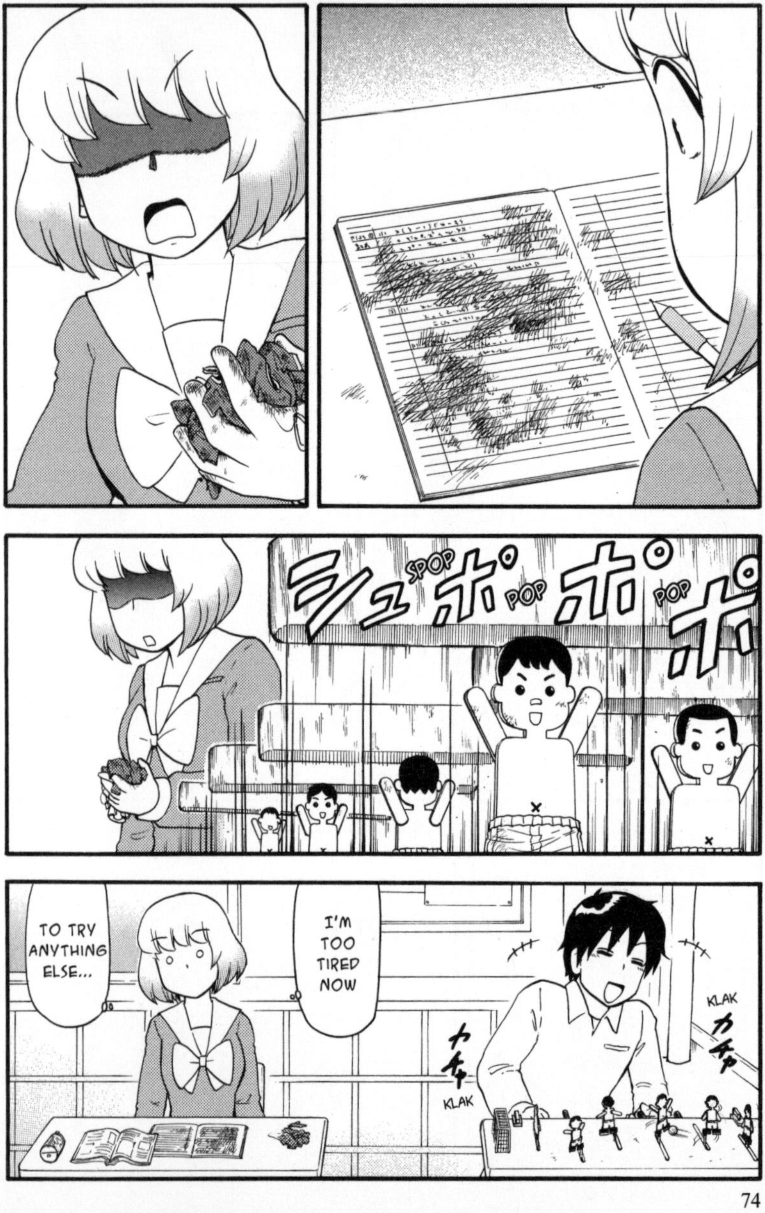
シュポ
SPOP
ポ
POP
ポ
POP
KLAK
カチャ
I'M TOO TIRED NOW
TO TRY ANYTHING ELSE...
カチャ
KLAK

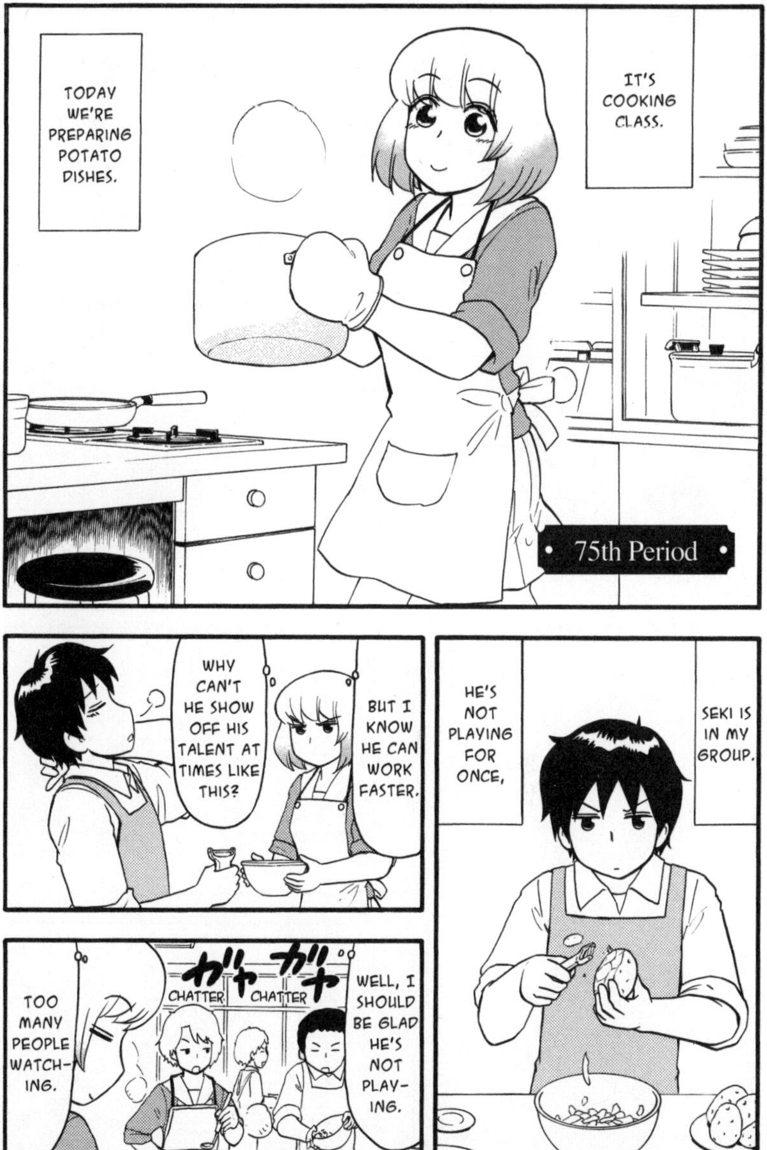
IT'S COOKING CLASS.
TODAY WE'RE PREPARING POTATO DISHES.
75th Period
SEKI IS IN MY GROUP.
HE'S NOT PLAYING FOR ONCE,
BUT I KNOW HE CAN WORK FASTER.
WHY CAN'T HE SHOW OFF HIS TALENT AT TIMES LIKE THIS?
WELL, I SHOULD BE GLAD HE'S NOT PLAY-ING.
ガヤ ガヤ
CHATTER CHATTER
TOO MANY PEOPLE WATCH-ING.

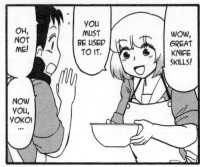

I'M DONE.
IS THIS HOW YOU WANTED THEM?
WOW, GREAT KNIFE SKILLS!
YOU MUST BE USED TO IT.
OH, NOT ME!
NOW YOU, YOKOI ...
I'M GLAD WE'RE GROUP MATES, GOTO!
FSH
HM?
DID SEKI JUST MAKE A STRANGELY SWIFT MOVE...?
BUB
HUB
SHADY.
DID HE TOUCH ...
THE BOILED EGGS FOR THE POTATO SALAD?
HMM ...
DID SEKI
Cake Flour

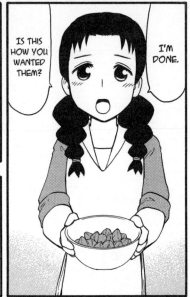

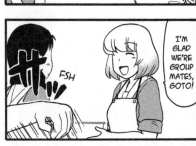

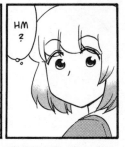

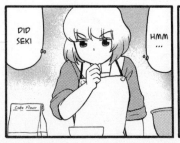

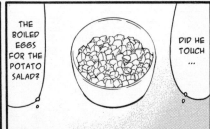

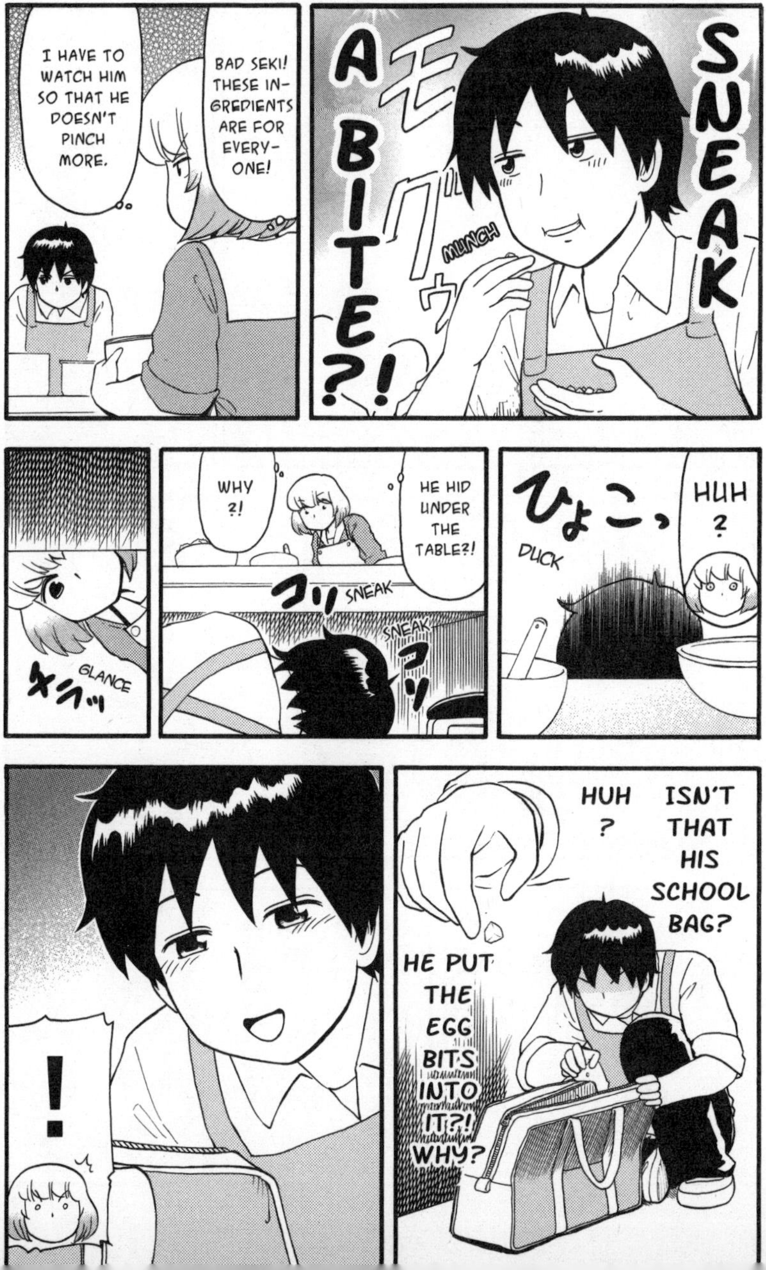
SNEAK
A BITE?!
MUNCH
BAD SEKI! THESE INGREDIENTS ARE FOR EVERYONE!
I HAVE TO WATCH HIM SO THAT HE DOESN'T PINCH MORE.
HUH?
ひょこっ
DUCK
HE HID UNDER THE TABLE?!
WHY?!
SNEAK
SNEAK
GLANCE
ISN'T THAT HIS SCHOOL BAG?
HUH?
HE PUT THE EGG BITS INTO IT?! WHY?
!

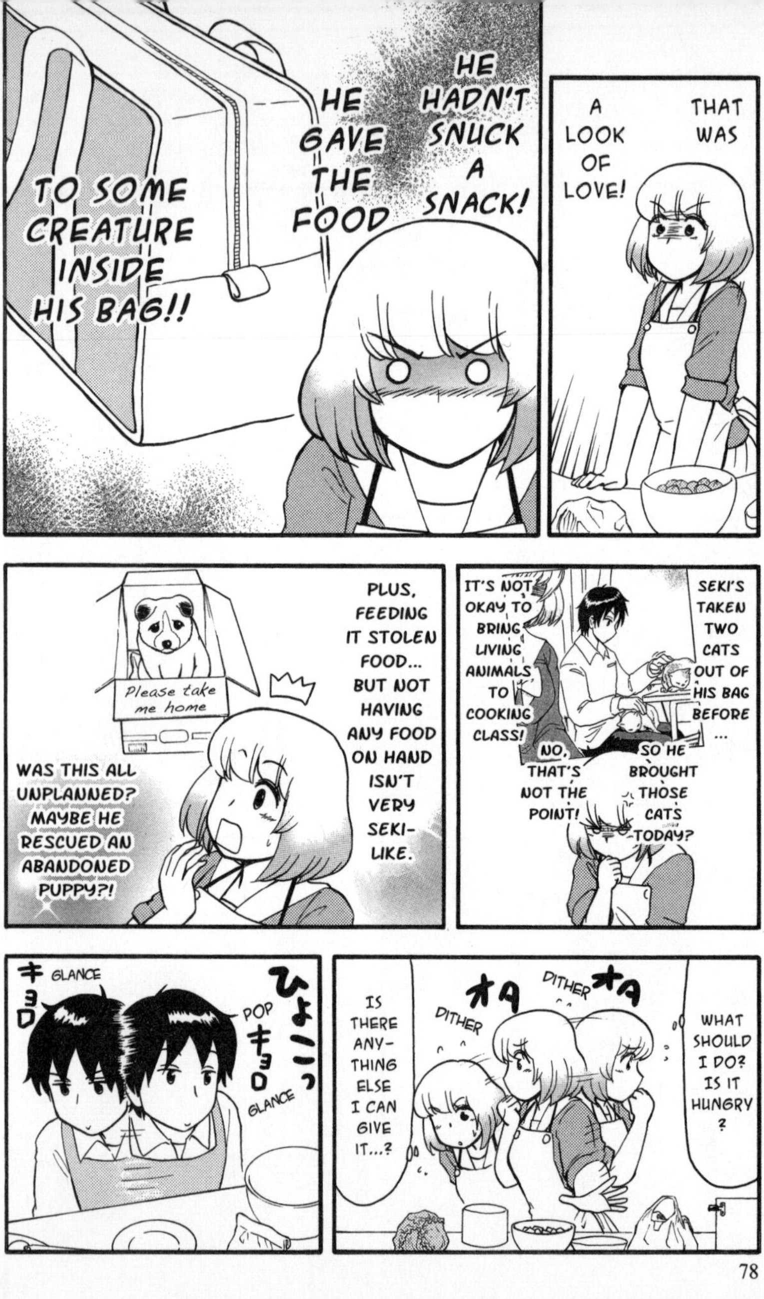
THAT WAS A LOOK OF LOVE!
HE HADN'T SNUCK A SNACK!
HE GAVE THE FOOD
TO SOME CREATURE INSIDE HIS BAG!!
SEKI'S TAKEN TWO CATS OUT OF HIS BAG BEFORE...
SO HE BROUGHT THOSE CATS TODAY?
IT'S NOT OKAY TO BRING LIVING ANIMALS TO COOKING CLASS!
NO, THAT'S NOT THE POINT!
PLUS, FEEDING IT STOLEN FOOD... BUT NOT HAVING ANY FOOD ON HAND ISN'T VERY SEKI-LIKE.
Please take me home
WAS THIS ALL UNPLANNED? MAYBE HE RESCUED AN ABANDONED PUPPY?!
WHAT SHOULD I DO? IS IT HUNGRY?
オタ
DITHER
オタ
DITHER
IS THERE ANY-THING ELSE I CAN GIVE IT...?
ひょこっ
POP
キョロ
GLANCE
キョロ
GLANCE

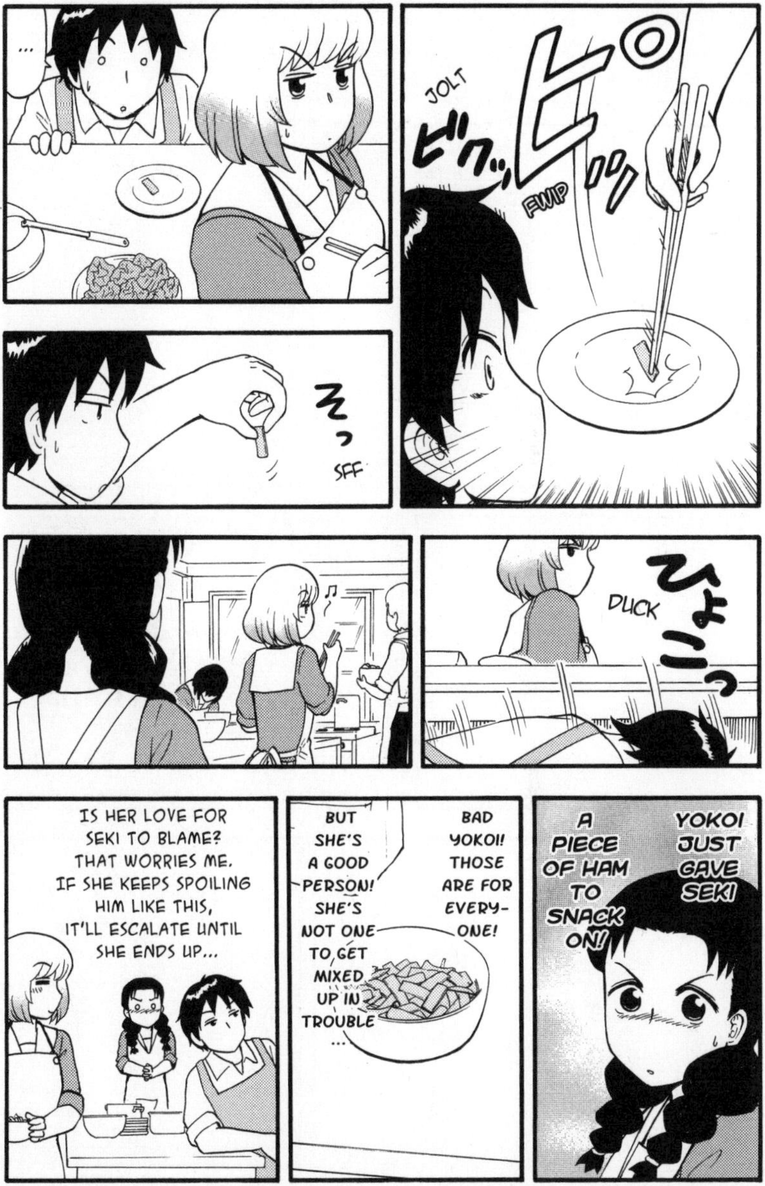
ビクッ
JOLT
ピッ
FWIP
...
そっ
SFF
ひょこっ
DUCK
YOKOI JUST GAVE SEKI
A PIECE OF HAM TO SNACK ON!
BAD YOKOI! THOSE ARE FOR EVERY-ONE!
BUT SHE'S A GOOD PERSON! SHE'S NOT ONE TO GET MIXED UP IN TROUBLE ...
IS HER LOVE FOR SEKI TO BLAME? THAT WORRIES ME. IF SHE KEEPS SPOILING HIM LIKE THIS, IT'LL ESCALATE UNTIL SHE ENDS UP...

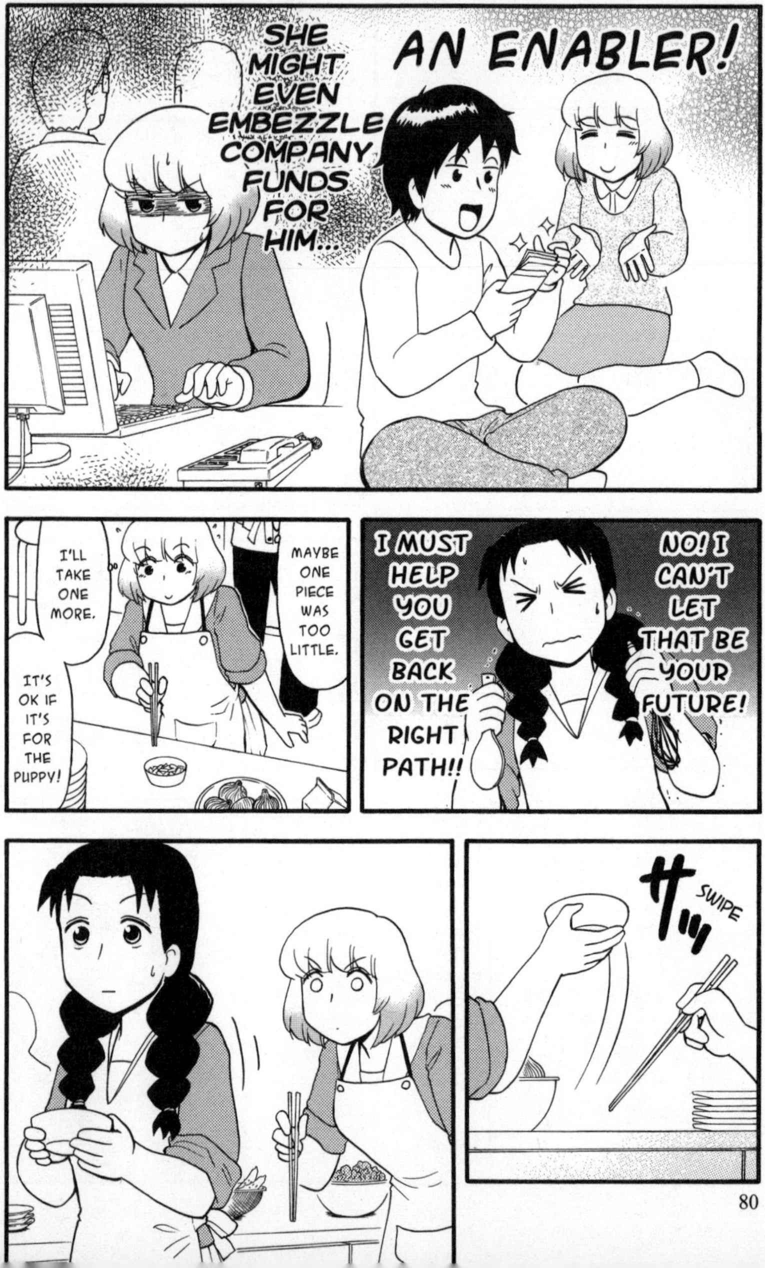
SHE MIGHT EVEN EMBEZZLE COMPANY FUNDS FOR HIM...
AN ENABLER!
I'LL TAKE ONE MORE.
IT'S OK IF IT'S FOR THE PUPPY!
MAYBE ONE PIECE WAS TOO LITTLE.
NO! I CAN'T LET THAT BE YOUR FUTURE!
I MUST HELP YOU GET BACK ON THE RIGHT PATH!!
SWIPE

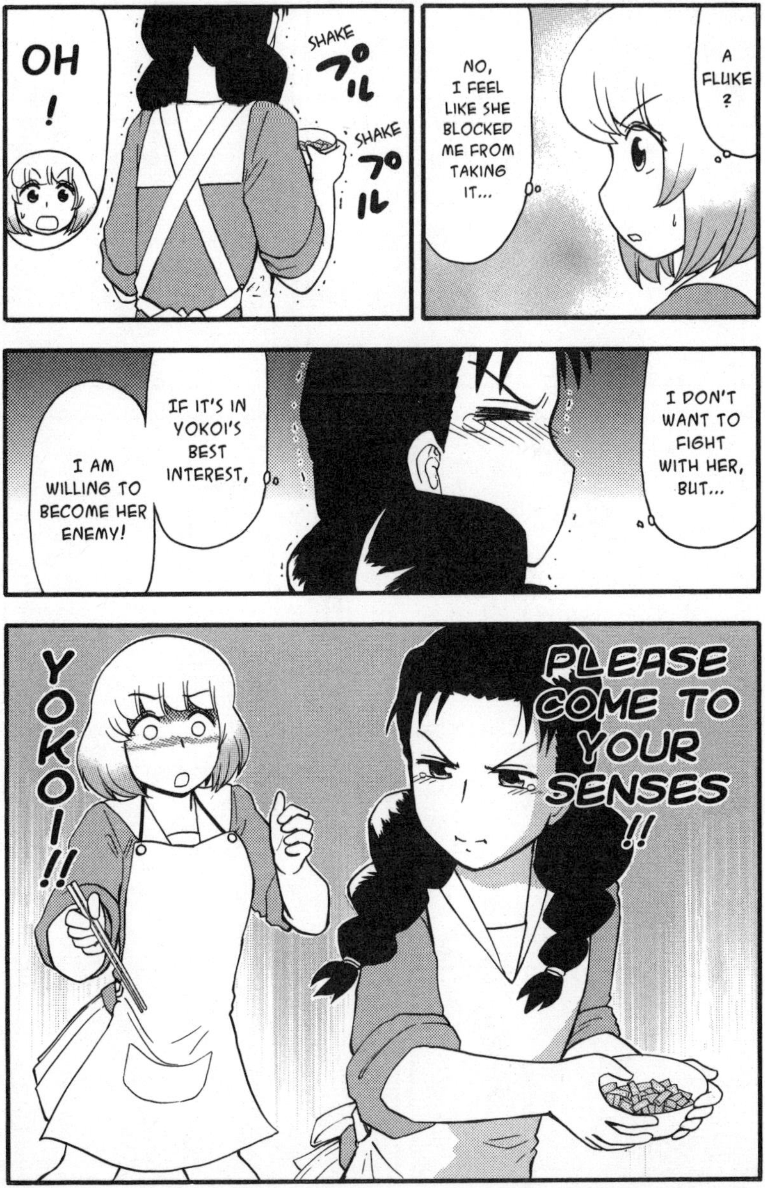
A FLUKE?
NO, I FEEL LIKE SHE BLOCKED ME FROM TAKING IT...
SHAKE プル
SHAKE プル
OH!
I DON'T WANT TO FIGHT WITH HER, BUT...
IF IT'S IN YOKOI'S BEST INTEREST,
I AM WILLING TO BECOME HER ENEMY!
PLEASE COME TO YOUR SENSES!!
YOKOI!!

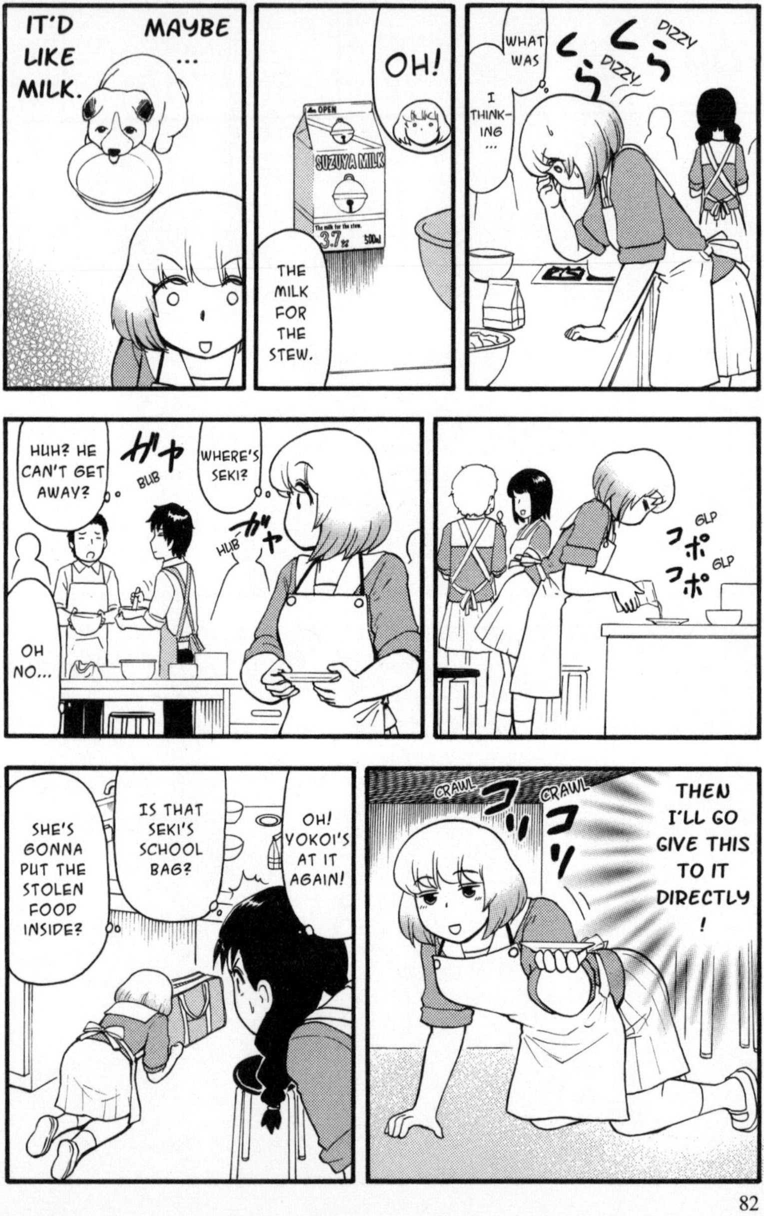
WHAT WAS I THINKING...
くら DIZZY
くら DIZZY
OH!
OPEN
SUZUYA MILK
The milk for the stew.
3.7
500ml
THE MILK FOR THE STEW.
MAYBE...
IT'D LIKE MILK.
コポ GLP
コポ GLP
WHERE'S SEKI?
ガヤ BUB
ガヤ HUB
HUH? HE CAN'T GET AWAY?
OH NO...
コソ CRAWL
コソ CRAWL
THEN I'LL GO GIVE THIS TO IT DIRECTLY!
OH! YOKOI'S AT IT AGAIN!
IS THAT SEKI'S SCHOOL BAG?
SHE'S GONNA PUT THE STOLEN FOOD INSIDE?

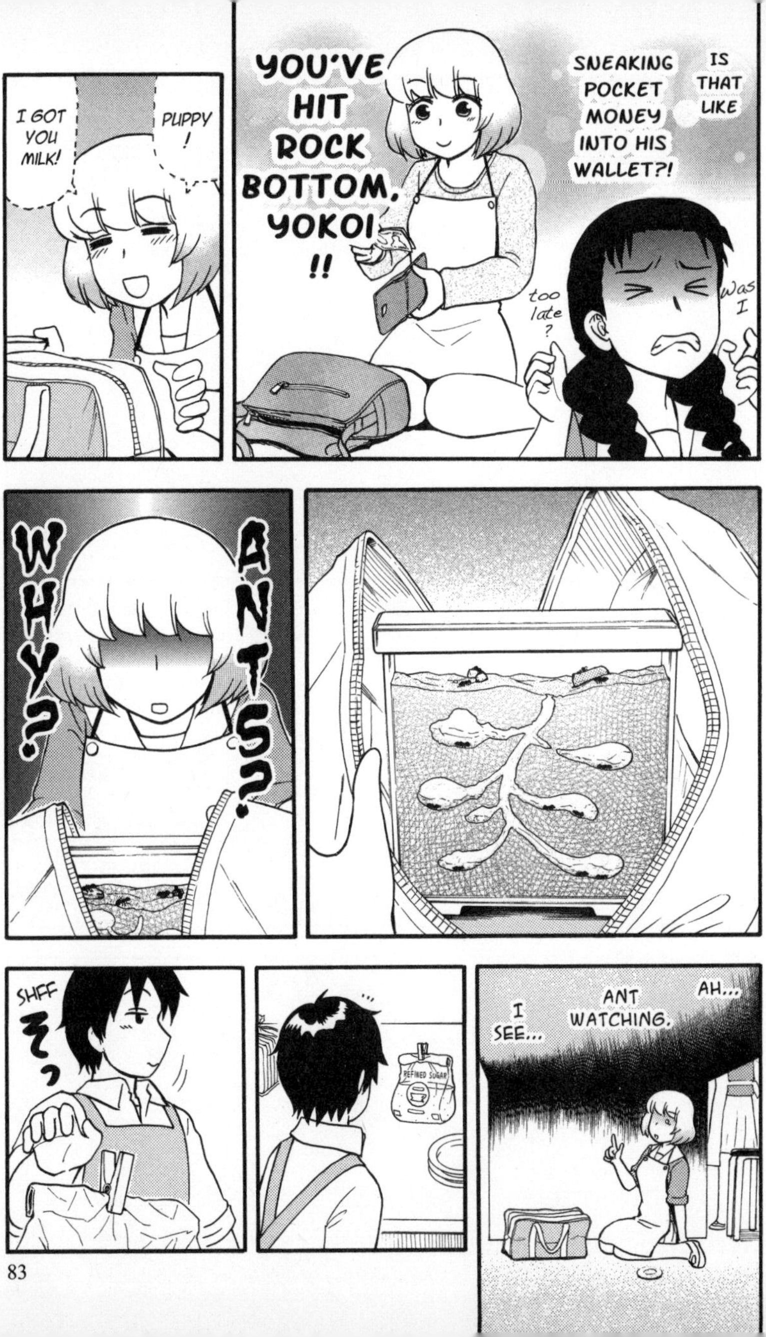
IS THAT LIKE
SNEAKING POCKET MONEY INTO HIS WALLET?!
YOU'VE HIT ROCK BOTTOM, YOKOI!!
Was I too late?
PUPPY!
I GOT YOU MILK!
ANTS?
WHY?
AH...
ANT WATCHING.
I SEE...
REFINED SUGAR
...
SHFF
そっ

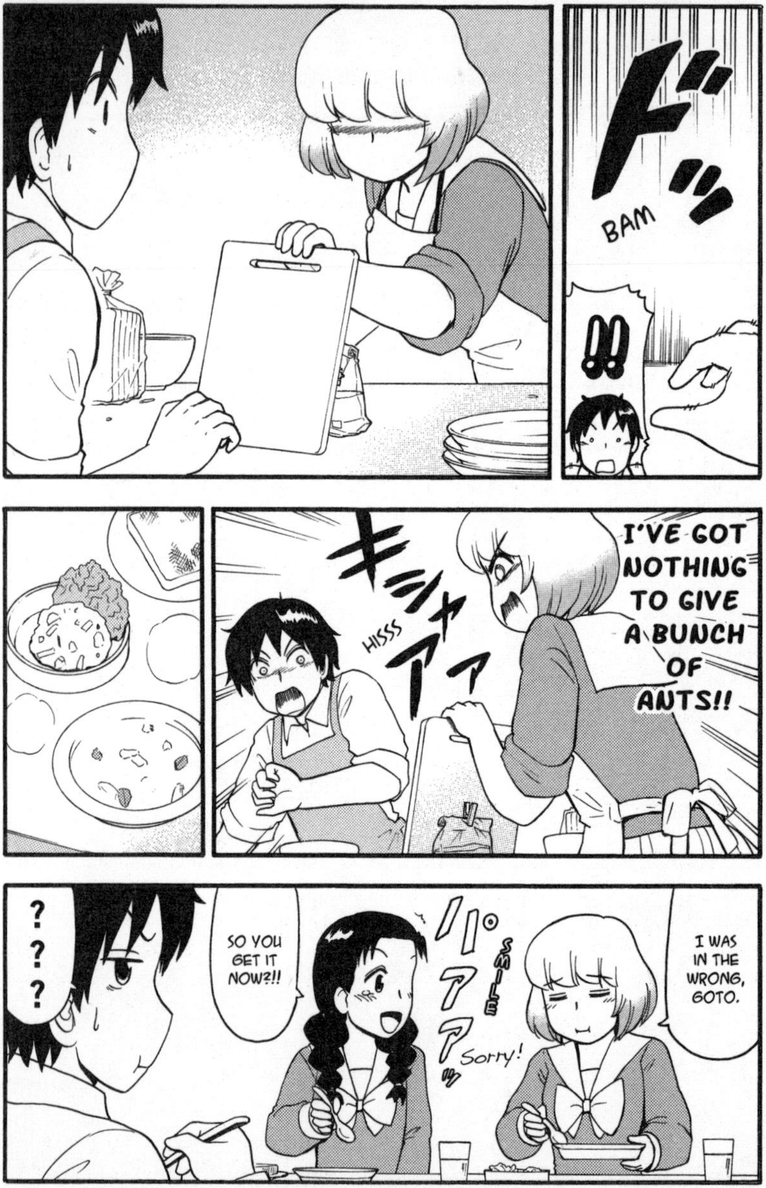
ドッ
BAM
!!
キシャア
HISSS
I'VE GOT NOTHING TO GIVE A BUNCH OF ANTS!!
I WAS IN THE WRONG, GOTO.
パアアッ
SMILE
Sorry!
SO YOU GET IT NOW?!!
???

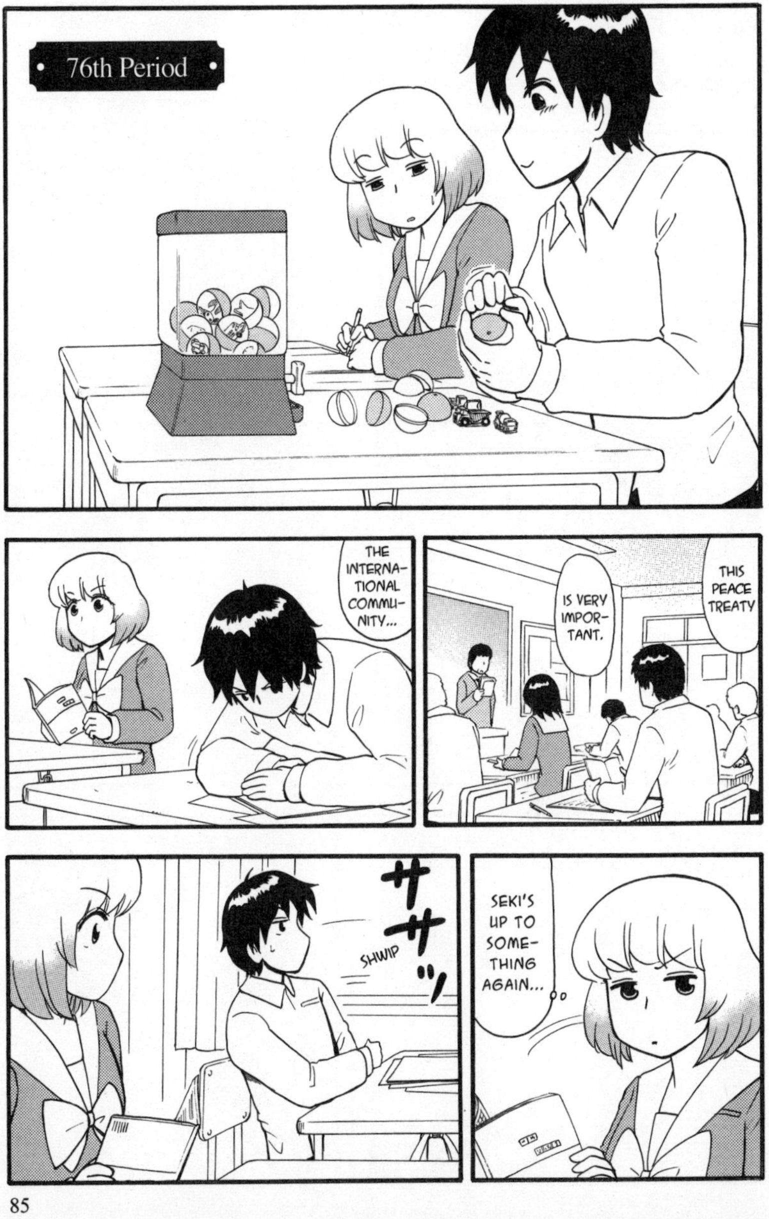
76th Period
THIS PEACE TREATY
IS VERY IMPORTANT.
THE INTERNATIONAL COMMUNITY...
SEKI'S UP TO SOMETHING AGAIN...
ササッ
SHWIP

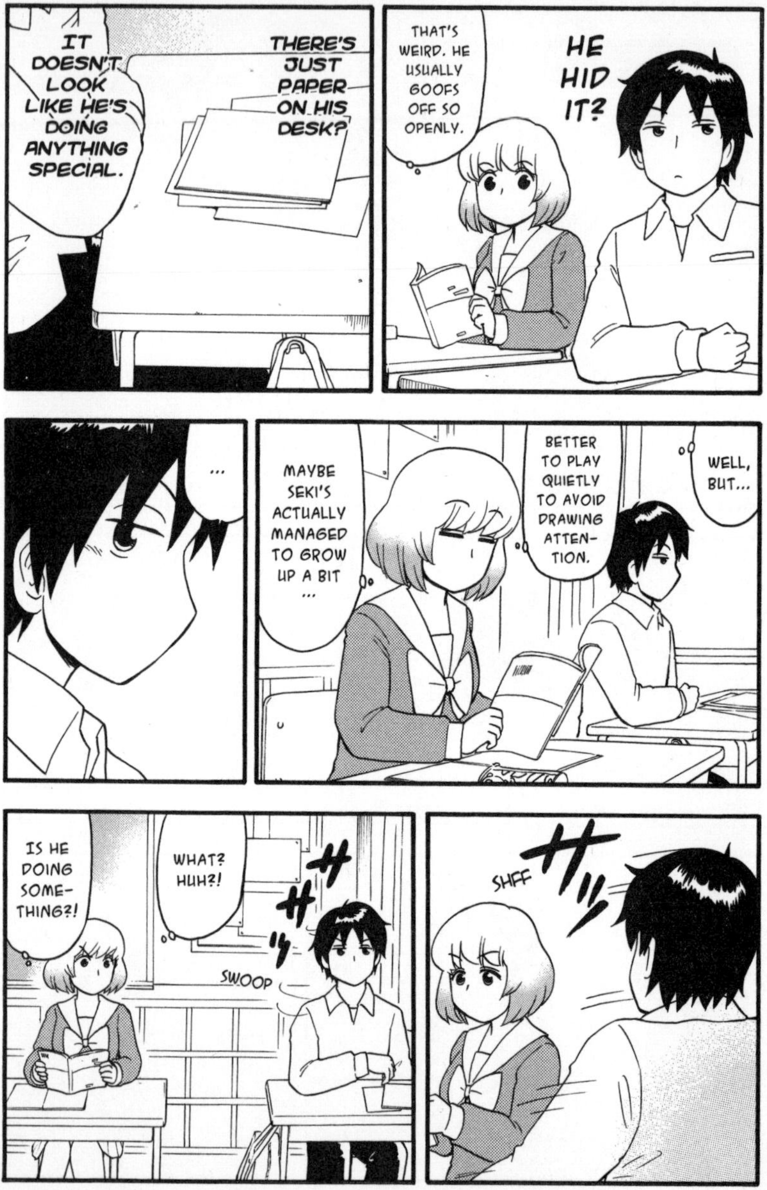
HE HID IT?
THAT'S WEIRD. HE USUALLY GOOFS OFF SO OPENLY.
THERE'S JUST PAPER ON HIS DESK?
IT DOESN'T LOOK LIKE HE'S DOING ANYTHING SPECIAL.
WELL, BUT...
BETTER TO PLAY QUIETLY TO AVOID DRAWING ATTENTION.
MAYBE SEKI'S ACTUALLY MANAGED TO GROW UP A BIT...
...
SHFF
WHAT? HUH?!
SWOOP
IS HE DOING SOMETHING?!

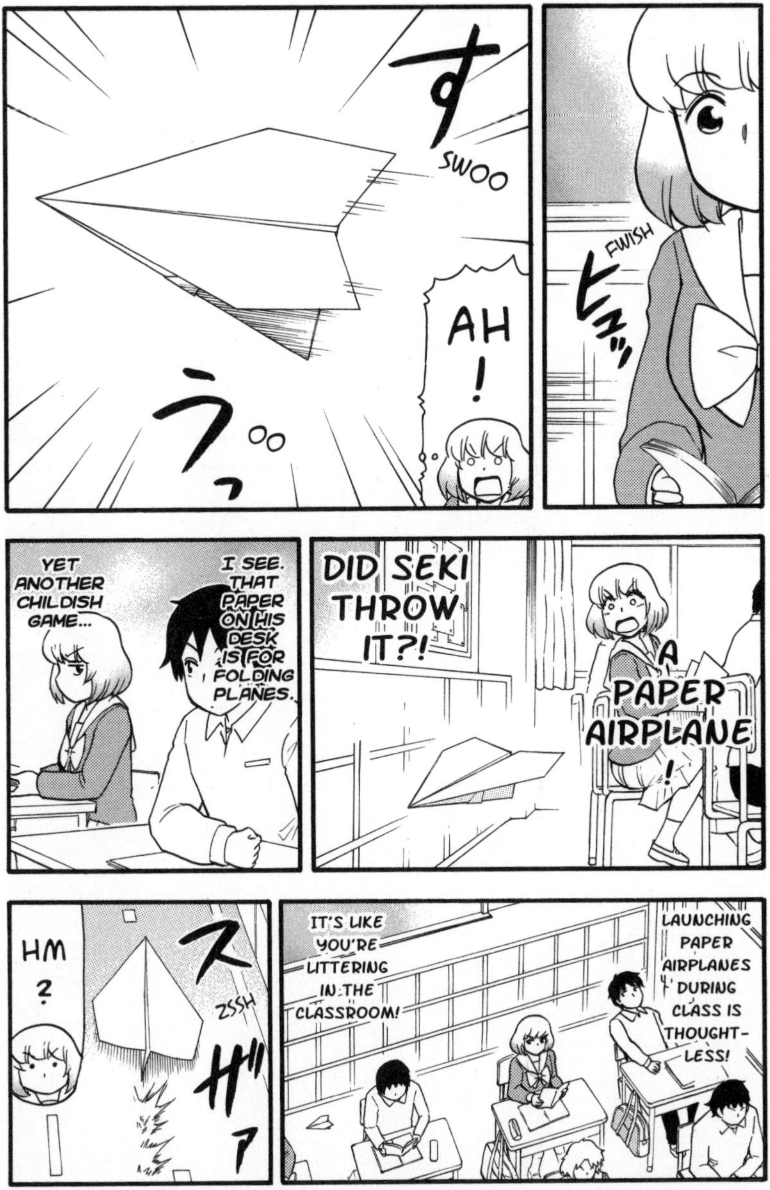
ヒュッ
FWISH
すうっ
SWOO
AH!
A PAPER AIRPLANE!
DID SEKI THROW IT?!
I SEE. THAT PAPER ON HIS DESK IS FOR FOLDING PLANES.
YET ANOTHER CHILDISH GAME...
LAUNCHING PAPER AIRPLANES DURING CLASS IS THOUGHTLESS!
IT'S LIKE YOU'RE LITTERING IN THE CLASSROOM!
スザァ
ZSSH
HM?

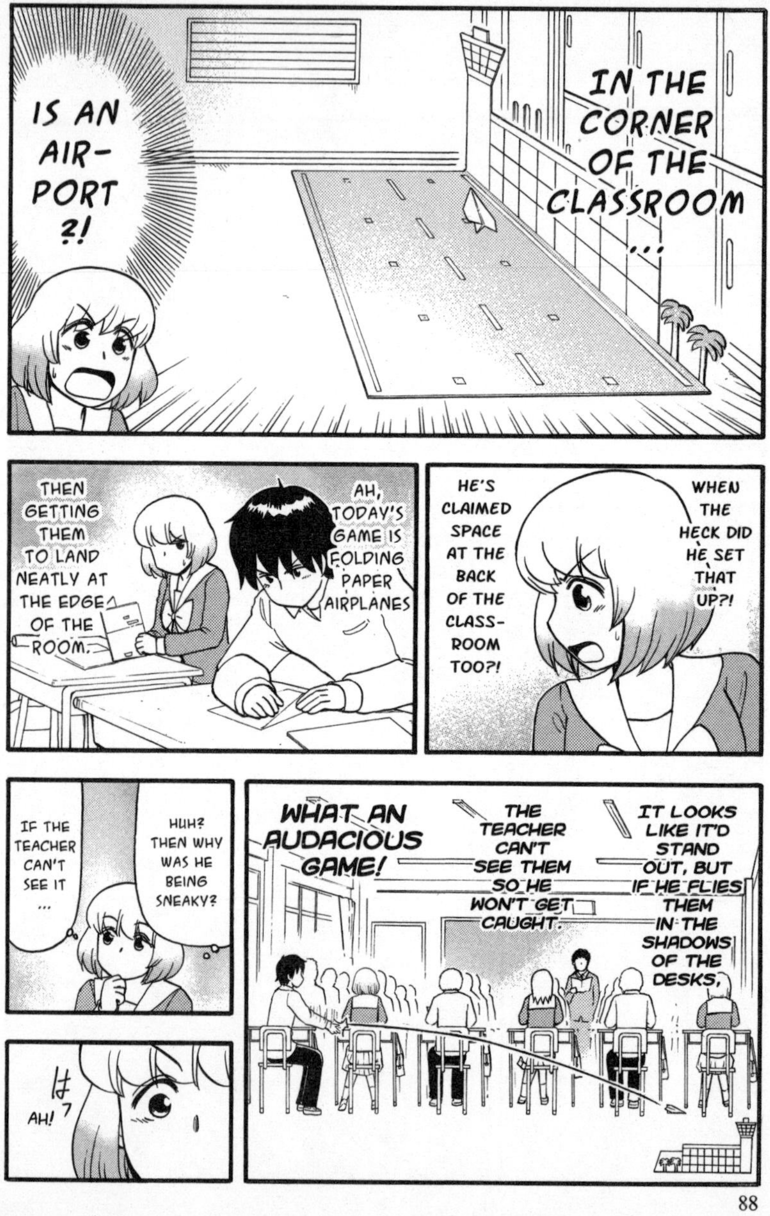
IN THE CORNER OF THE CLASSROOM...
IS AN AIR-PORT ?!
WHEN THE HECK DID HE SET THAT UP?!
HE'S CLAIMED SPACE AT THE BACK OF THE CLASS-ROOM TOO?!
AH, TODAY'S GAME IS FOLDING PAPER AIRPLANES
THEN GETTING THEM TO LAND NEATLY AT THE EDGE OF THE ROOM.
IT LOOKS LIKE IT'D STAND OUT, BUT IF HE FLIES THEM IN THE SHADOWS OF THE DESKS,
THE TEACHER CAN'T SEE THEM SO HE WON'T GET CAUGHT.
WHAT AN AUDACIOUS GAME!
HUH? THEN WHY WAS HE BEING SNEAKY?
IF THE TEACHER CAN'T SEE IT ...
は
AH!

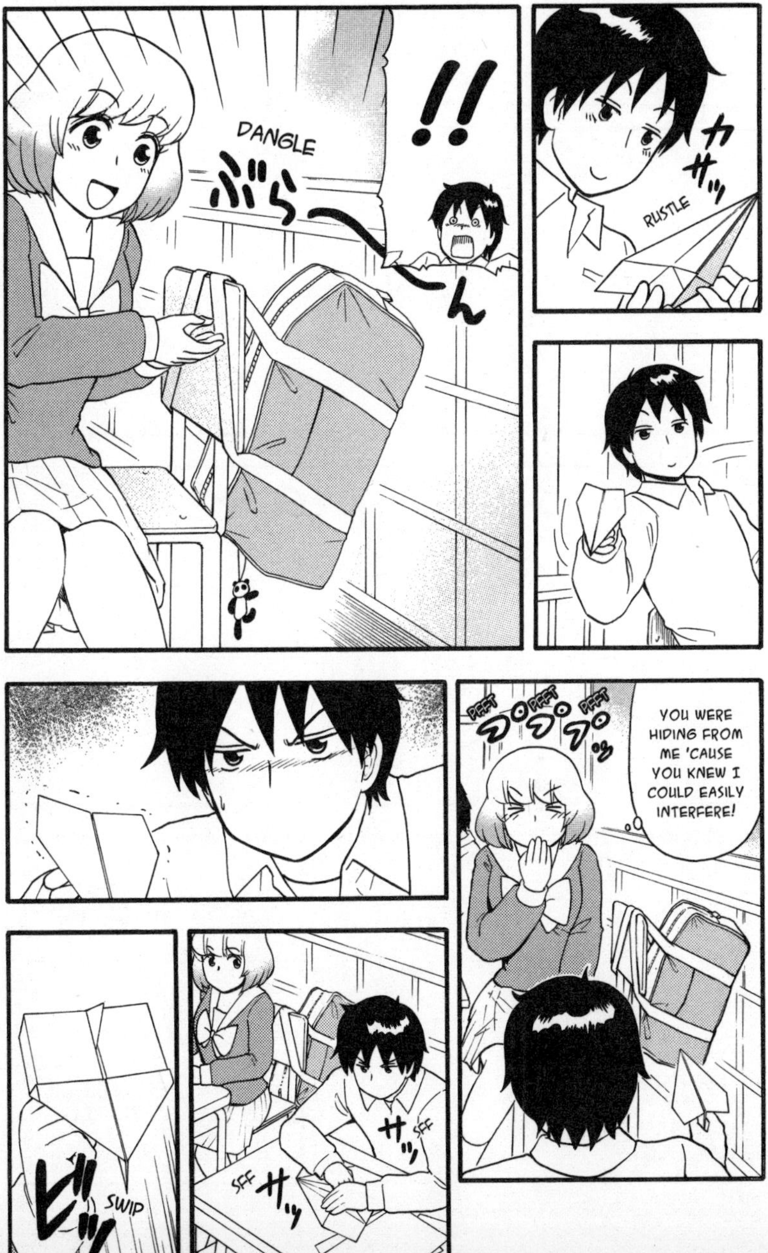

カサッ
RUSTLE
!!
DANGLE
ぶら〜〜ん
PFFT PFFT PFFT
プププ
YOU WERE HIDING FROM ME 'CAUSE YOU KNEW I COULD EASILY INTERFERE!
SFF
サッ
SFF
サッ
ビッ
SWIP

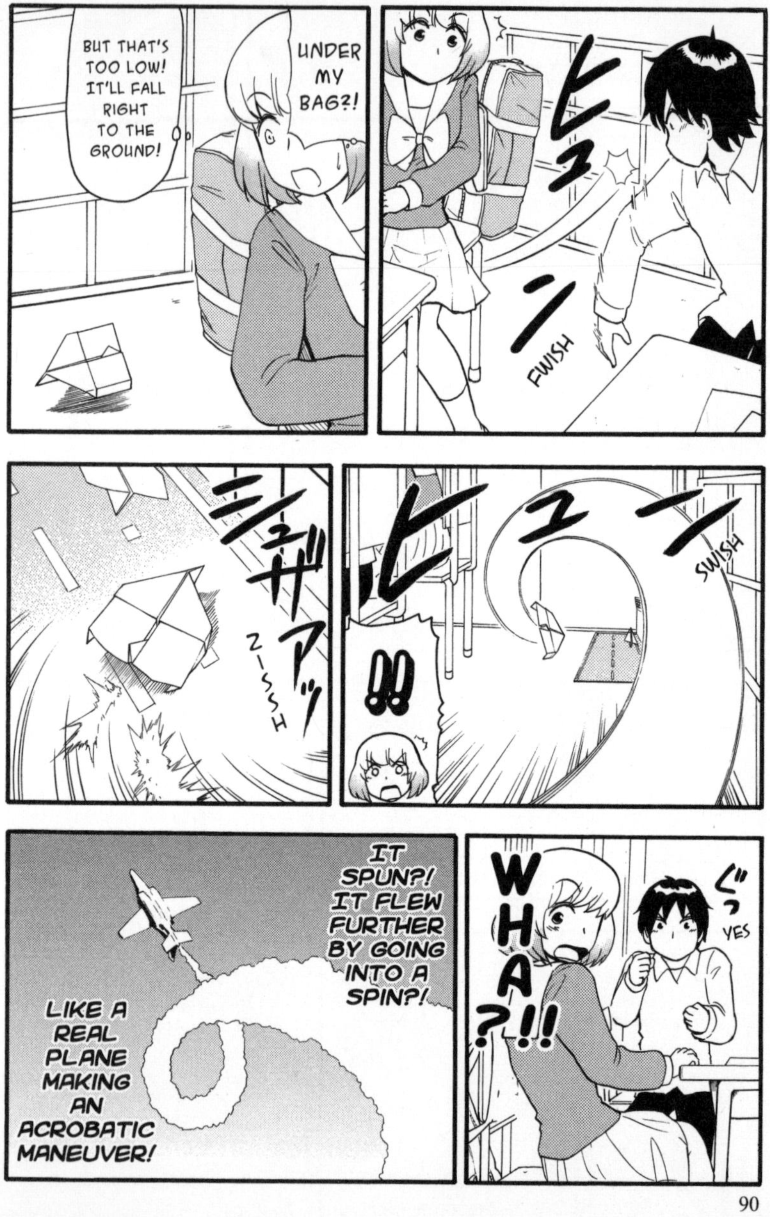

ヒュン
FWISH
UNDER MY BAG?!
BUT THAT'S TOO LOW! IT'LL FALL RIGHT TO THE GROUND!
ヒュン
SWISH
!!
シュザアッ
Z-SSSH
WHA?!!
ぐっ
YES
IT SPUN?! IT FLEW FURTHER BY GOING INTO A SPIN?!
LIKE A REAL PLANE MAKING AN ACROBATIC MANEUVER!

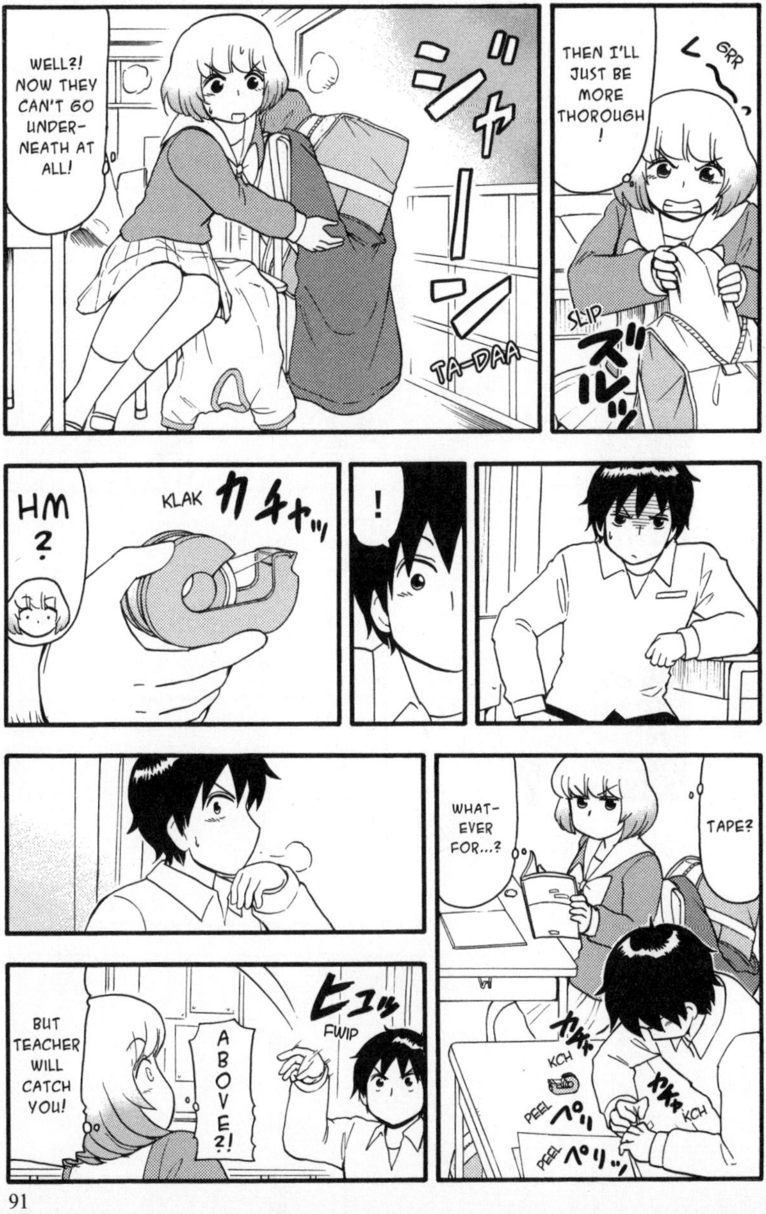
GRR
THEN I'LL JUST BE MORE THOROUGH!
SLIP
WELL?! NOW THEY CAN'T GO UNDERNEATH AT ALL!
TA-DAA
!
KLAK
HM?
TAPE?
WHATEVER FOR...?
KCH
KCH
PEEL
PEEL
FWIP
ABOVE?!
BUT TEACHER WILL CATCH YOU!

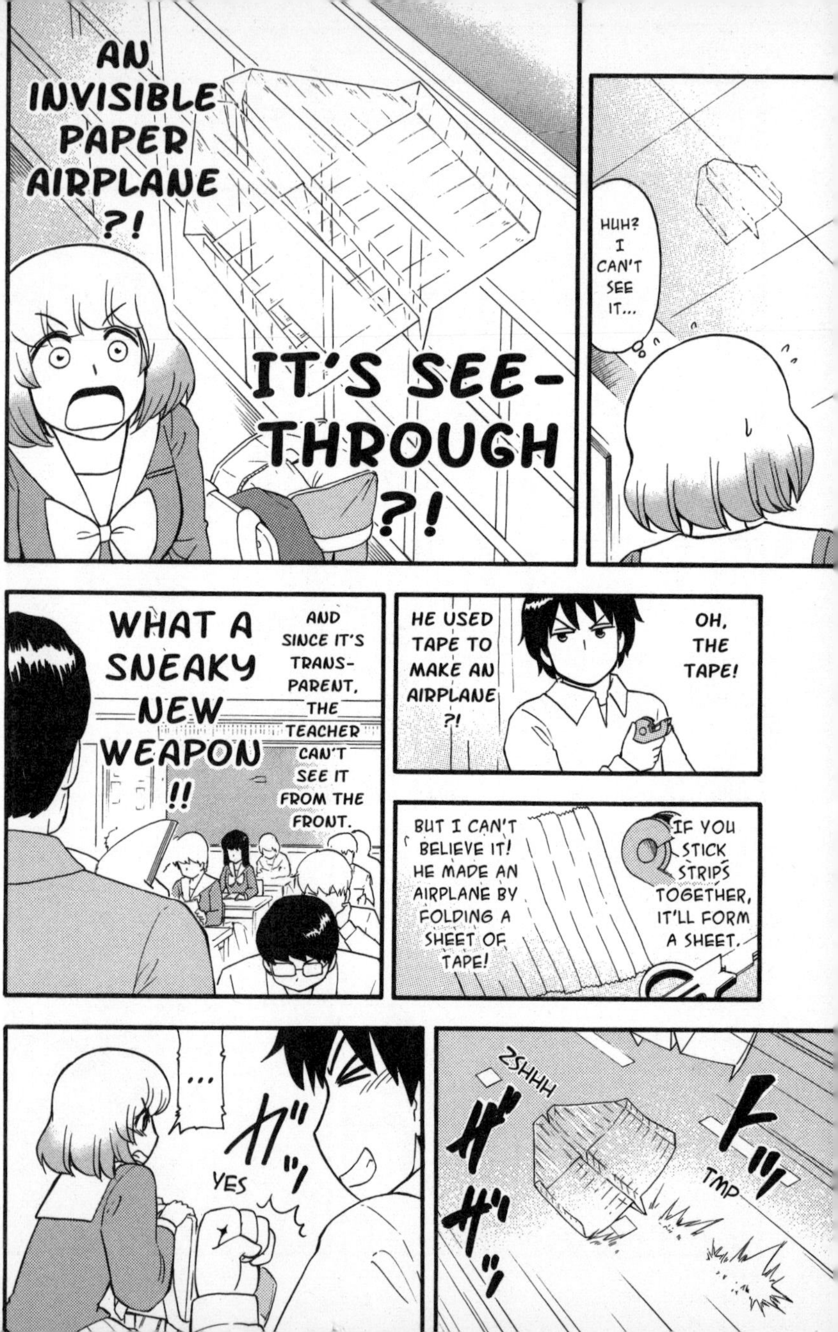
HUH? I CAN'T SEE IT...
AN INVISIBLE PAPER AIRPLANE ?!
IT'S SEE-THROUGH ?!
OH, THE TAPE!
HE USED TAPE TO MAKE AN AIRPLANE ?!
IF YOU STICK STRIPS TOGETHER, IT'LL FORM A SHEET.
BUT I CAN'T BELIEVE IT! HE MADE AN AIRPLANE BY FOLDING A SHEET OF TAPE!
AND SINCE IT'S TRANS-PARENT, THE TEACHER CAN'T SEE IT FROM THE FRONT.
WHAT A SNEAKY NEW WEAPON !!
TMP
ZSHHH
YES
...

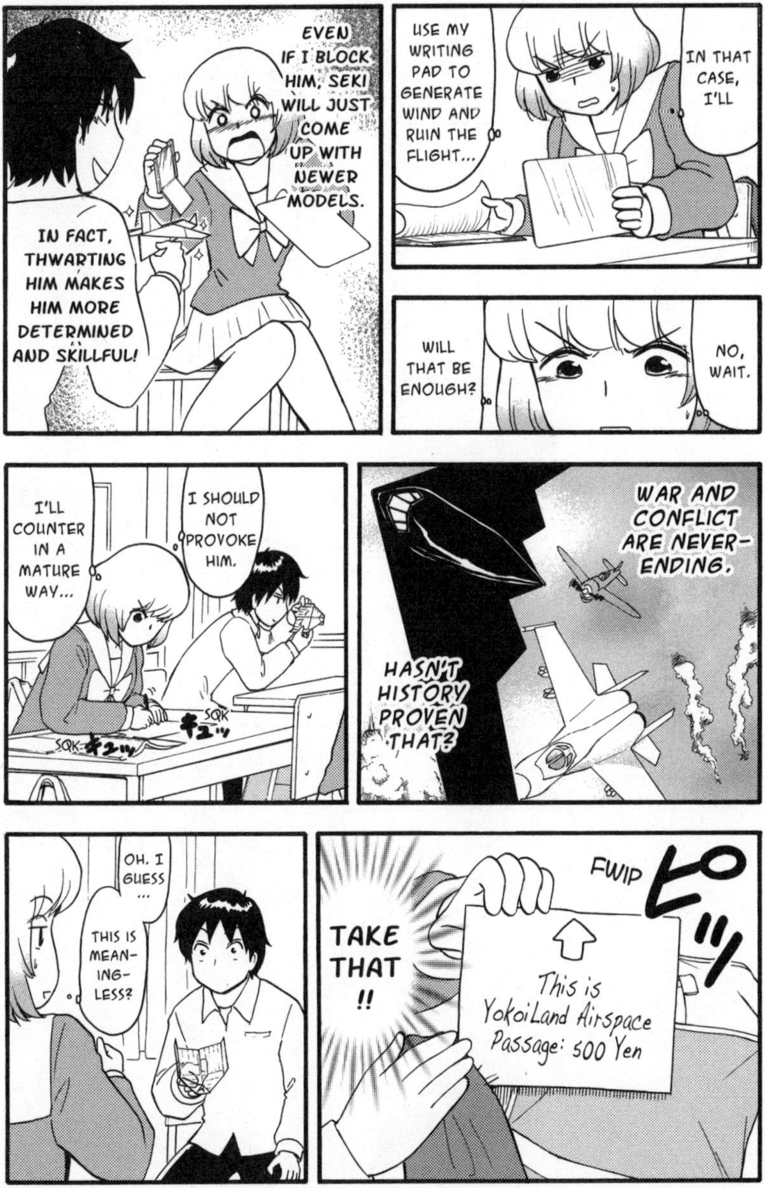
IN THAT CASE, I'LL
USE MY WRITING PAD TO GENERATE WIND AND RUIN THE FLIGHT...
NO, WAIT.
WILL THAT BE ENOUGH?
EVEN IF I BLOCK HIM, SEKI WILL JUST COME UP WITH NEWER MODELS.
IN FACT, THWARTING HIM MAKES HIM MORE DETERMINED AND SKILLFUL!
WAR AND CONFLICT ARE NEVER-ENDING.
HASN'T HISTORY PROVEN THAT?
I SHOULD NOT PROVOKE HIM.
I'LL COUNTER IN A MATURE WAY...
SQK
SQK
FWIP
TAKE THAT !!
This is YokoiLand Airspace
Passage: 500 Yen
OH. I GUESS ...
THIS IS MEAN-ING-LESS?

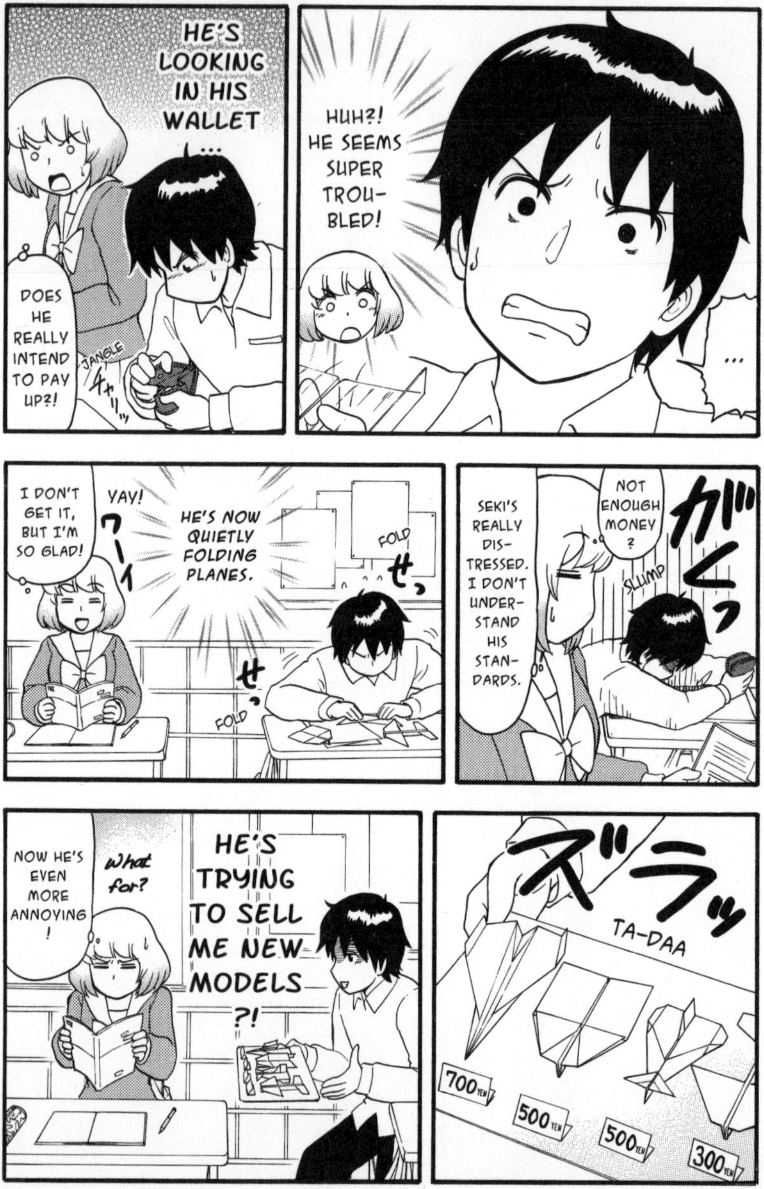
HUH?! HE SEEMS SUPER TROUBLED!
...
HE'S LOOKING IN HIS WALLET ...
DOES HE REALLY INTEND TO PAY UP?!
JANGLE
ガクッ
NOT ENOUGH MONEY?
SLUMP
SEKI'S REALLY DISTRESSED. I DON'T UNDERSTAND HIS STANDARDS.
HE'S NOW QUIETLY FOLDING PLANES.
FOLD
せっ
YAY!
ワーイ
I DON'T GET IT, BUT I'M SO GLAD!
せっ
FOLD
ズラッ
TA-DAA
700 YEN
500 YEN
500 YEN
300 YEN
HE'S TRYING TO SELL ME NEW MODELS?!
what for?
NOW HE'S EVEN MORE ANNOYING!

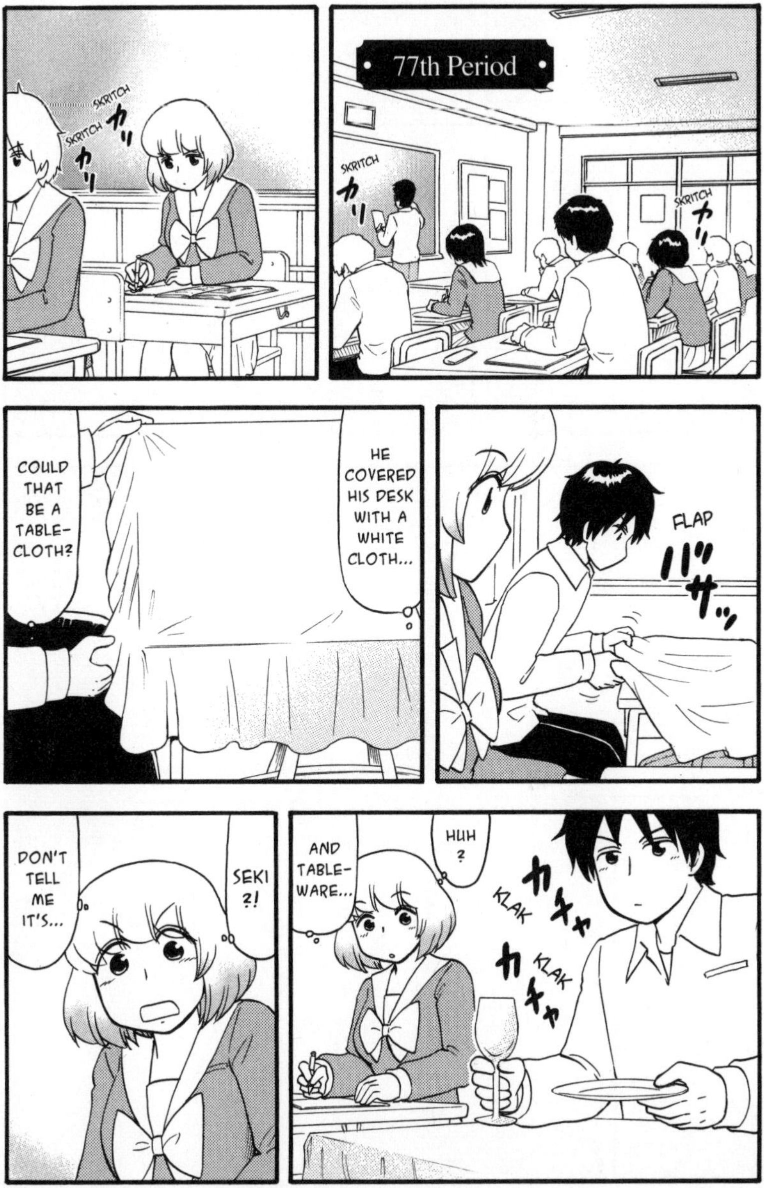
77th Period
SKRITCH
SKRITCH
SKRITCH
SKRITCH
FLAP
HE COVERED HIS DESK WITH A WHITE CLOTH...
COULD THAT BE A TABLE-CLOTH?
HUH?
KLAK
KLAK
AND TABLE-WARE...
SEKI?!
DON'T TELL ME IT'S...

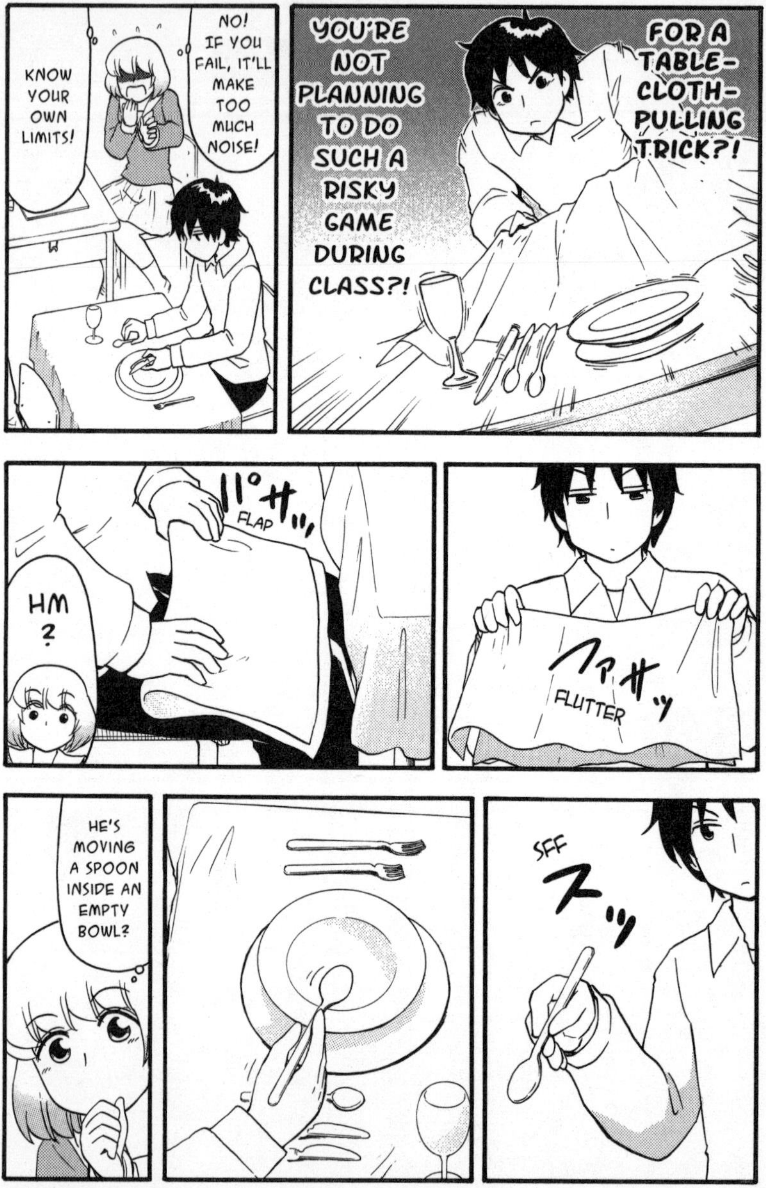
FOR A TABLE-CLOTH-PULLING TRICK?!
YOU'RE NOT PLANNING TO DO SUCH A RISKY GAME DURING CLASS?!
NO! IF YOU FAIL, IT'LL MAKE TOO MUCH NOISE!
KNOW YOUR OWN LIMITS!
ファサッ
FLUTTER
パサッ
FLAP
HM?
スッ
SFF
HE'S MOVING A SPOON INSIDE AN EMPTY BOWL?

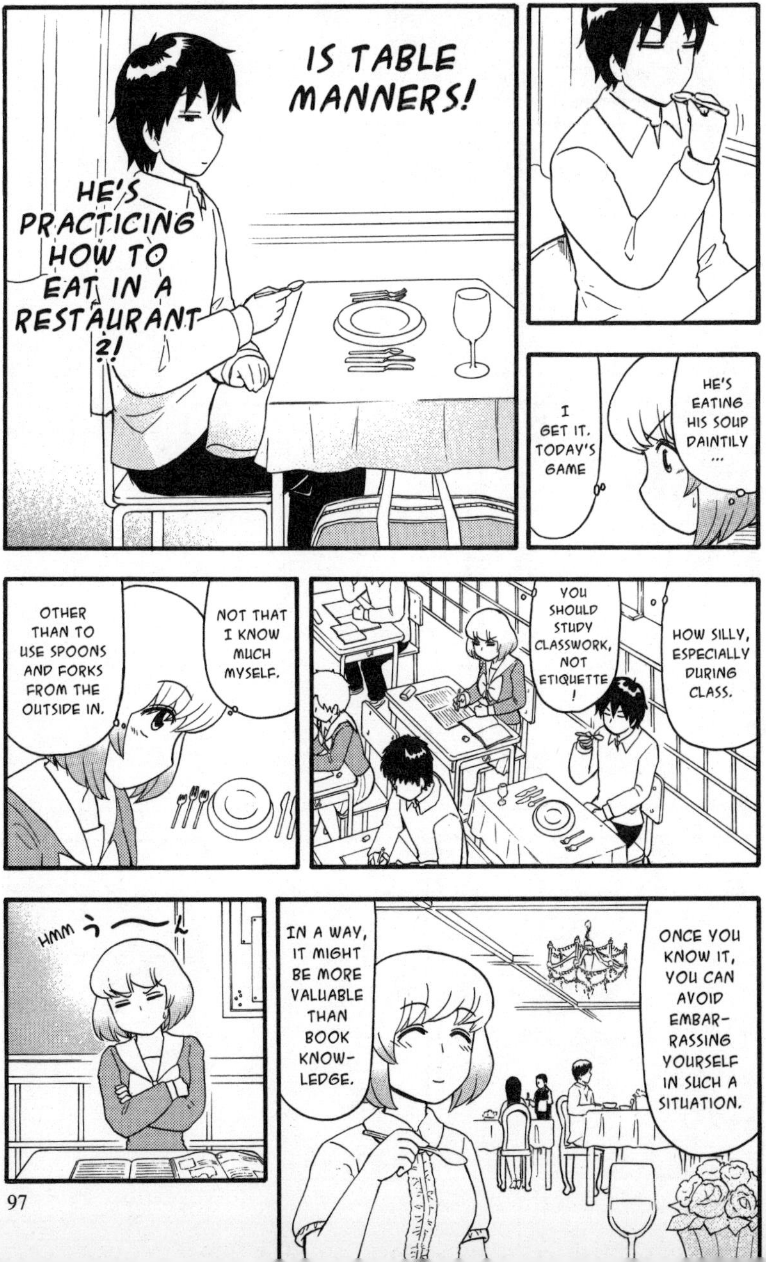
HE'S EATING HIS SOUP DAINTILY ...
I GET IT. TODAY'S GAME
IS TABLE MANNERS!
HE'S PRACTICING HOW TO EAT IN A RESTAURANT ?!
HOW SILLY, ESPECIALLY DURING CLASS.
YOU SHOULD STUDY CLASSWORK, NOT ETIQUETTE!
NOT THAT I KNOW MUCH MYSELF.
OTHER THAN TO USE SPOONS AND FORKS FROM THE OUTSIDE IN.
ONCE YOU KNOW IT, YOU CAN AVOID EMBAR-RASSING YOURSELF IN SUCH A SITUATION.
IN A WAY, IT MIGHT BE MORE VALUABLE THAN BOOK KNOW-LEDGE.
HMM うーーん

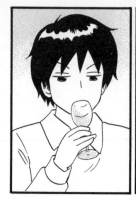

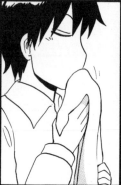

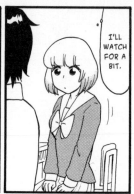

I'LL WATCH FOR A BIT.
LEAVE IT TO SEKI.
Whoa
THERE'S REFINEMENT IN EVERY GESTURE.
HUH?
SEKI'S TOUCHING THE TIP OF THE SPOON TO HIS MOUTH?
THAT LOOKS HARD TO USE!
NORMALLY, YOU SIP FROM THE SIDE!
NO, SEKI LIKELY DID RESEARCH IN PREP FOR TODAY.
SO THE POSITION OF THAT SPOON MIGHT BE RIGHT...
BUT IT'S NEWS TO ME...

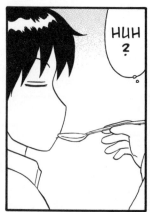

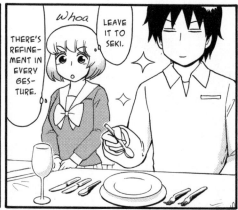

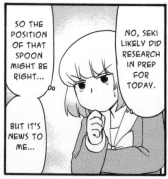

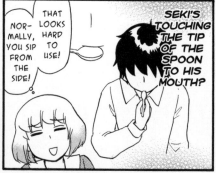

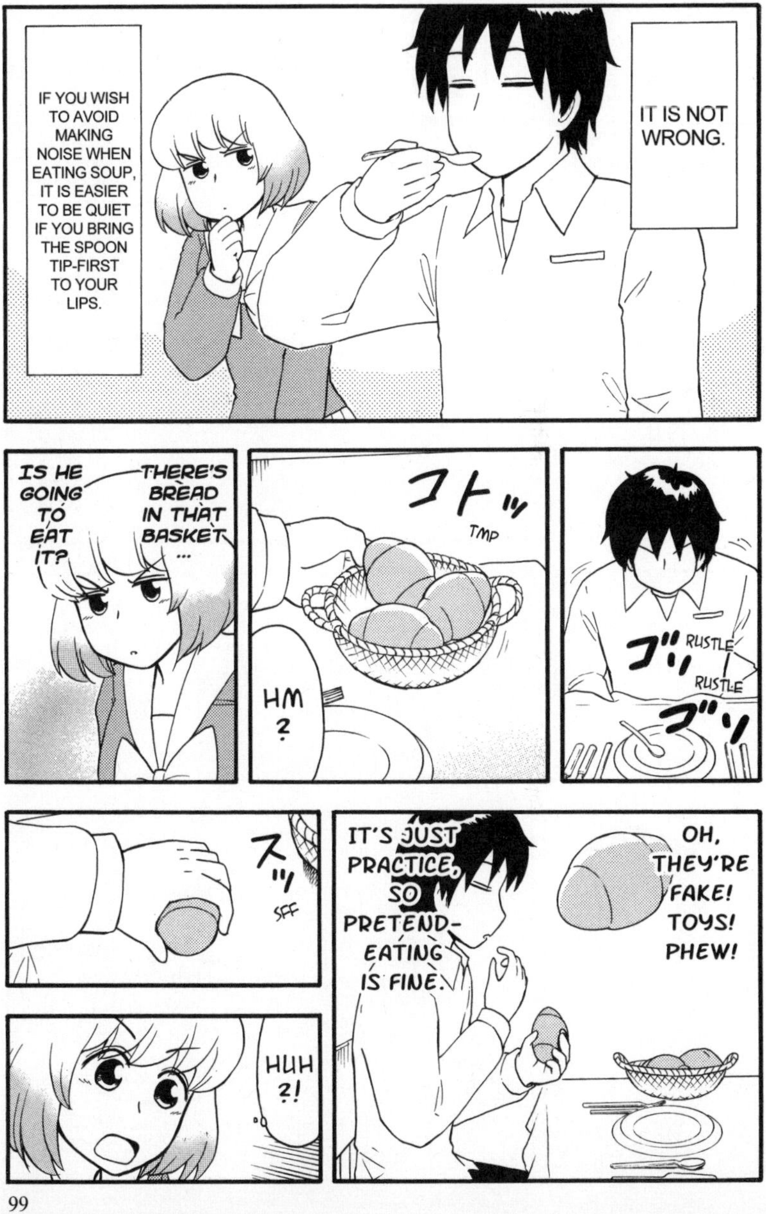
IT IS NOT WRONG.
IF YOU WISH TO AVOID MAKING NOISE WHEN EATING SOUP, IT IS EASIER TO BE QUIET IF YOU BRING THE SPOON TIP-FIRST TO YOUR LIPS.
ゴソ RUSTLE
RUSTLE ゴソ
コトッ TMP
HM ?
THERE'S BREAD IN THAT BASKET ...
IS HE GOING TO EAT IT?
OH, THEY'RE FAKE! TOYS! PHEW!
IT'S JUST PRACTICE, SO PRETEND-EATING IS FINE.
スッ SFF
HUH ?!

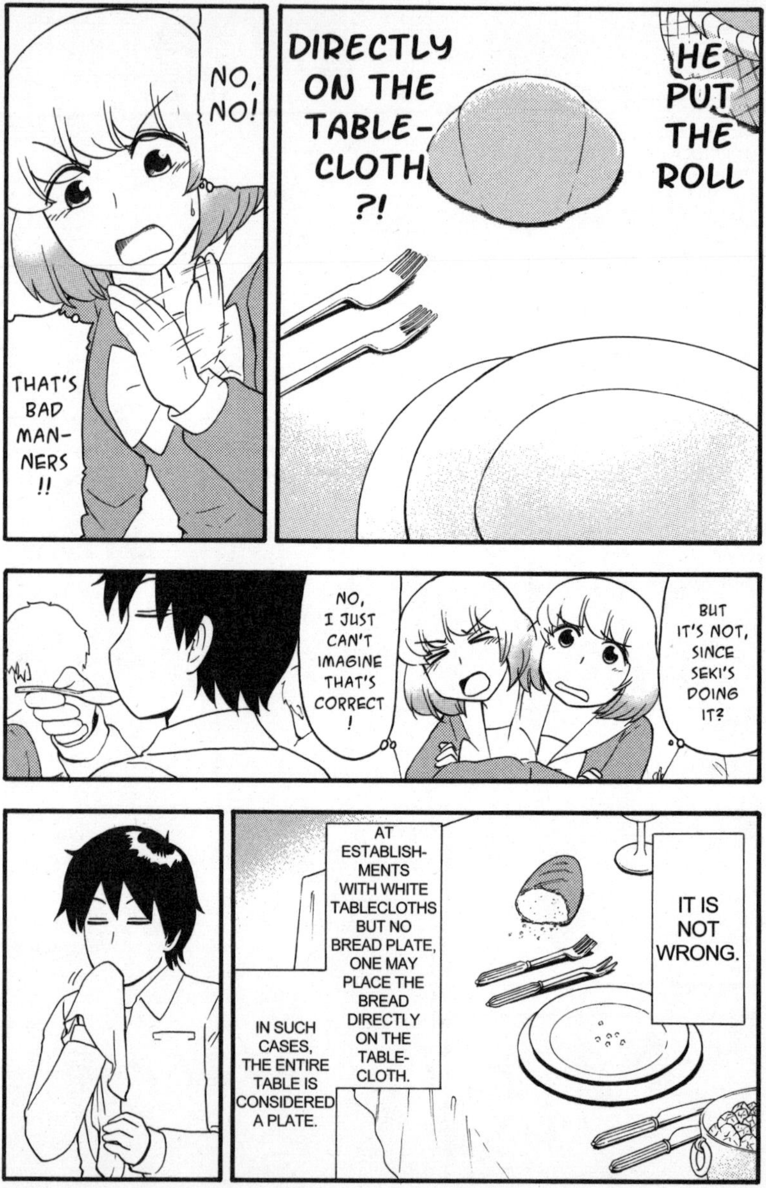
HE PUT THE ROLL
DIRECTLY ON THE TABLE-CLOTH ?!
NO, NO!
THAT'S BAD MAN-NERS !!
BUT IT'S NOT, SINCE SEKI'S DOING IT?
NO, I JUST CAN'T IMAGINE THAT'S CORRECT!
IT IS NOT WRONG.
AT ESTABLISH-MENTS WITH WHITE TABLECLOTHS BUT NO BREAD PLATE, ONE MAY PLACE THE BREAD DIRECTLY ON THE TABLE-CLOTH.
IN SUCH CASES, THE ENTIRE TABLE IS CONSIDERED A PLATE.

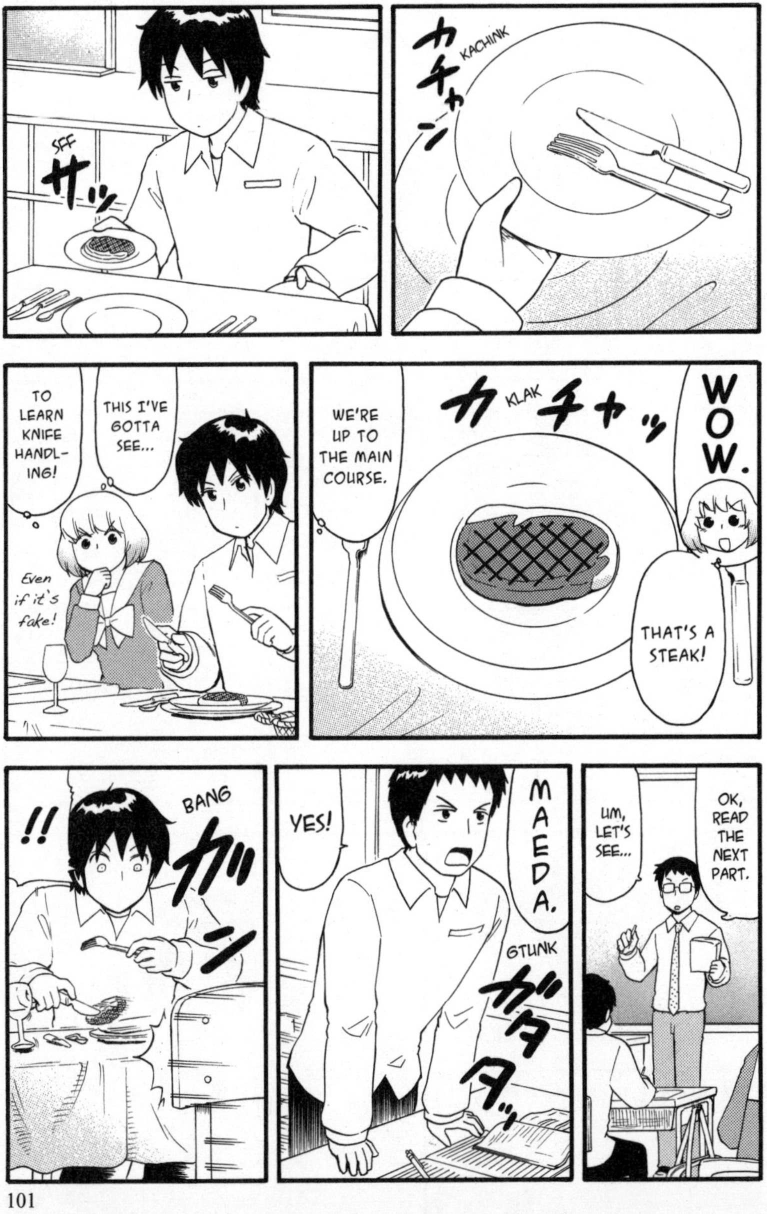
カチャン
KACHINK
サッ
SFF
WOW.
THAT'S A STEAK!
カチャッ
KLAK
WE'RE UP TO THE MAIN COURSE.
THIS I'VE GOTTA SEE...
TO LEARN KNIFE HANDLING!
Even if it's fake!
OK, READ THE NEXT PART.
UM, LET'S SEE...
MAEDA.
YES!
ガタタッ
GTUNK
ガン
BANG
!!

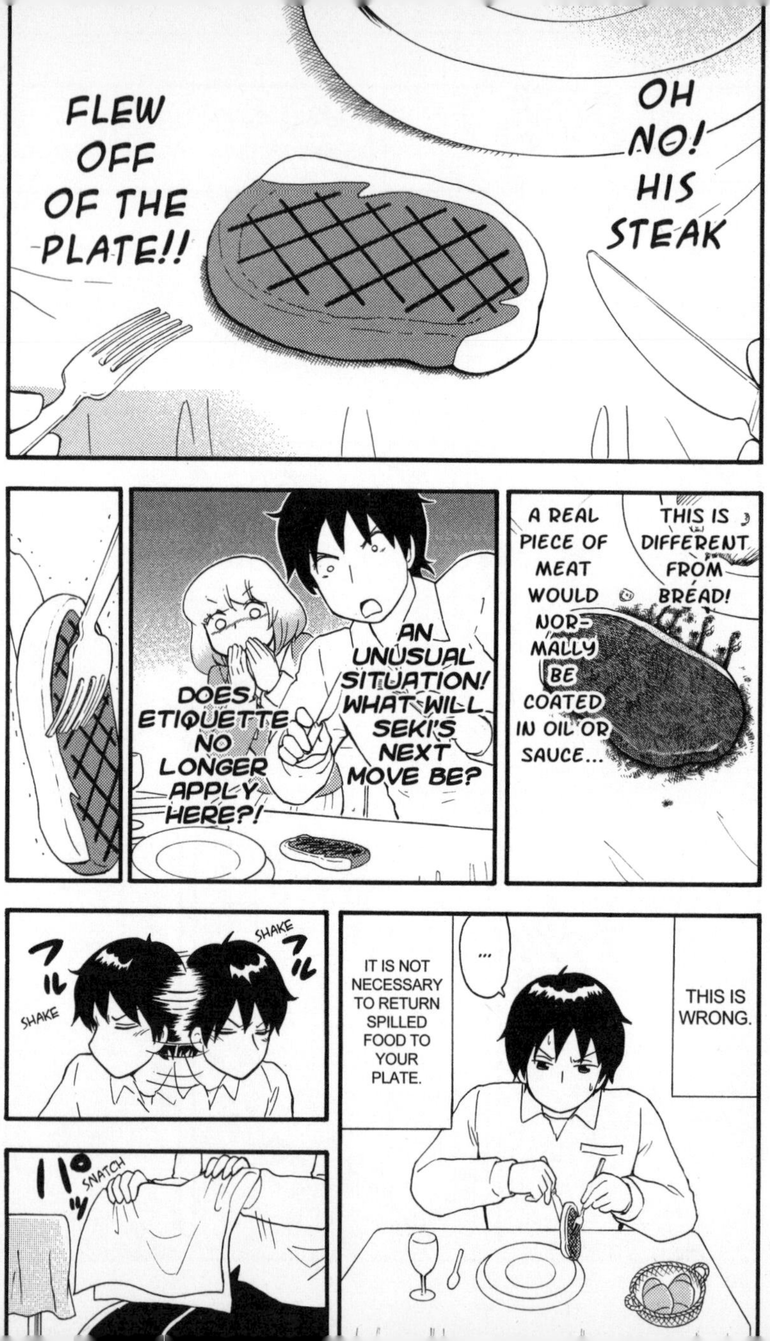
OH NO! HIS STEAK
FLEW OFF OF THE PLATE!!
THIS IS DIFFERENT FROM BREAD!
A REAL PIECE OF MEAT WOULD NOR-MALLY BE COATED IN OIL OR SAUCE...
AN UNUSUAL SITUATION! WHAT WILL SEKI'S NEXT MOVE BE?
DOES ETIQUETTE NO LONGER APPLY HERE?!
THIS IS WRONG.
...
IT IS NOT NECESSARY TO RETURN SPILLED FOOD TO YOUR PLATE.
フル
SHAKE
フル
SHAKE
パッ
SNATCH

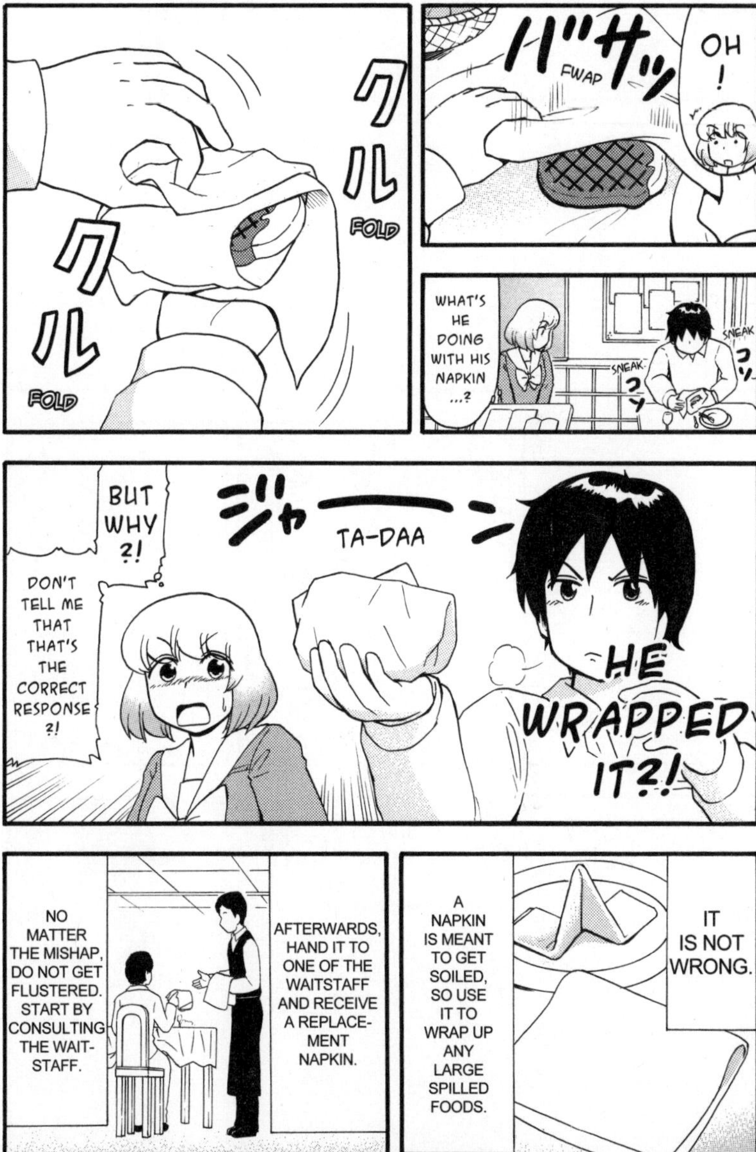
バサッ
FWAP
OH!
WHAT'S HE DOING WITH HIS NAPKIN ...?
コソ
SNEAK
コソ
SNEAK
クル
FOLD
クル
FOLD
ジャーーン
TA-DAA
HE WRAPPED IT?!
DON'T TELL ME THAT THAT'S THE CORRECT RESPONSE ?!
BUT WHY ?!
IT IS NOT WRONG.
A NAPKIN IS MEANT TO GET SOILED, SO USE IT TO WRAP UP ANY LARGE SPILLED FOODS.
NO MATTER THE MISHAP, DO NOT GET FLUSTERED. START BY CONSULTING THE WAIT-STAFF.
AFTERWARDS, HAND IT TO ONE OF THE WAITSTAFF AND RECEIVE A REPLACE-MENT NAPKIN.

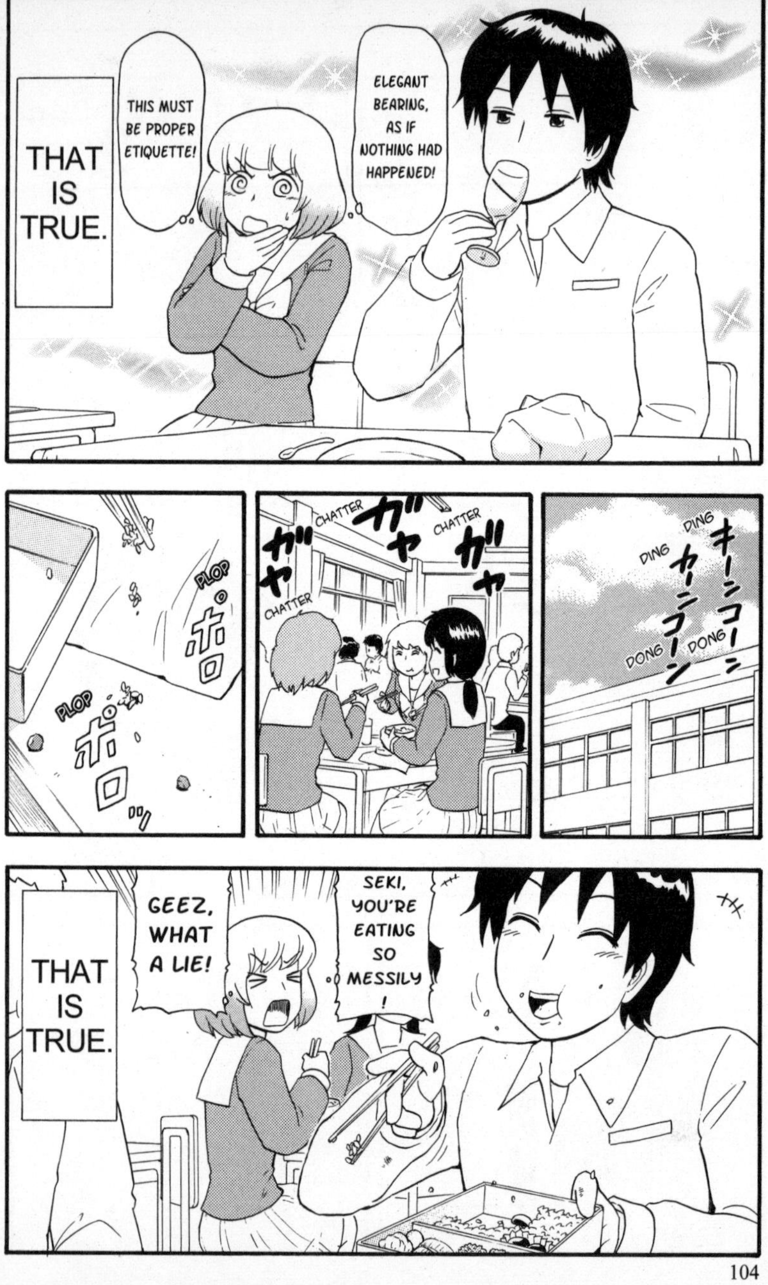
ELEGANT BEARING, AS IF NOTHING HAD HAPPENED!
THIS MUST BE PROPER ETIQUETTE!
THAT IS TRUE.
DING DING
キーンコーン
DONG DONG
カーンコーン
CHATTER
ガヤ
CHATTER
ガヤ
CHATTER
PLOP
ポロ
PLOP
ポロッ
SEKI, YOU'RE EATING SO MESSILY!
GEEZ, WHAT A LIE!
THAT IS TRUE.

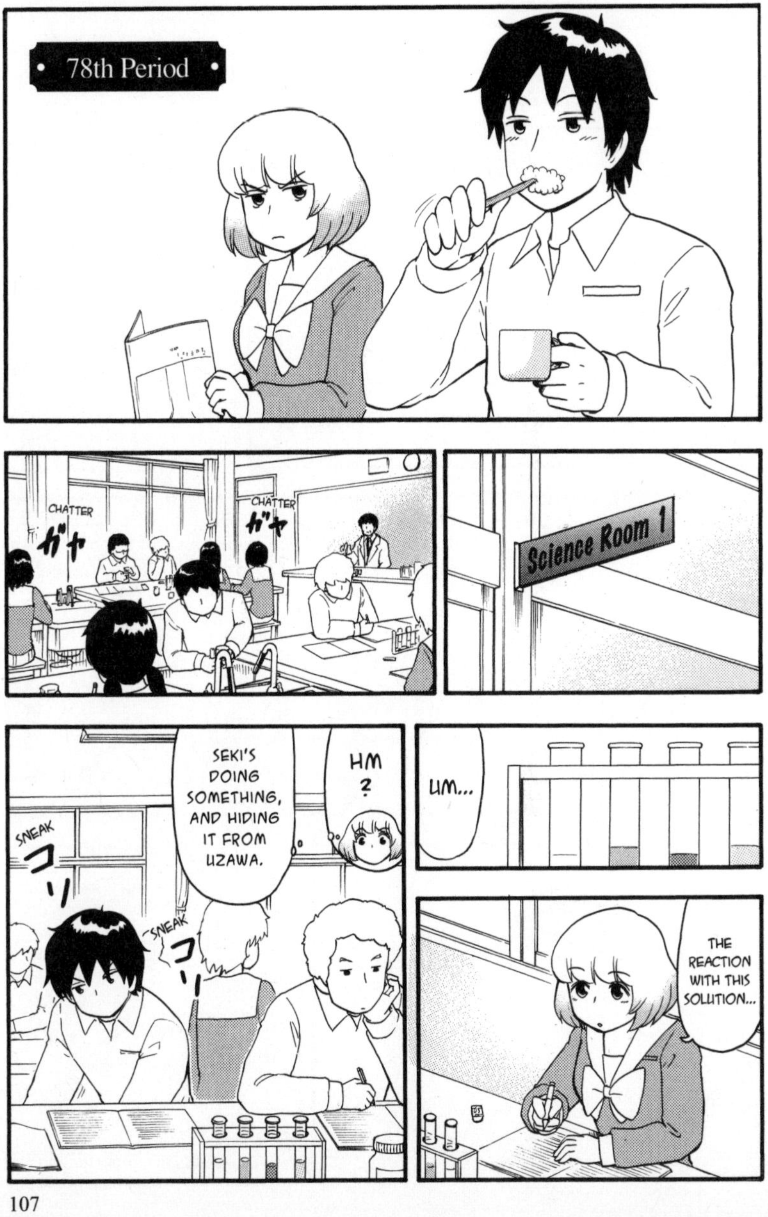
78th Period
Science Room 1
CHATTER
ガヤ
CHATTER
ガヤ
UM...
THE REACTION WITH THIS SOLUTION...
HM ?
SEKI'S DOING SOMETHING, AND HIDING IT FROM UZAWA.
SNEAK
コソ
SNEAK
コソ

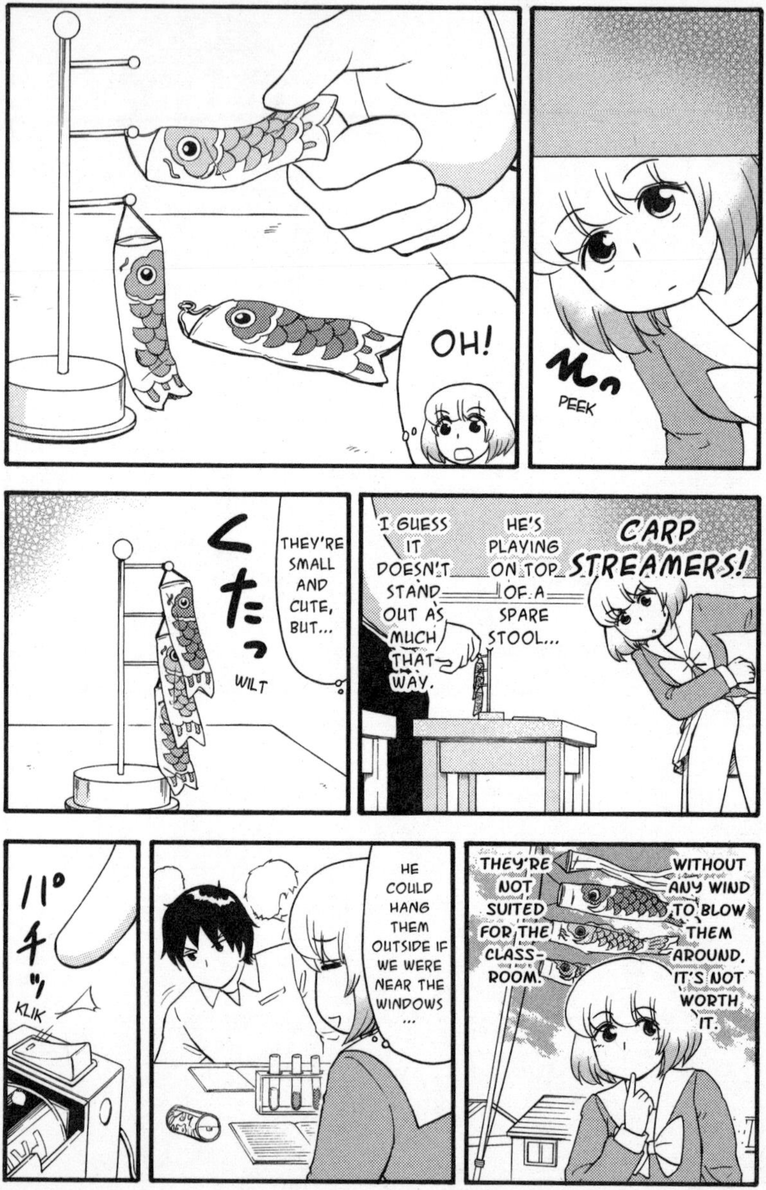
PEEK
OH!
CARP STREAMERS!
HE'S PLAYING ON TOP OF A SPARE STOOL...
I GUESS IT DOESN'T STAND OUT AS MUCH THAT WAY.
THEY'RE SMALL AND CUTE, BUT...
くたっ
WILT
WITHOUT ANY WIND TO BLOW THEM AROUND, IT'S NOT WORTH IT.
THEY'RE NOT SUITED FOR THE CLASSROOM.
HE COULD HANG THEM OUTSIDE IF WE WERE NEAR THE WINDOWS ...
パチッ
KLIK

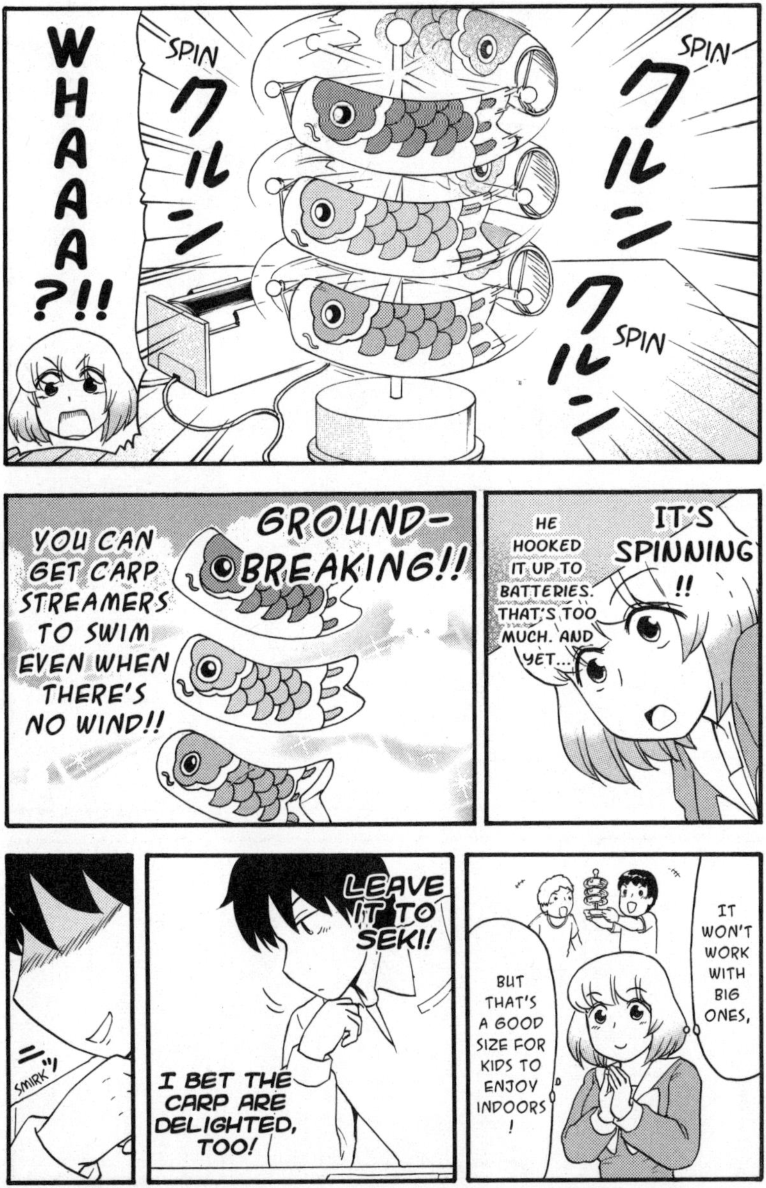
SPIN
クルン
SPIN
クルン
SPIN
クルン
WHAAAA?!!
IT'S SPINNING!!
HE HOOKED IT UP TO BATTERIES. THAT'S TOO MUCH. AND YET...
GROUND-BREAKING!!
YOU CAN GET CARP STREAMERS TO SWIM EVEN WHEN THERE'S NO WIND!!
IT WON'T WORK WITH BIG ONES,
BUT THAT'S A GOOD SIZE FOR KIDS TO ENJOY INDOORS!
LEAVE IT TO SEKI!
I BET THE CARP ARE DELIGHTED, TOO!
ニッ
SMIRK

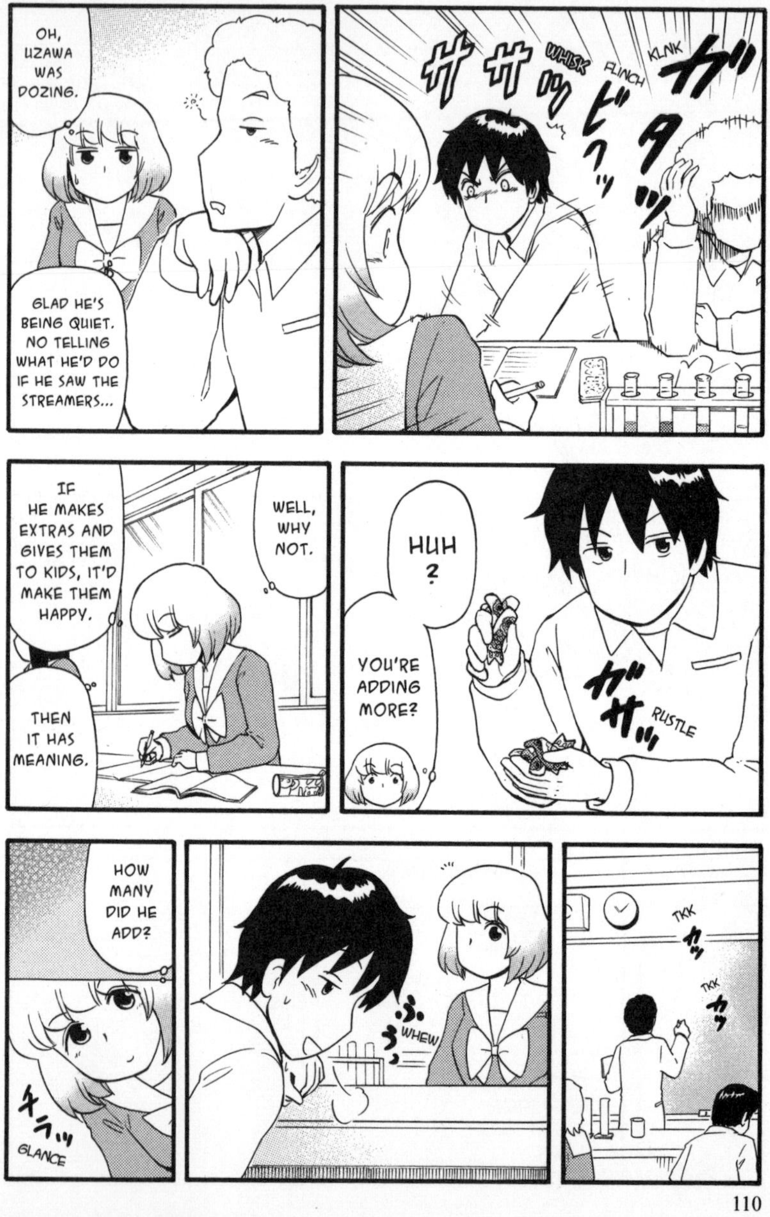
KLNK
ガタッ
FLINCH
ビクッ
WHISK
ササッ
OH, UZAWA WAS DOZING.
GLAD HE'S BEING QUIET. NO TELLING WHAT HE'D DO IF HE SAW THE STREAMERS...
HUH?
ガサッ
RUSTLE
YOU'RE ADDING MORE?
WELL, WHY NOT.
IF HE MAKES EXTRAS AND GIVES THEM TO KIDS, IT'D MAKE THEM HAPPY.
THEN IT HAS MEANING.
TKK
カッ
TKK
カッ
ふぅっ
WHEW
HOW MANY DID HE ADD?
チラッ
GLANCE

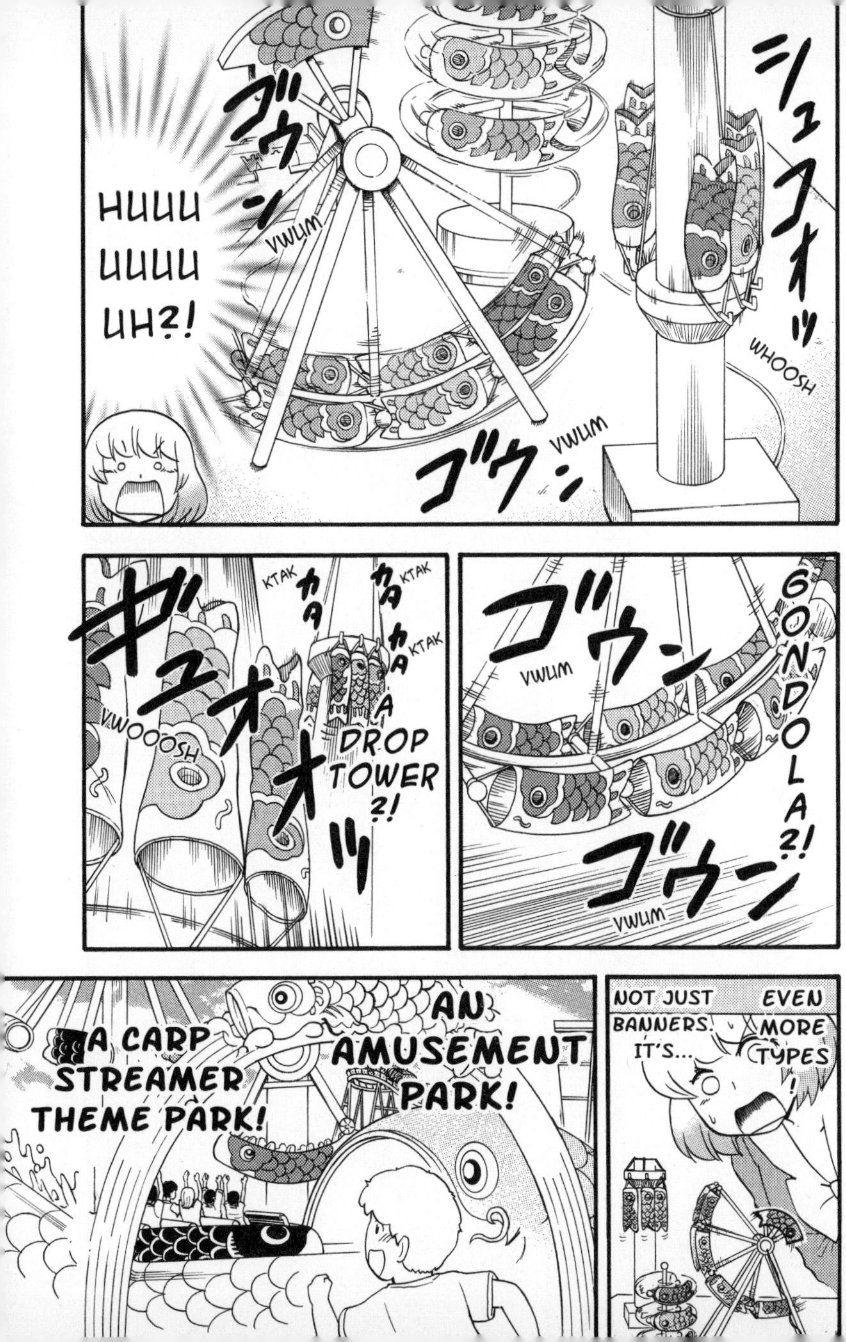
シュコオッ
WHOOSH
ゴウン
VWUM
HUUUUUUUUUUH?!
ゴウン
VWUM
GONDOLA?!
ゴウン
VWUM
ゴウン
VWUM
カタ
KTAK
カタ
KTAK
A DROP TOWER?!
ギュオオッ
VWOOOSH
EVEN MORE TYPES!
NOT JUST BANNERS. IT'S...
AN AMUSEMENT PARK!
A CARP STREAMER THEME PARK!

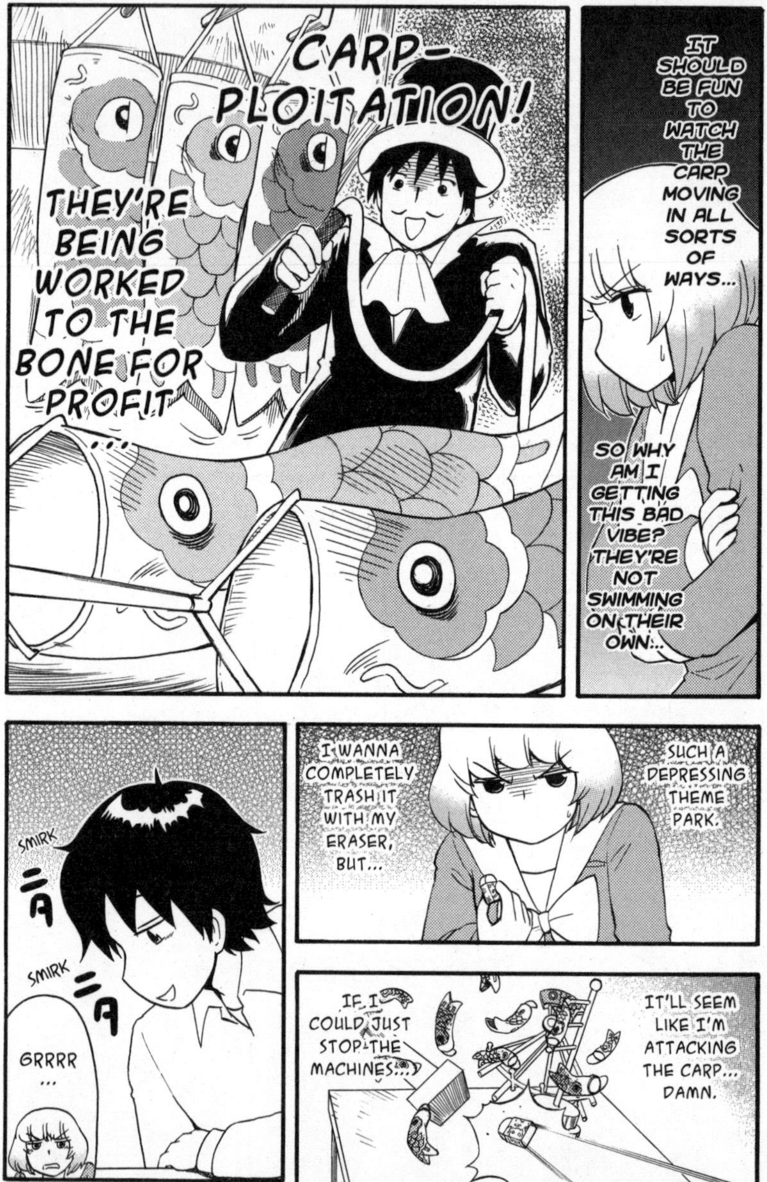
IT SHOULD BE FUN TO WATCH THE CARP MOVING IN ALL SORTS OF WAYS...
SO WHY AM I GETTING THIS BAD VIBE? THEY'RE NOT SWIMMING ON THEIR OWN...
CARP-PLOITATION!
THEY'RE BEING WORKED TO THE BONE FOR PROFIT
...
SUCH A DEPRESSING THEME PARK.
I WANNA COMPLETELY TRASH IT WITH MY ERASER, BUT...
IT'LL SEEM LIKE I'M ATTACKING THE CARP... DAMN.
IF I COULD JUST STOP THE MACHINES...
SMIRK
SMIRK
GRRRR ...

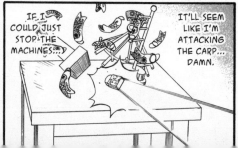

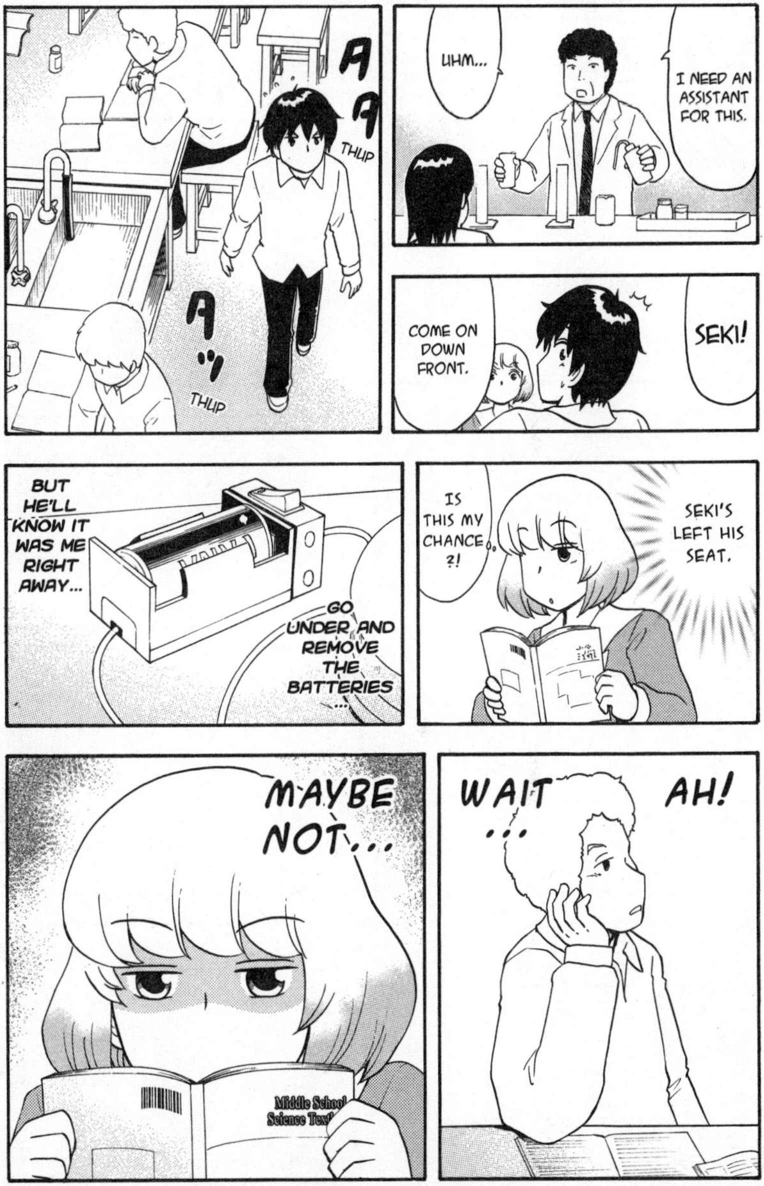
I NEED AN ASSISTANT FOR THIS.
UHM...
SEKI!
COME ON DOWN FRONT.
タタ
THUP
タッ
THUP
SEKI'S LEFT HIS SEAT.
IS THIS MY CHANCE?!
GO UNDER AND REMOVE THE BATTERIES...
BUT HE'LL KNOW IT WAS ME RIGHT AWAY...
AH!
WAIT...
MAYBE NOT...
Middle School Science Text

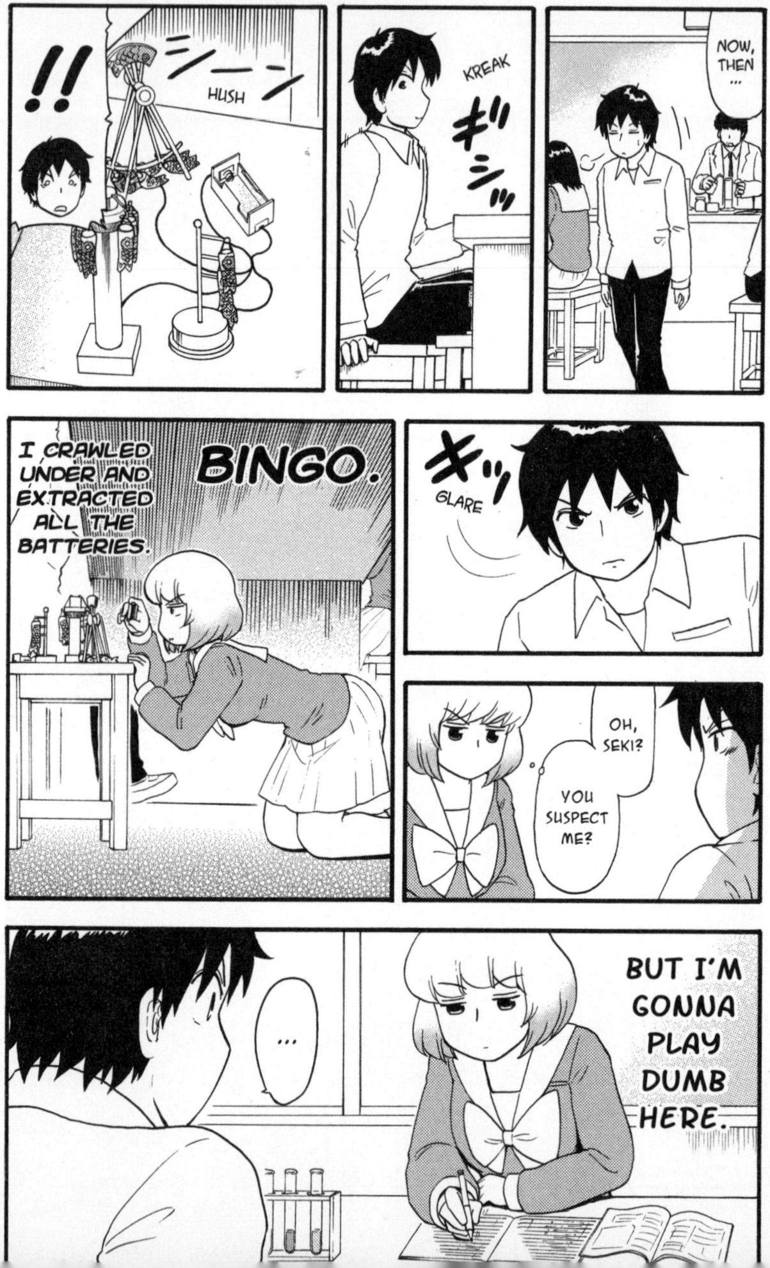

NOW, THEN ...
KREAK
ギシッ
!!
HUSH
GLARE
キッ
OH, SEKI?
YOU SUSPECT ME?
BINGO.
I CRAWLED UNDER AND EXTRACTED ALL THE BATTERIES.
BUT I'M GONNA PLAY DUMB HERE.
...

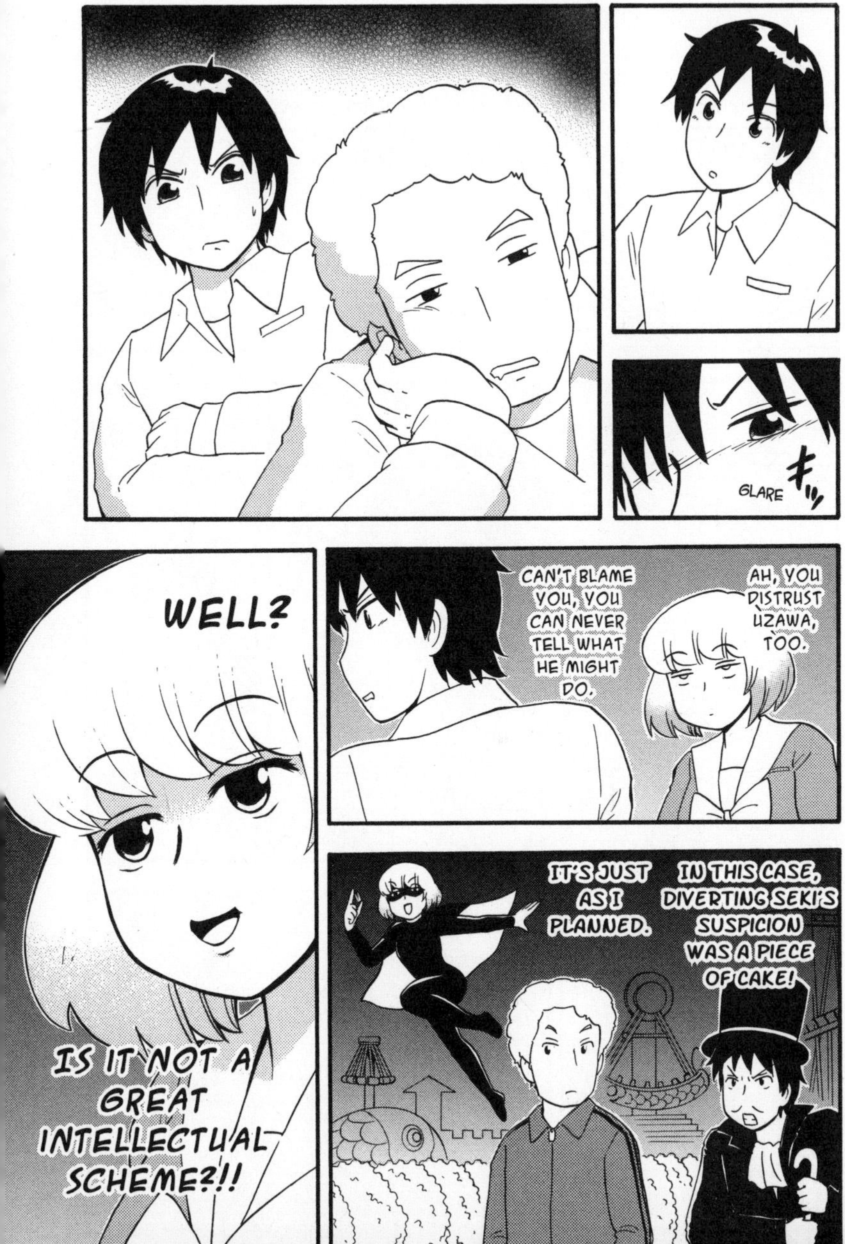
GLARE
AH, YOU DISTRUST UZAWA, TOO.
CAN'T BLAME YOU, YOU CAN NEVER TELL WHAT HE MIGHT DO.
IN THIS CASE, DIVERTING SEKI'S SUSPICION WAS A PIECE OF CAKE!
IT'S JUST AS I PLANNED.
WELL?
IS IT NOT A GREAT INTELLECTUAL SCHEME?!!

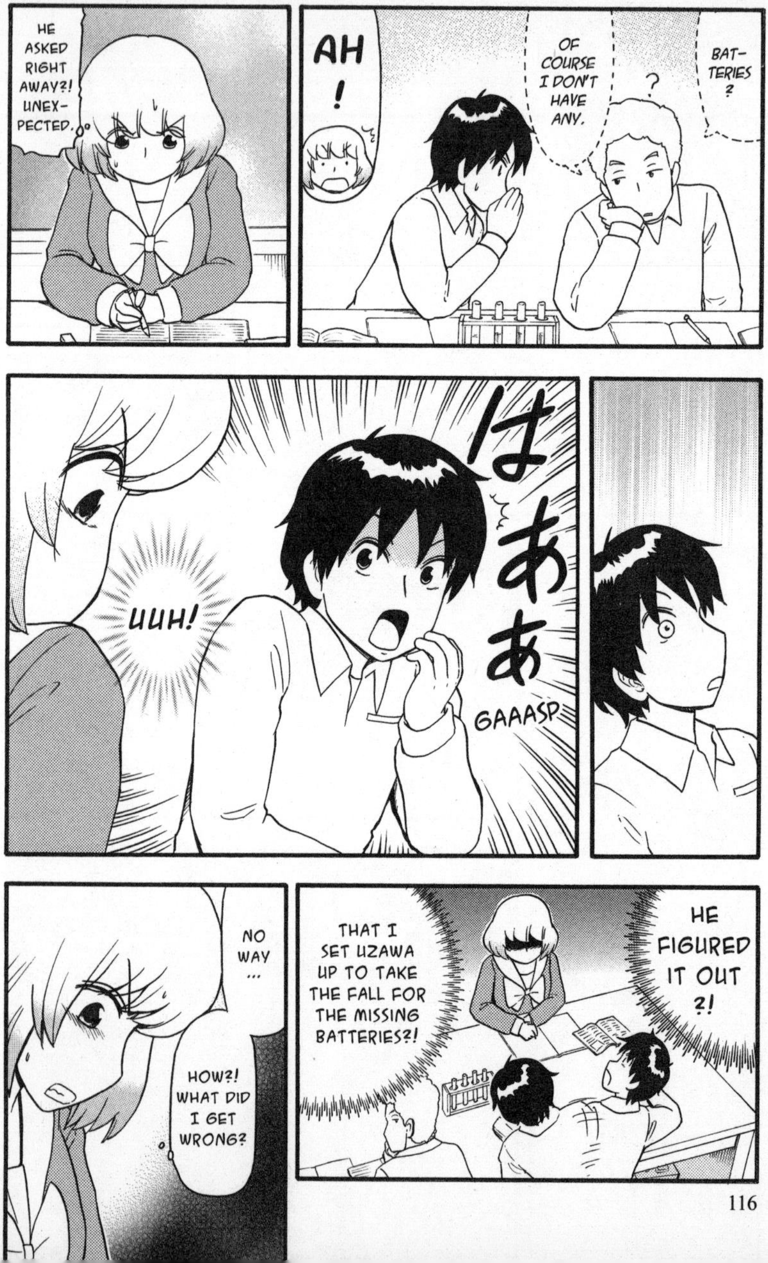
BAT-TERIES?
?
OF COURSE I DON'T HAVE ANY.
AH!
HE ASKED RIGHT AWAY?! UNEXPECTED.
はあぁ
GAAASP
UUH!
HE FIGURED IT OUT?!
THAT I SET UZAWA UP TO TAKE THE FALL FOR THE MISSING BATTERIES?!
NO WAY...
HOW?! WHAT DID I GET WRONG?

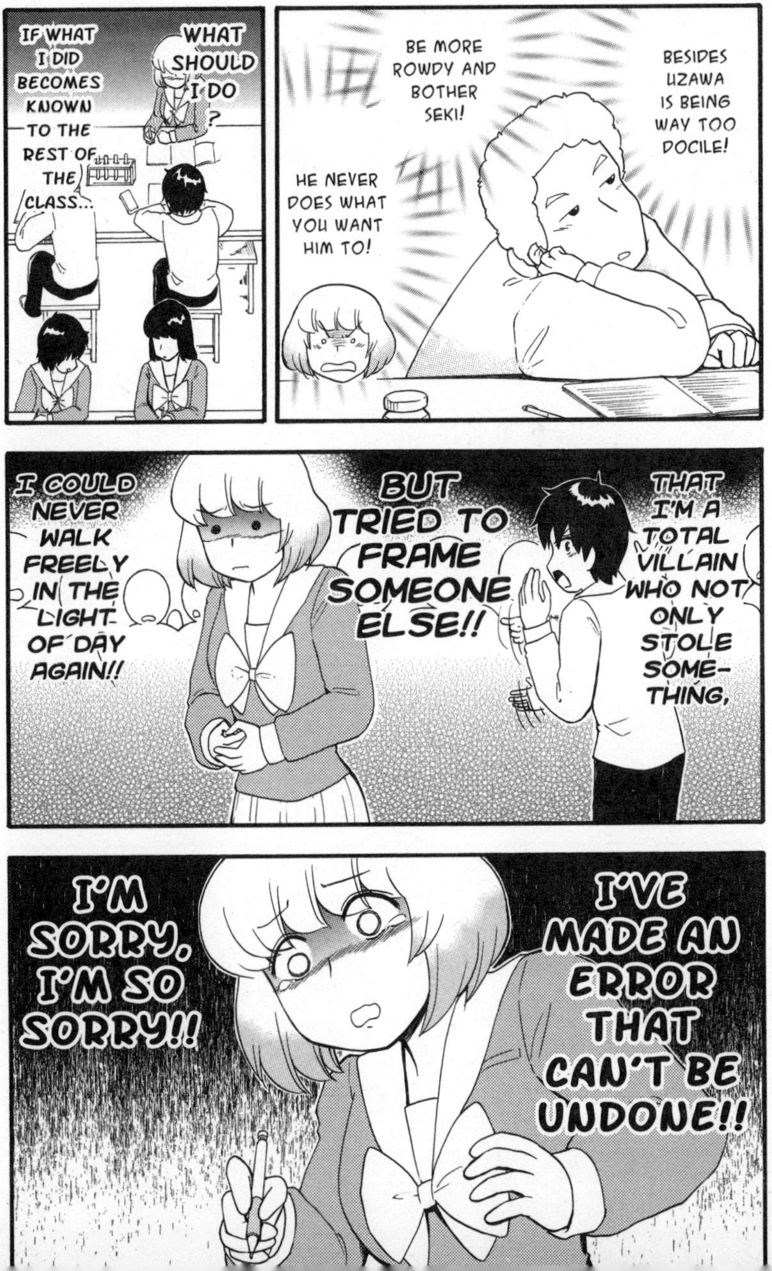
BESIDES UZAWA IS BEING WAY TOO DOCILE!
BE MORE ROWDY AND BOTHER SEKI!
HE NEVER DOES WHAT YOU WANT HIM TO!
WHAT SHOULD I DO?
IF WHAT I DID BECOMES KNOWN TO THE REST OF THE CLASS...
THAT I'M A TOTAL VILLAIN WHO NOT ONLY STOLE SOMETHING,
BUT TRIED TO FRAME SOMEONE ELSE!!
I COULD NEVER WALK FREELY IN THE LIGHT OF DAY AGAIN!!
I'VE MADE AN ERROR THAT CAN'T BE UNDONE!!
I'M SORRY, I'M SO SORRY!!

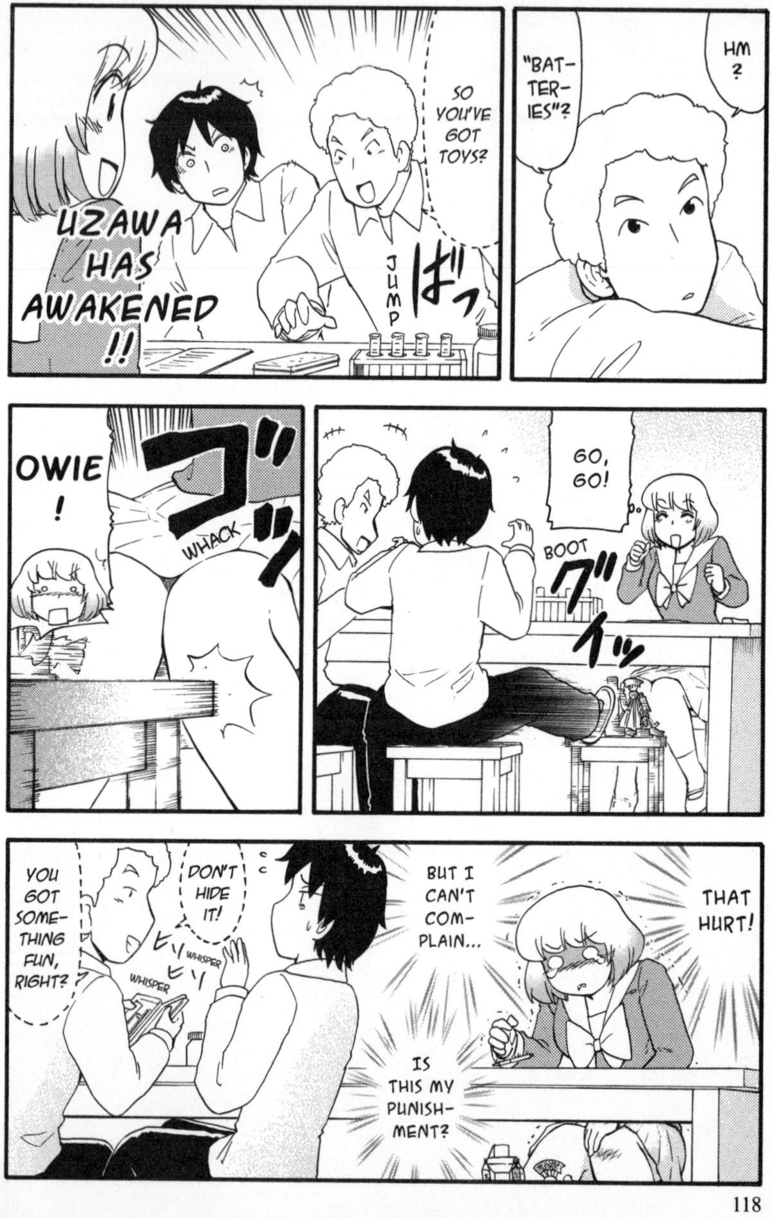
HM?
"BAT-TER-IES"?
SO YOU'VE GOT TOYS?
ばっ
JUMP
UZAWA HAS AWAKENED!!
GO, GO!
BOOT
グイッ
ゴッ
WHACK
OWIE!
THAT HURT!
BUT I CAN'T COM-PLAIN...
IS THIS MY PUNISH-MENT?
DON'T HIDE IT!
ヒソヒソ
WHISPER
WHISPER
YOU GOT SOME-THING FUN, RIGHT?

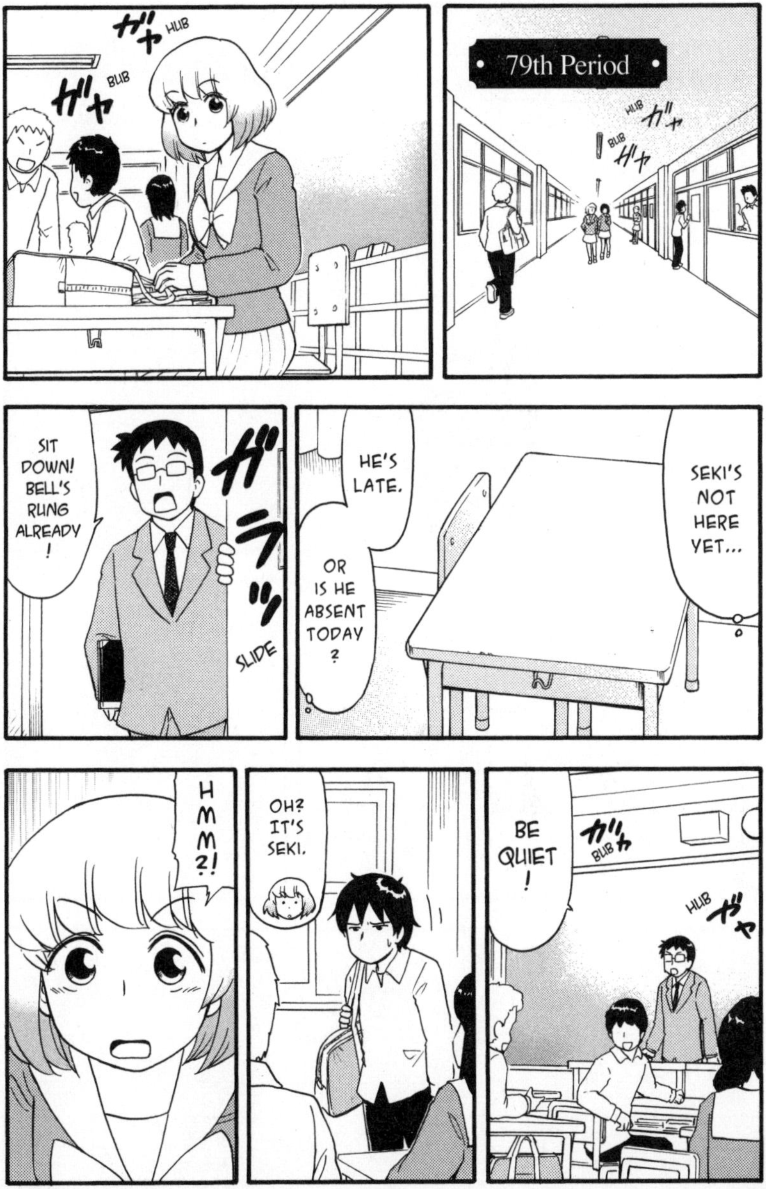
79th Period
HUB ガヤ
BUB ガヤ
ガヤ HUB
ガヤ BUB
SEKI'S NOT HERE YET...
HE'S LATE.
OR IS HE ABSENT TODAY?
ガラッ
SLIDE
SIT DOWN! BELL'S RUNG ALREADY!
BE QUIET!
ガヤ BUB
HUB ガヤ
OH? IT'S SEKI.
HMM?!

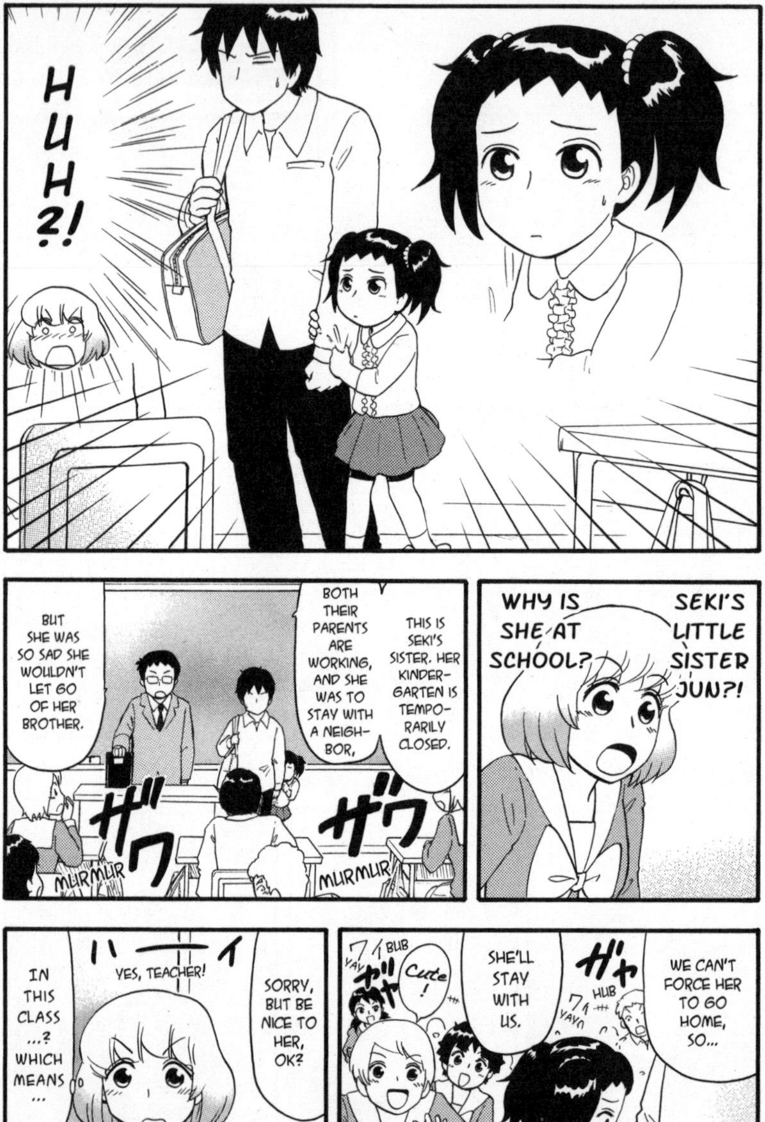
HUH?!
SEKI'S LITTLE SISTER JUN?!
WHY IS SHE AT SCHOOL?
THIS IS SEKI'S SISTER. HER KINDERGARTEN IS TEMPORARILY CLOSED.
BOTH THEIR PARENTS ARE WORKING, AND SHE WAS TO STAY WITH A NEIGHBOR,
BUT SHE WAS SO SAD SHE WOULDN'T LET GO OF HER BROTHER.
ザワ
MURMUR
ザワ
MURMUR
WE CAN'T FORCE HER TO GO HOME, SO...
ガヤ
HUB
ワイ
YAY
SHE'LL STAY WITH US.
ワイ
YAY
ガヤ
BUB
Cute!
SORRY, BUT BE NICE TO HER, OK?
ハーイ
YES, TEACHER!
IN THIS CLASS...? WHICH MEANS...

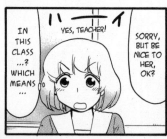

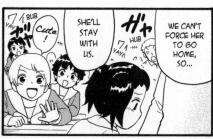

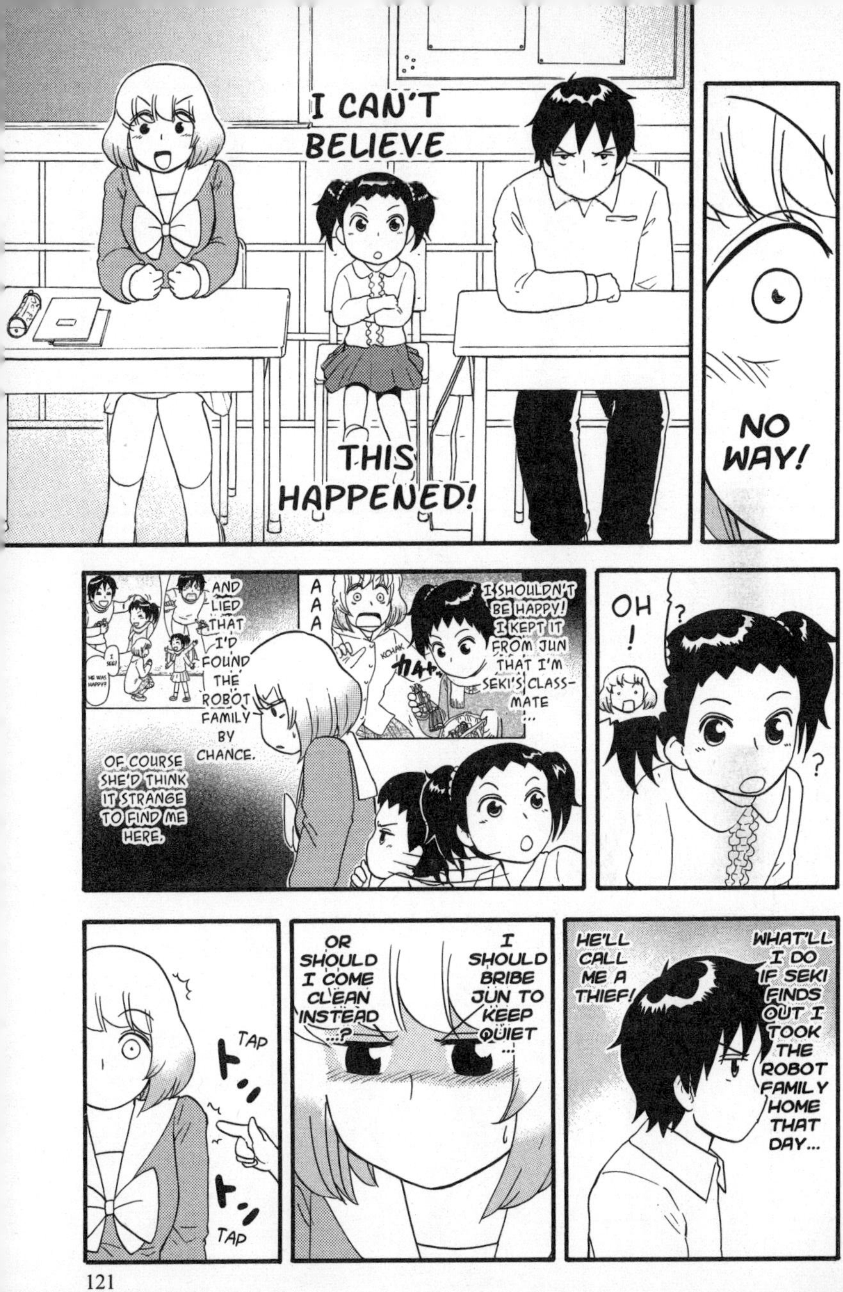
NO WAY!
I CAN'T BELIEVE
THIS HAPPENED!
OH!
I SHOULDN'T BE HAPPY! I KEPT IT FROM JUN THAT I'M SEKI'S CLASSMATE ...
AAA
KOHAK
AND LIED THAT I'D FOUND THE ROBOT FAMILY BY CHANCE.
OF COURSE SHE'D THINK IT STRANGE TO FIND ME HERE.
WHAT'LL I DO IF SEKI FINDS OUT I TOOK THE ROBOT FAMILY HOME THAT DAY...
HE'LL CALL ME A THIEF!
I SHOULD BRIBE JUN TO KEEP QUIET ...
OR SHOULD I COME CLEAN INSTEAD ...?
TAP
TAP

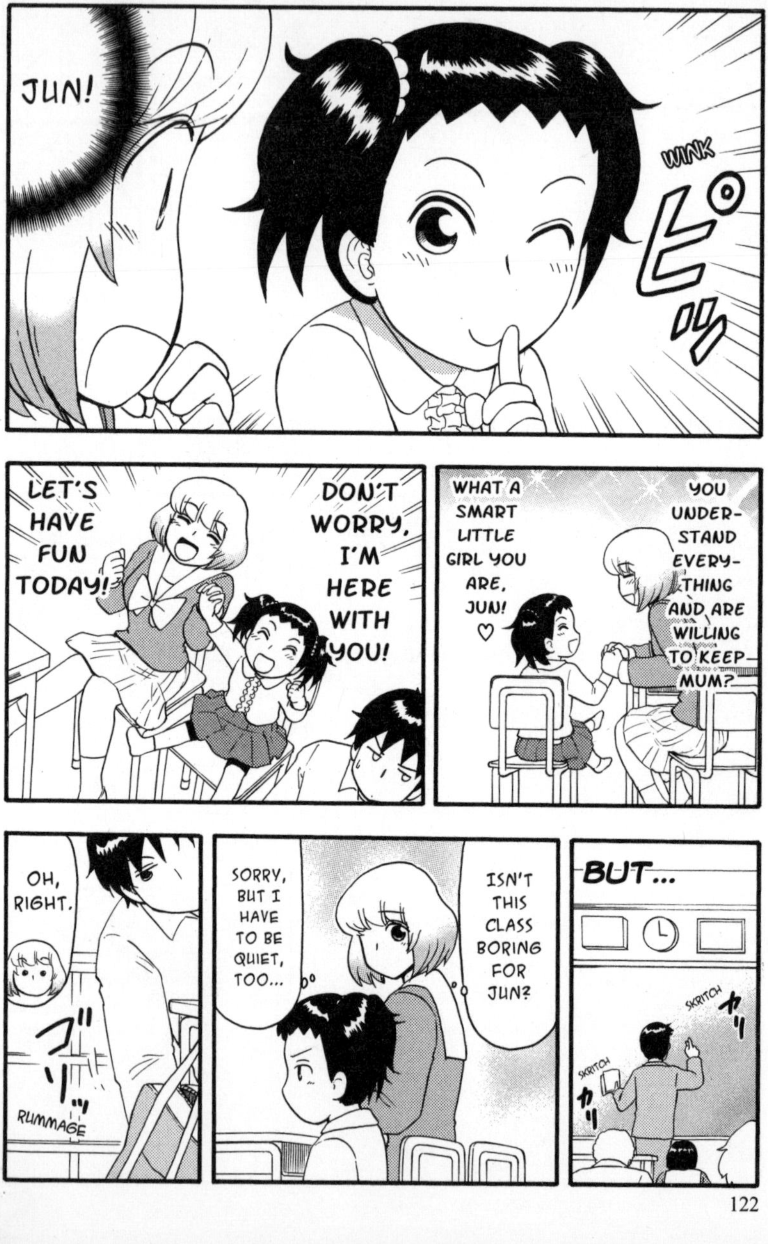
JUN!
WINK
ピッ
YOU UNDER-STAND EVERY-THING AND ARE WILLING TO KEEP MUM?
WHAT A SMART LITTLE GIRL YOU ARE, JUN! ♡
DON'T WORRY, I'M HERE WITH YOU!
LET'S HAVE FUN TODAY!
BUT...
SKRITCH
SKRITCH
ISN'T THIS CLASS BORING FOR JUN?
SORRY, BUT I HAVE TO BE QUIET, TOO...
OH, RIGHT.
RUMMAGE

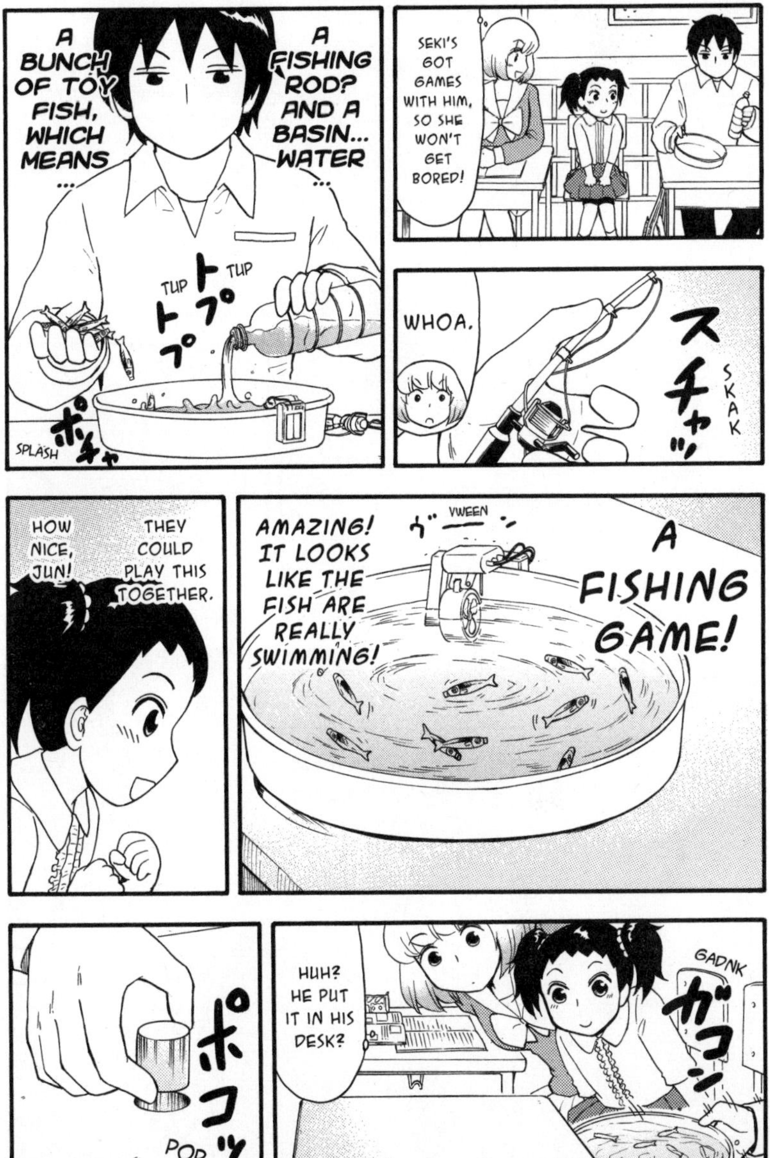
SEKI'S GOT GAMES WITH HIM, SO SHE WON'T GET BORED!
WHOA.
SKAK
A FISHING ROD? AND A BASIN... WATER ...
A BUNCH OF TOY FISH, WHICH MEANS ...
TUP TUP
SPLASH
A FISHING GAME!
VWEEN
AMAZING! IT LOOKS LIKE THE FISH ARE REALLY SWIMMING!
THEY COULD PLAY THIS TOGETHER.
HOW NICE, JUN!
GADNK
HUH? HE PUT IT IN HIS DESK?
POP

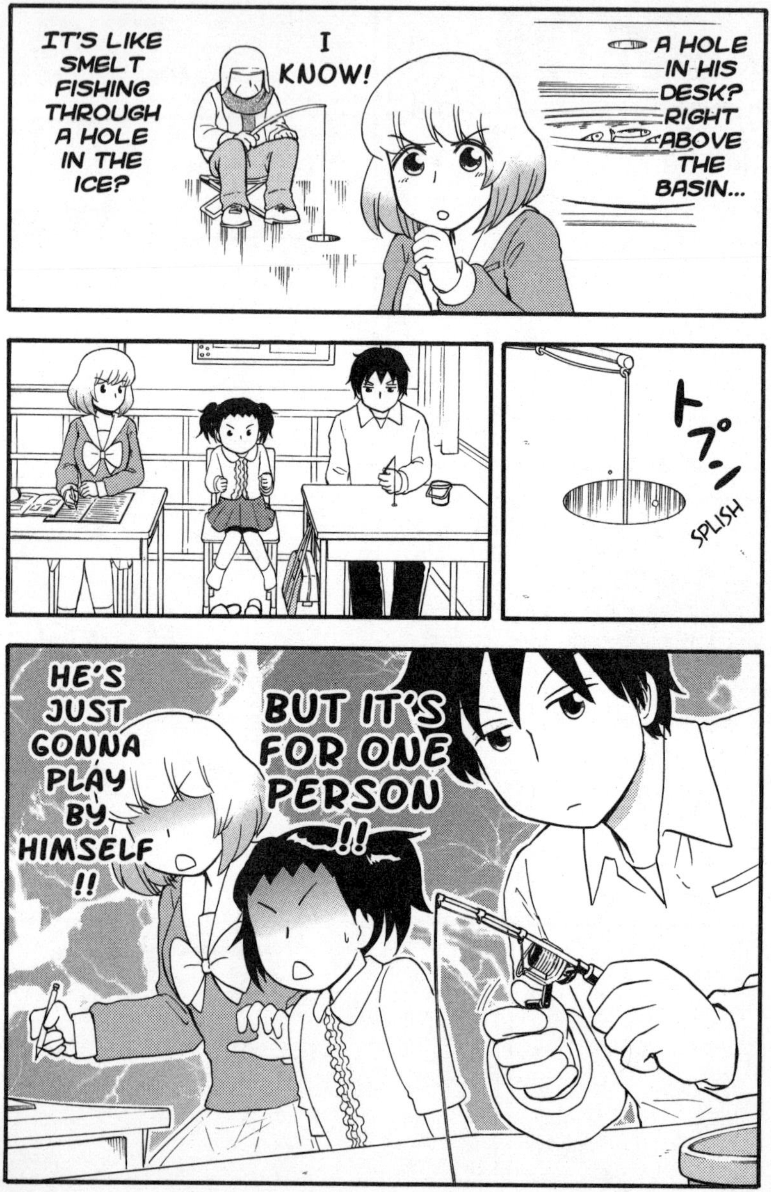
A HOLE IN HIS DESK? RIGHT ABOVE THE BASIN...
I KNOW!
IT'S LIKE SMELT FISHING THROUGH A HOLE IN THE ICE?
トプン
SPLISH
BUT IT'S FOR ONE PERSON!!
HE'S JUST GONNA PLAY BY HIMSELF!!

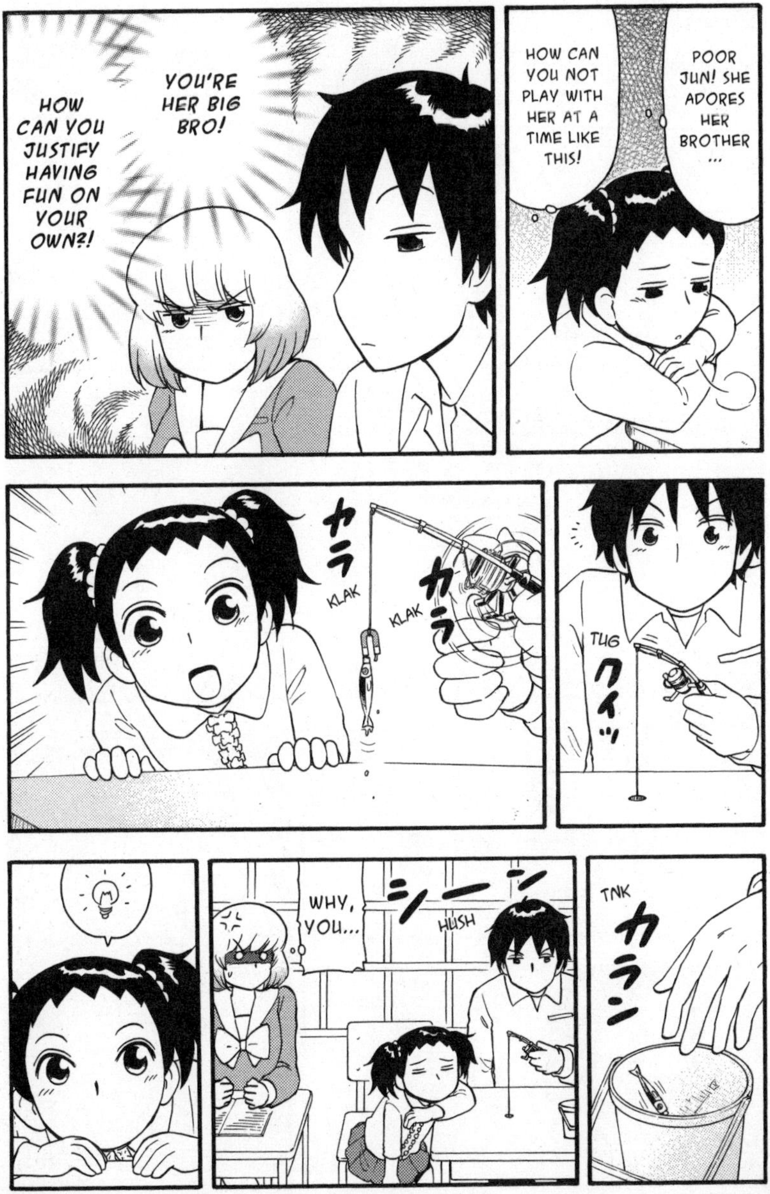
POOR JUN! SHE ADORES HER BROTHER ...
HOW CAN YOU NOT PLAY WITH HER AT A TIME LIKE THIS!
YOU'RE HER BIG BRO!
HOW CAN YOU JUSTIFY HAVING FUN ON YOUR OWN?!
TUG
クイッ
カラ
KLAK
カラ
KLAK
TNK
カラン
シーン
HUSH
WHY, YOU...

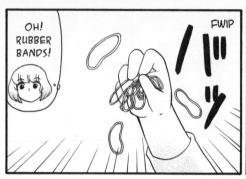

RUSTLE
RUSTLE
FWIP
OH! RUBBER BANDS!
DOES SEKI'S ENTIRE FAMILY CARRY THOSE?
FW
SHE TIED THEM TOGETHER TO FORM A NET?!
HAP
SWSH
SPLASH
JUN'S GONNA TRY TO CATCH FISH WITH THAT NET.
I SEE.
SHE'S AS SKILLED AS HER MOM WITH RUBBER BANDS!

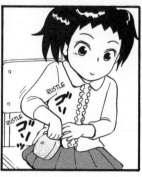

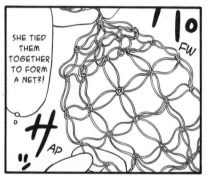

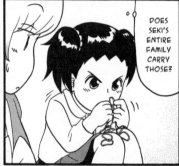

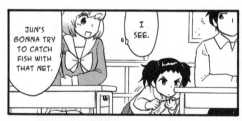

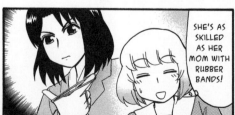

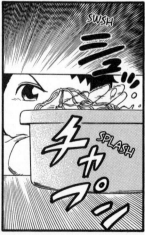

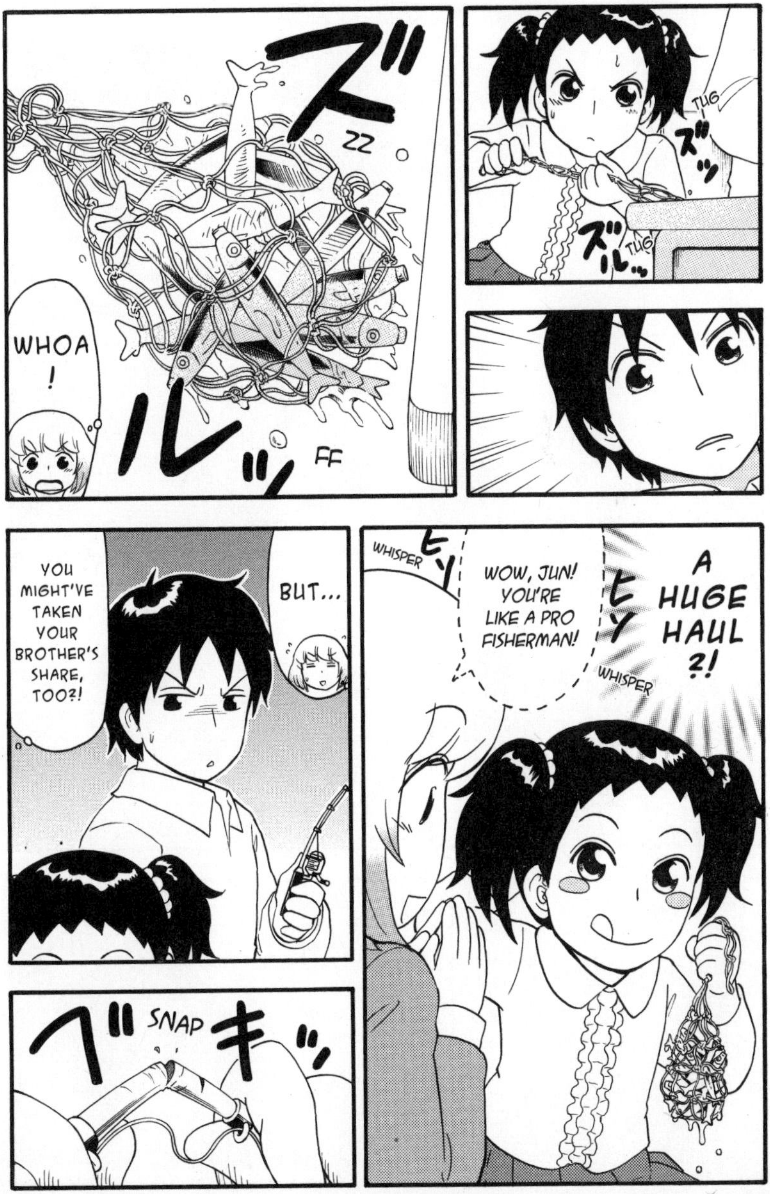

TUG
ズッ
ズル…
TUG
ズズルッ
ZZ
FF
WHOA!
A HUGE HAUL?!
ヒソ
WHISPER
WOW, JUN! YOU'RE LIKE A PRO FISHERMAN!
ヒソ
WHISPER
BUT...
YOU MIGHT'VE TAKEN YOUR BROTHER'S SHARE, TOO?!
ベキッ
SNAP

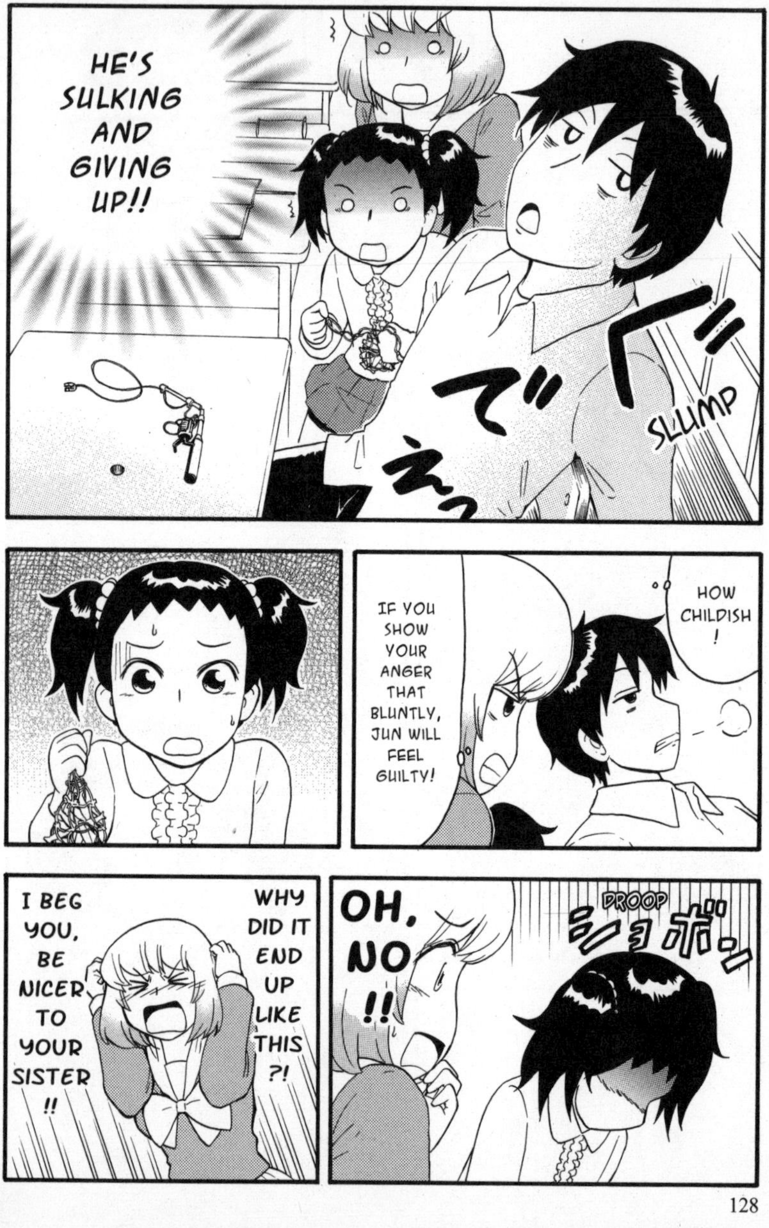
HE'S SULKING AND GIVING UP!!
SLUMP
HOW CHILDISH!
IF YOU SHOW YOUR ANGER THAT BLUNTLY, JUN WILL FEEL GUILTY!
DROOP
OH, NO!!
WHY DID IT END UP LIKE THIS?!
I BEG YOU, BE NICER TO YOUR SISTER!!

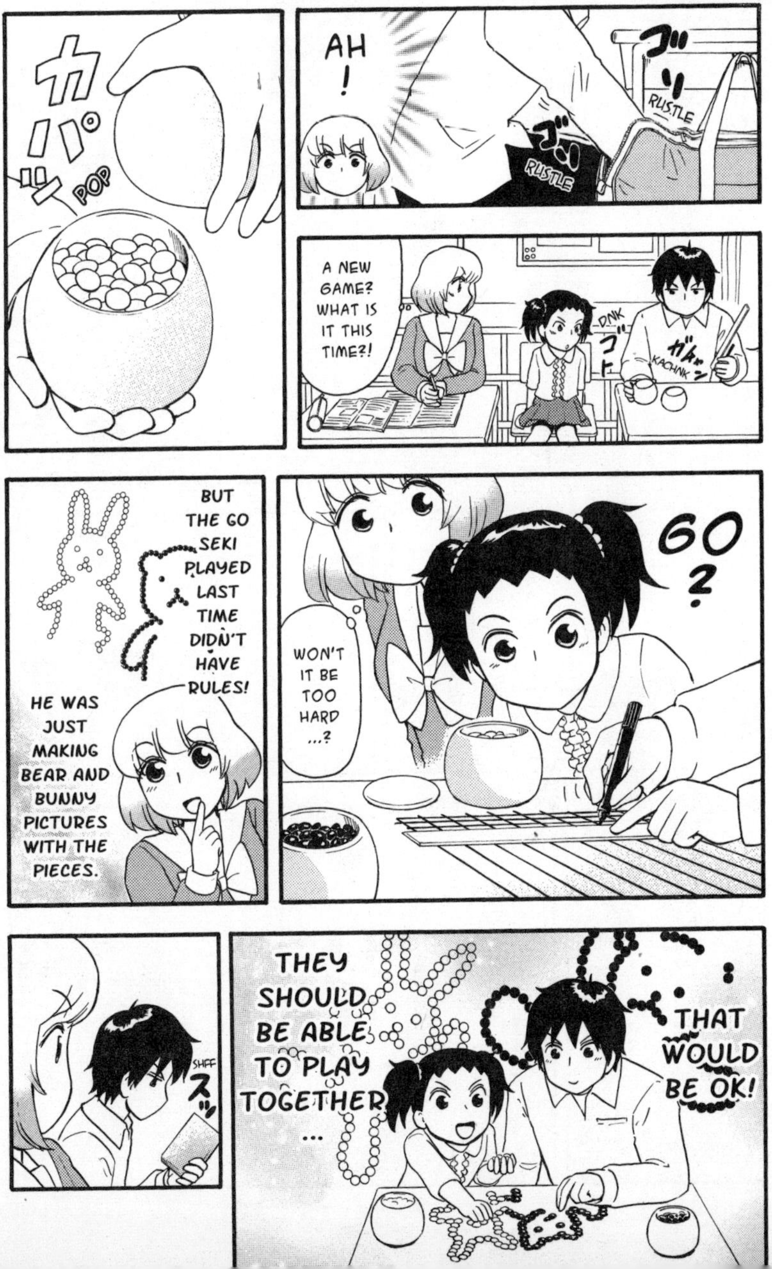
RUSTLE
RUSTLE
AH!
DNK
KACHNK
A NEW GAME? WHAT IS IT THIS TIME?!
POP
GO?
WON'T IT BE TOO HARD ...?
BUT THE GO SEKI PLAYED LAST TIME DIDN'T HAVE RULES!
HE WAS JUST MAKING BEAR AND BUNNY PICTURES WITH THE PIECES.
THAT WOULD BE OK!
THEY SHOULD BE ABLE TO PLAY TOGETHER ...
SHFF

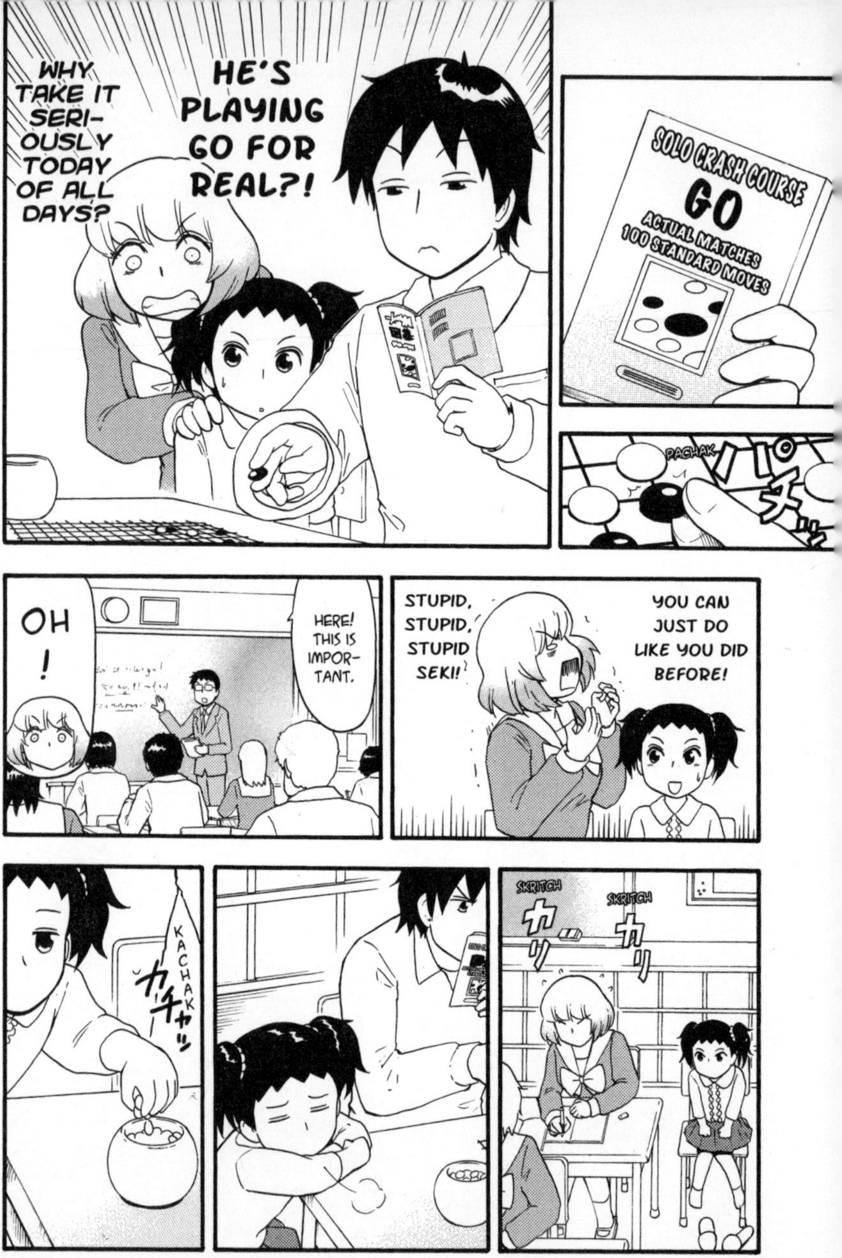
SOLO CRASH COURSE
GO
ACTUAL MATCHES
100 STANDARD MOVES
PACHAK
HE'S PLAYING GO FOR REAL?!
WHY TAKE IT SERIOUSLY TODAY OF ALL DAYS?
YOU CAN JUST DO LIKE YOU DID BEFORE!
STUPID, STUPID, STUPID SEKI!
HERE! THIS IS IMPORTANT.
OH!
SKRITCH
SKRITCH
KACHAK

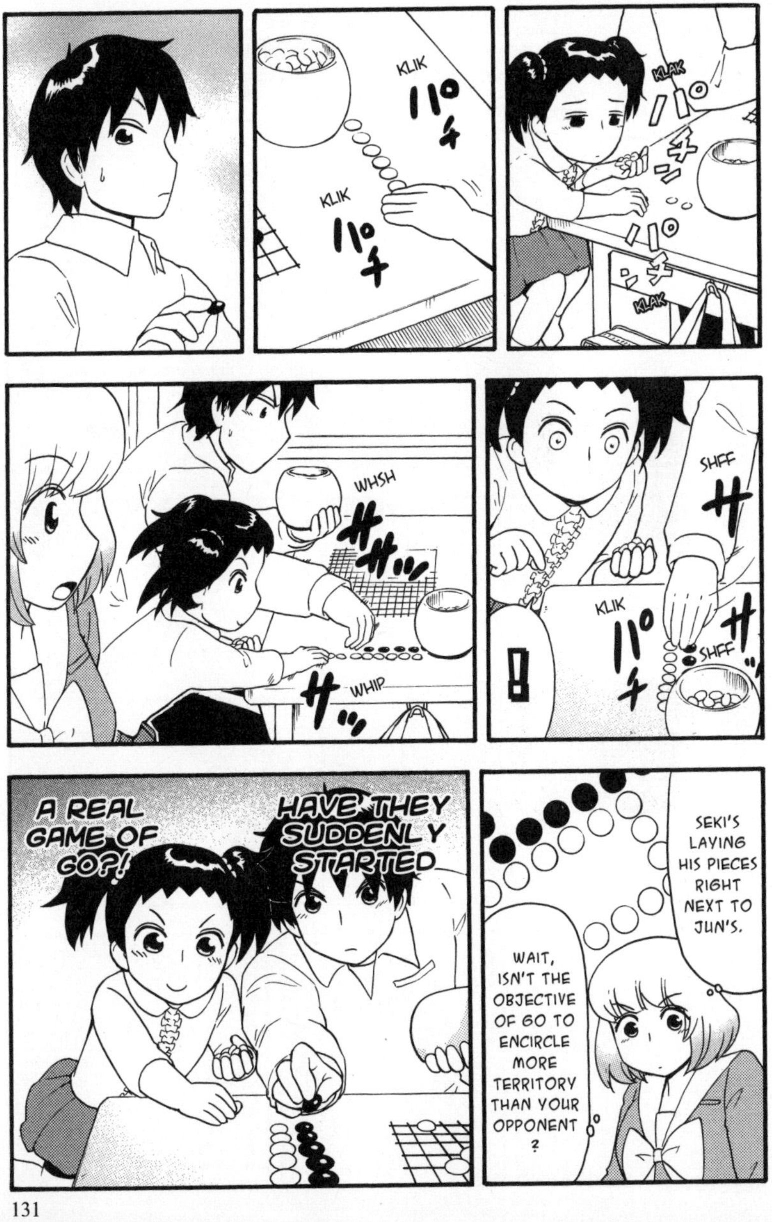
KLAK
KLAK
KLIK
パチ
KLIK
パチ
SHFF
サ
KLIK
パチ
SHFF
!
WHSH
WHIP
SEKI'S LAYING HIS PIECES RIGHT NEXT TO JUN'S.
WAIT, ISN'T THE OBJECTIVE OF GO TO ENCIRCLE MORE TERRITORY THAN YOUR OPPONENT?
HAVE THEY SUDDENLY STARTED
A REAL GAME OF GO?!

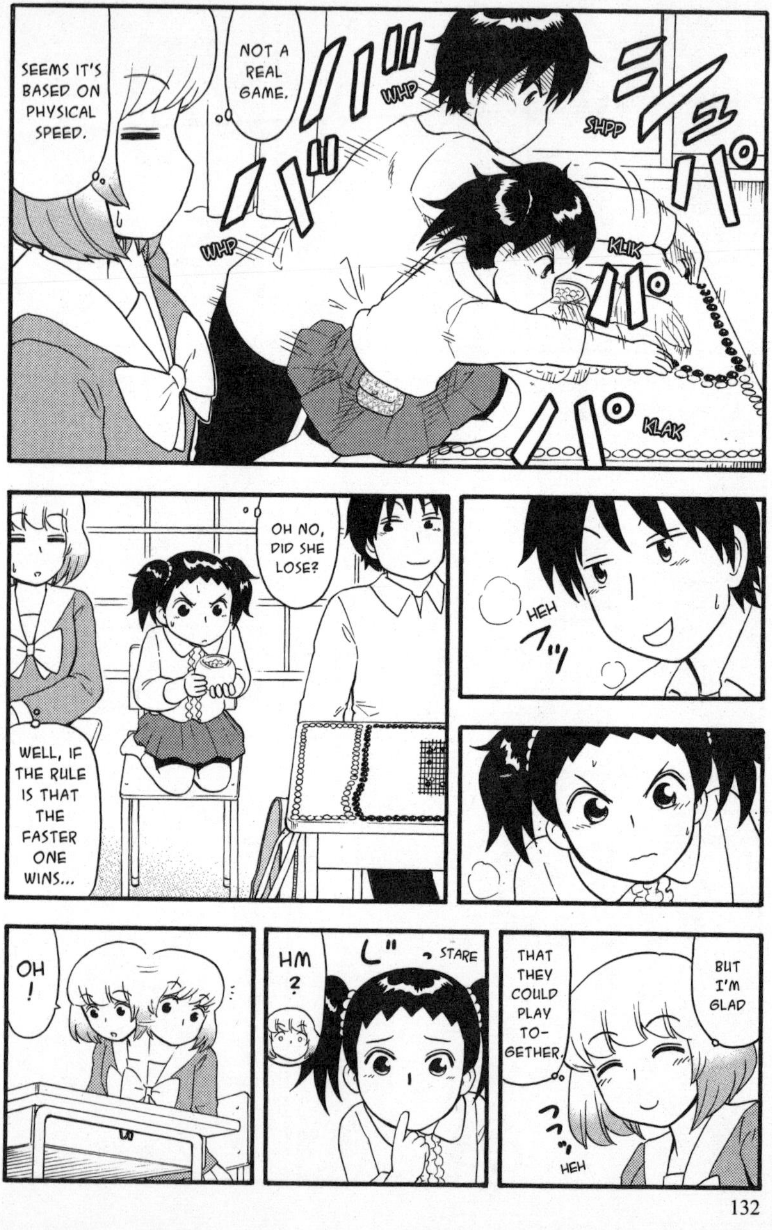
SHPP
WHP
NOT A REAL GAME.
SEEMS IT'S BASED ON PHYSICAL SPEED.
KLIK
WHP
KLAK
HEH
OH NO, DID SHE LOSE?
WELL, IF THE RULE IS THAT THE FASTER ONE WINS...
BUT I'M GLAD
THAT THEY COULD PLAY TO-GETHER.
HEH
STARE
HM ?
OH !

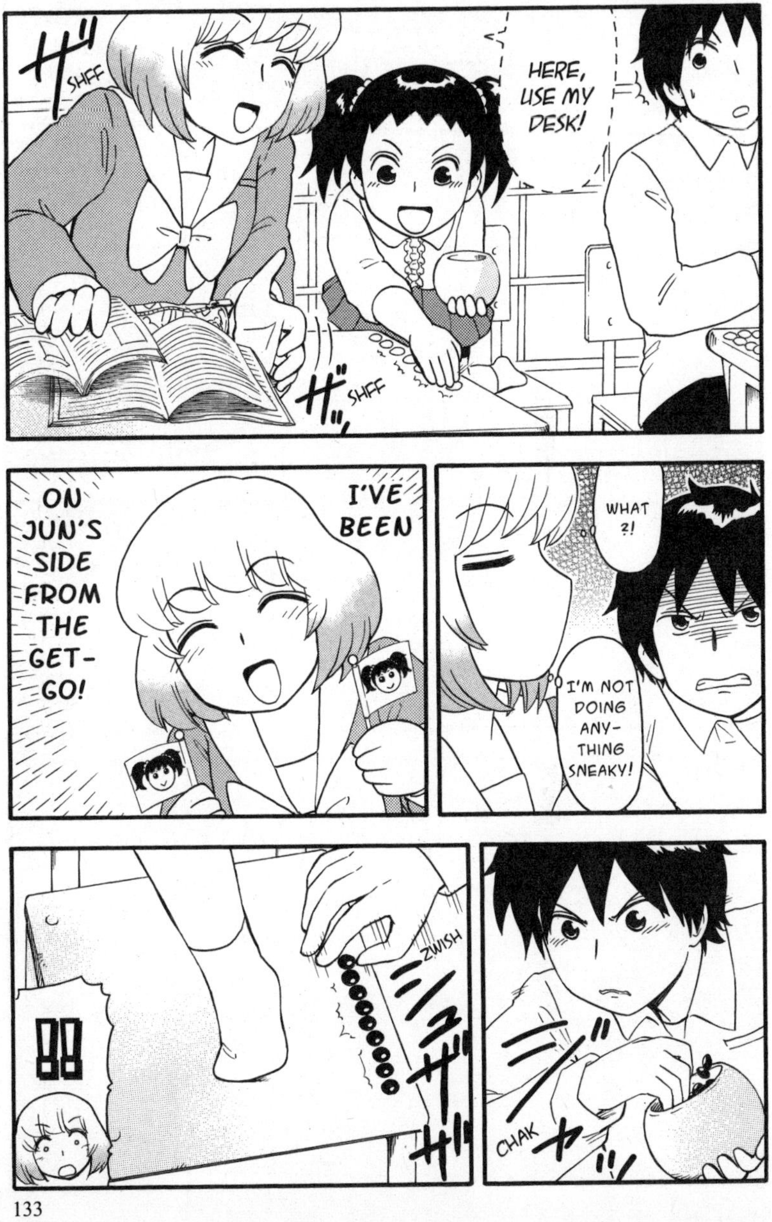
HERE, USE MY DESK!
SHFF
SHFF
WHAT?!
I'M NOT DOING ANYTHING SNEAKY!
I'VE BEEN
ON JUN'S SIDE FROM THE GET-GO!
CHAK
ZWISH
!!

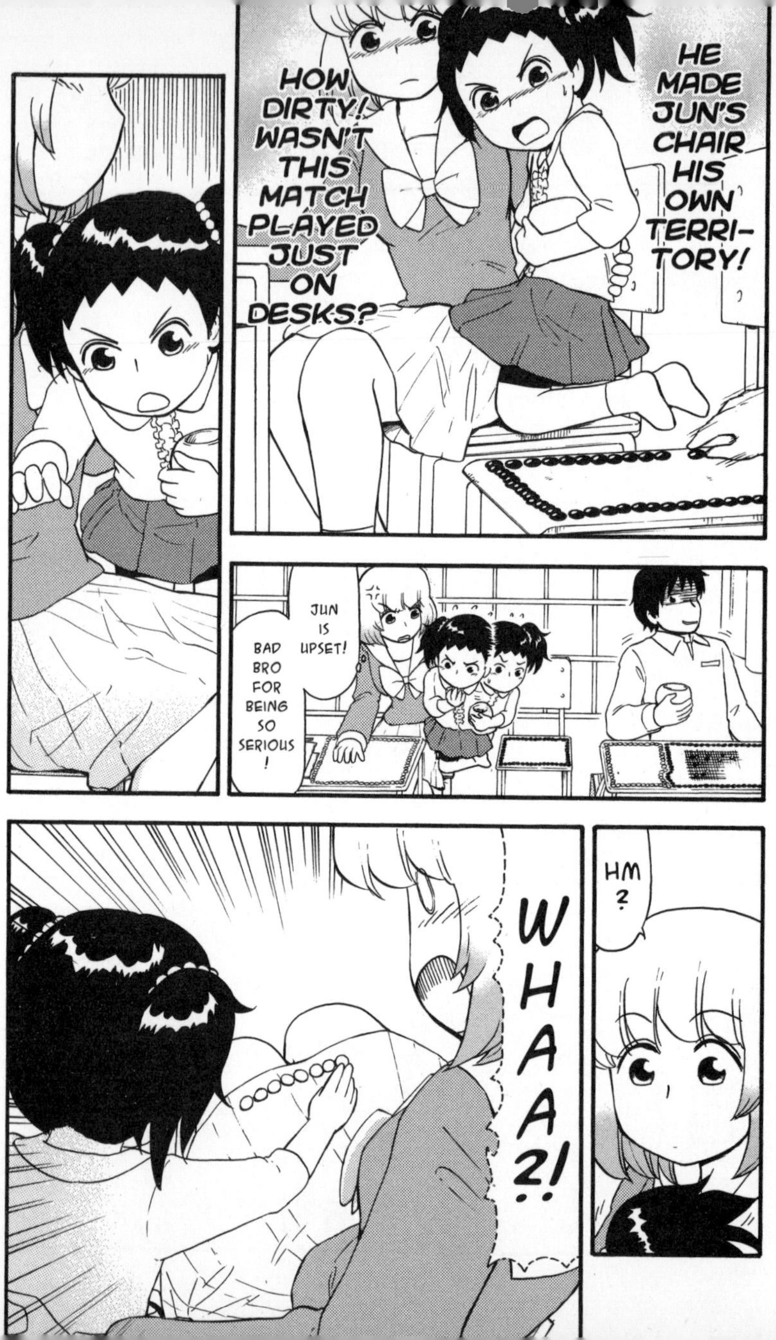
HE MADE JUN'S CHAIR HIS OWN TERRITORY!
HOW DIRTY! WASN'T THIS MATCH PLAYED JUST ON DESKS?
JUN IS UPSET!
BAD BRO FOR BEING SO SERIOUS!
HM?
WHAA?!

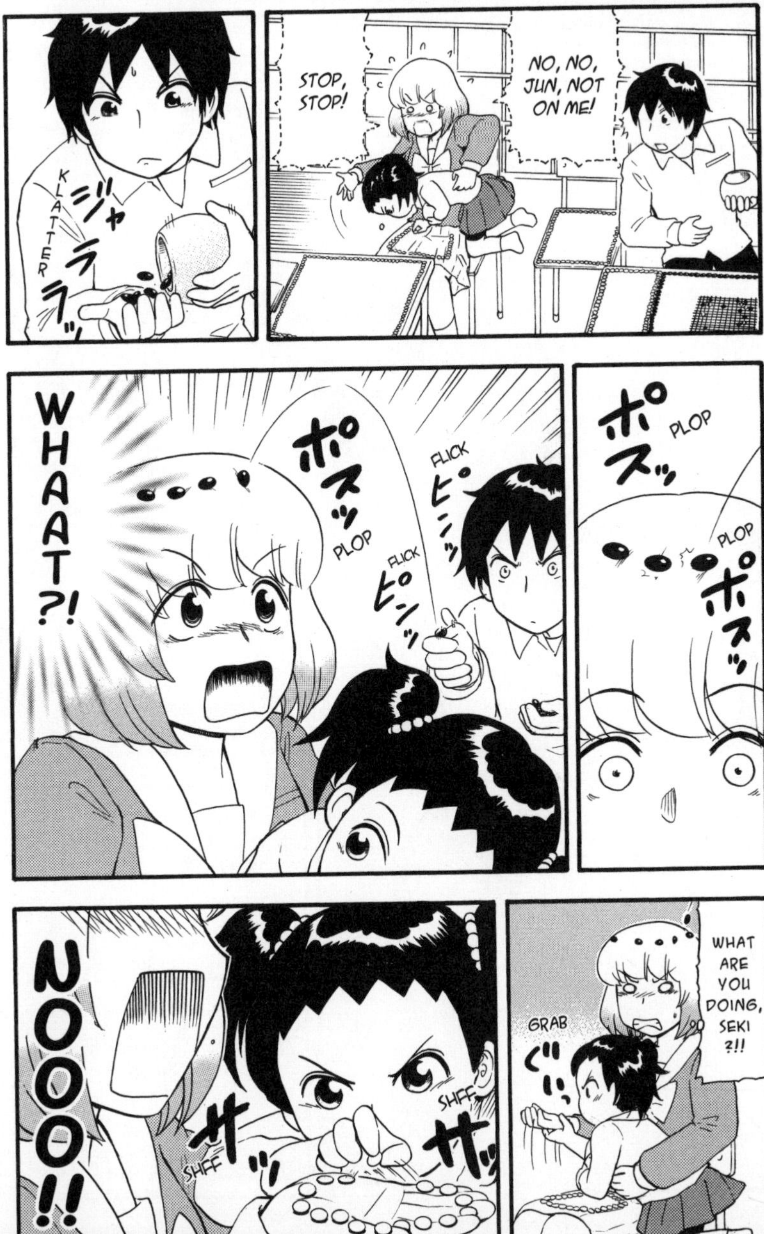

NO, NO, JUN, NOT ON ME!
STOP, STOP!
ジャララッ
KLATTER
ポスッ
PLOP
PLOP
ポスッ
ピンッ
FLICK
ピンッ
FLICK
ポスッ
PLOP
WHAAAT?!
WHAT ARE YOU DOING, SEKI?!!
ぐいっ
GRAB
サッ
SHFF
サッ
SHFF
NOOOO!!

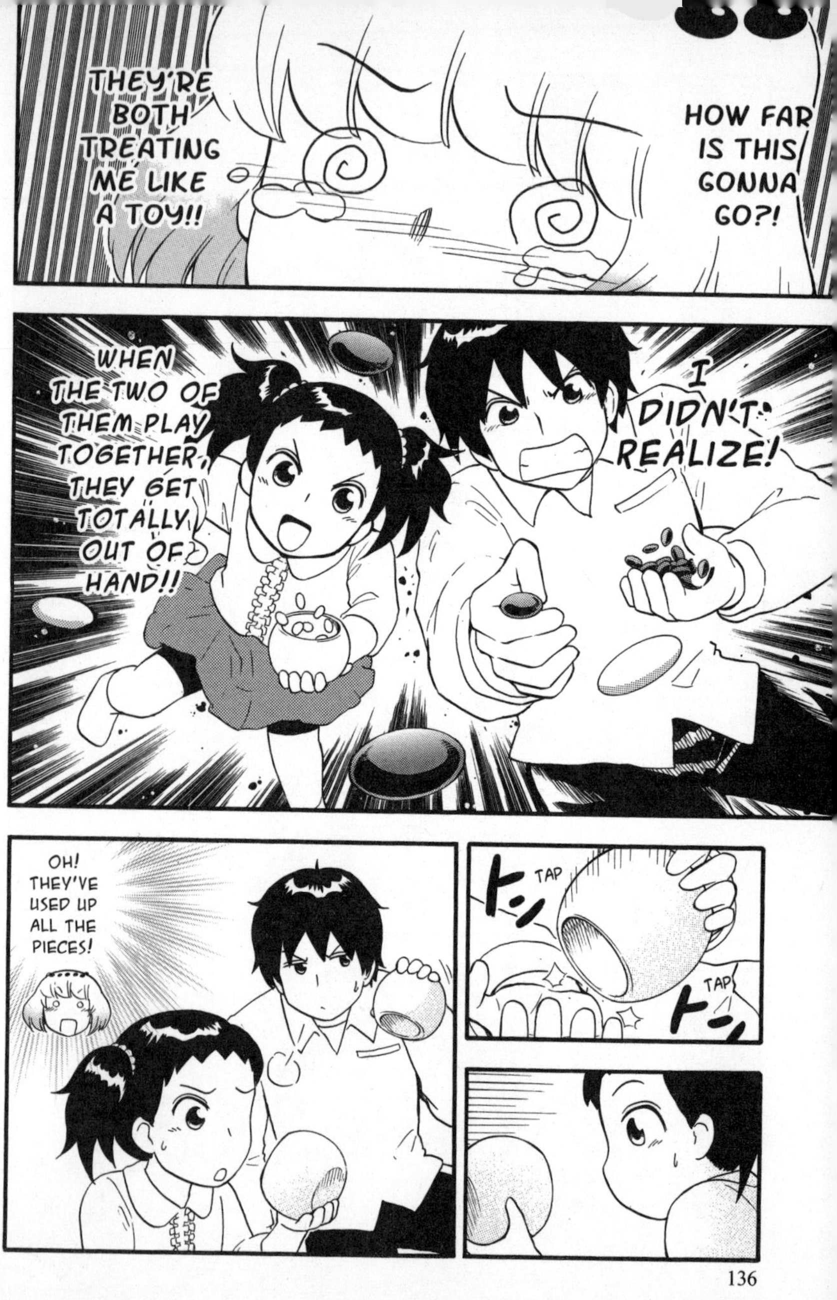
HOW FAR IS THIS GONNA GO?!
THEY'RE BOTH TREATING ME LIKE A TOY!!
I DIDN'T REALIZE!
WHEN THE TWO OF THEM PLAY TOGETHER, THEY GET TOTALLY OUT OF HAND!!
TAP
TAP
OH! THEY'VE USED UP ALL THE PIECES!

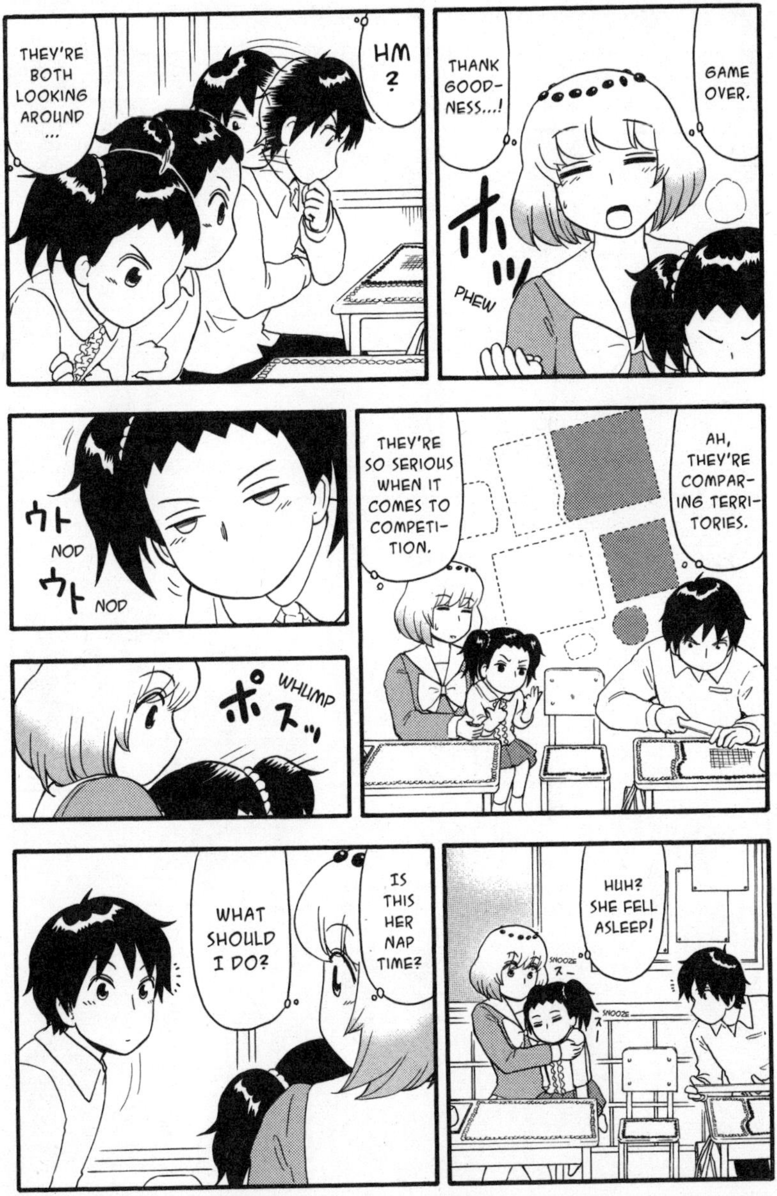
GAME OVER.
THANK GOODNESS...!
ホッ
PHEW
HM?
THEY'RE BOTH LOOKING AROUND...
AH, THEY'RE COMPARING TERRITORIES.
THEY'RE SO SERIOUS WHEN IT COMES TO COMPETITION.
ウト
NOD
ウト
NOD
ポスッ
WHUMP
HUH? SHE FELL ASLEEP!
SNOOZE
スー
SNOOZE
スー
IS THIS HER NAP TIME?
WHAT SHOULD I DO?

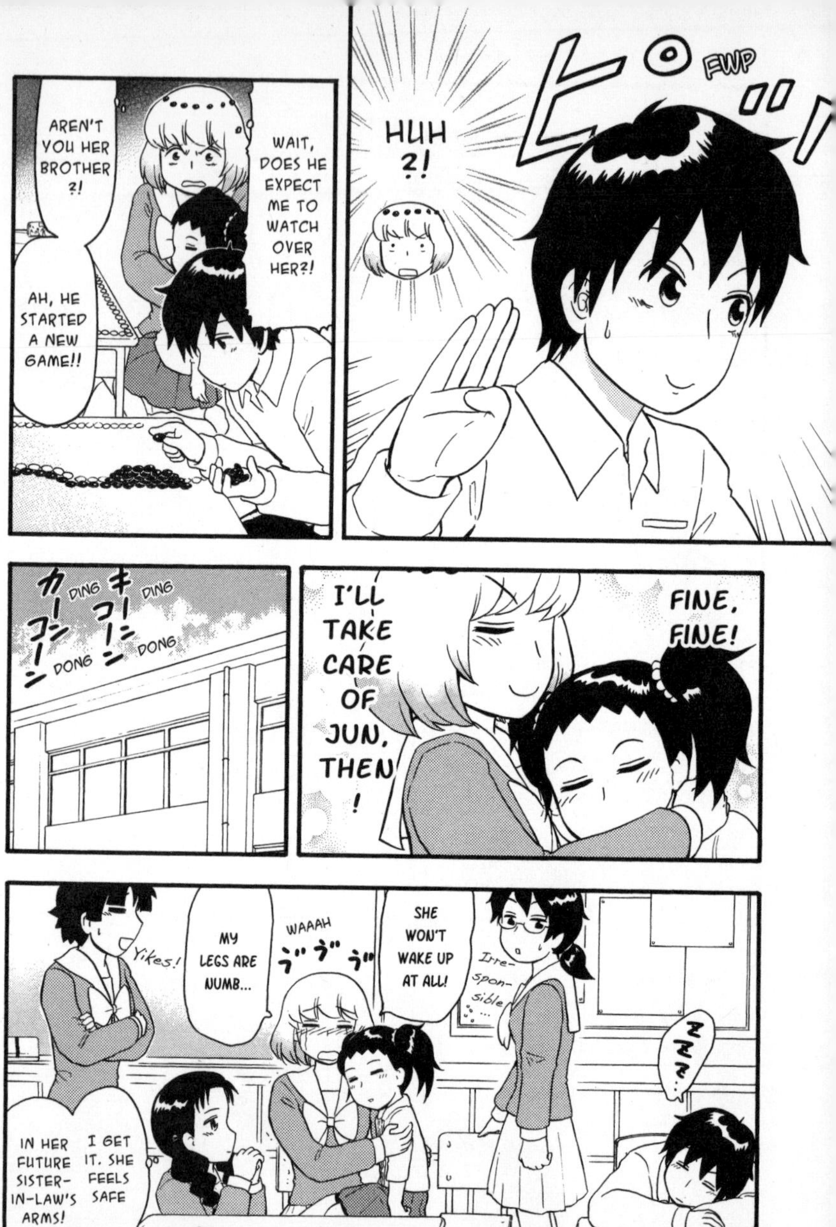
FWP
HUH ?!
WAIT, DOES HE EXPECT ME TO WATCH OVER HER?!
AREN'T YOU HER BROTHER ?!
AH, HE STARTED A NEW GAME!!
FINE, FINE!
I'LL TAKE CARE OF JUN, THEN !
DING DING
DONG DONG
SHE WON'T WAKE UP AT ALL!
Irre-spon-sible...
WAAAH
MY LEGS ARE NUMB...
Yikes!
I GET IT. SHE FEELS SAFE
IN HER FUTURE SISTER-IN-LAW'S ARMS!

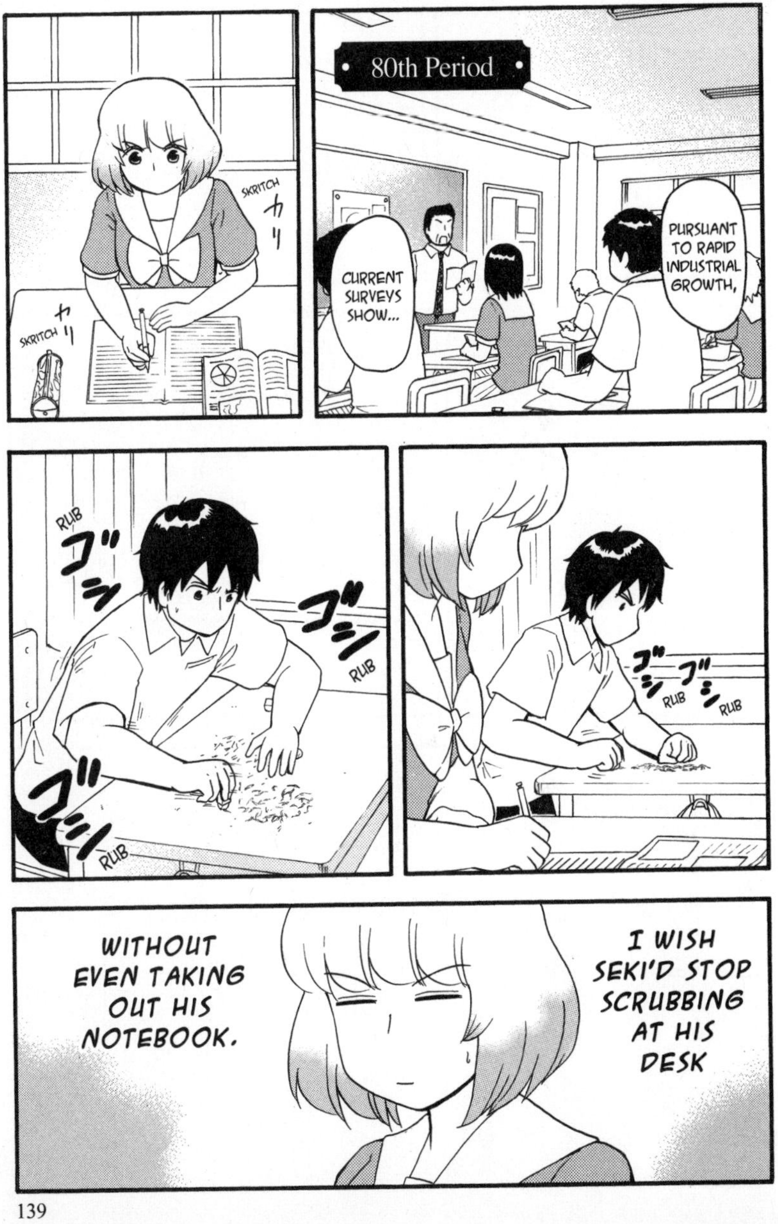
80th Period
PURSUANT TO RAPID INDUSTRIAL GROWTH,
CURRENT SURVEYS SHOW...
SKRITCH カリ
SKRITCH カリ
RUB ゴシ
RUB ゴシ
RUB ゴシ
RUB ゴシ
RUB ゴシ
RUB ゴシ
I WISH SEKI'D STOP SCRUBBING AT HIS DESK
WITHOUT EVEN TAKING OUT HIS NOTEBOOK.

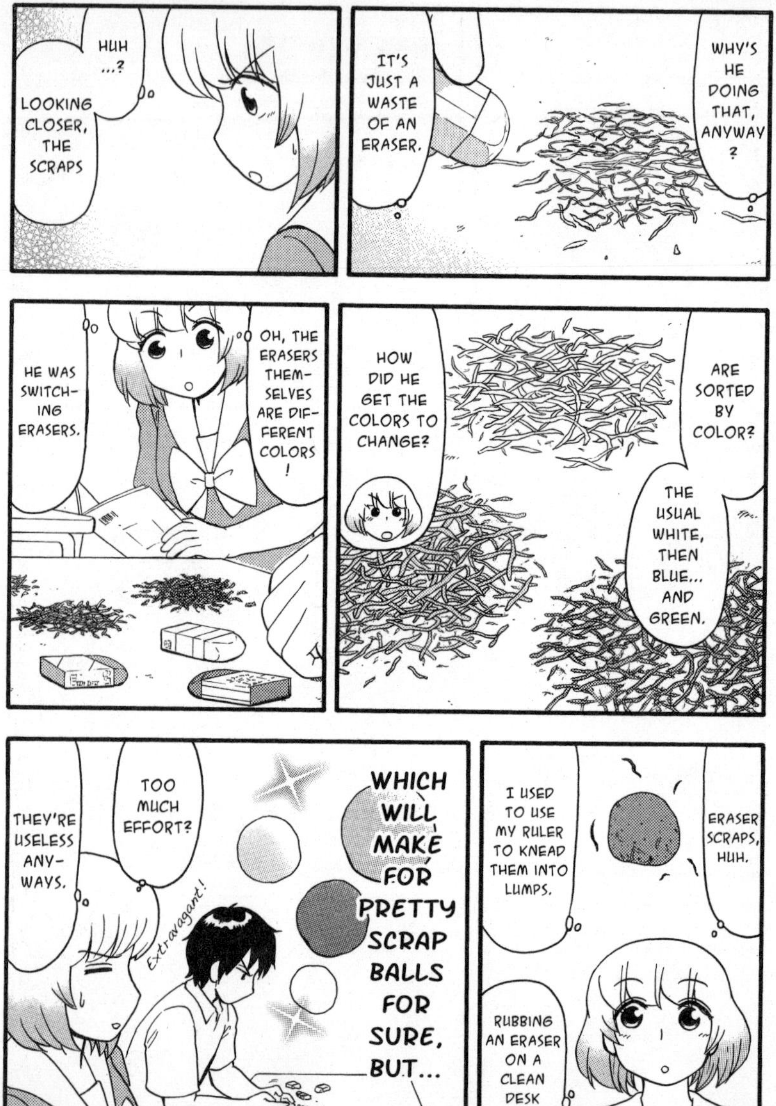

WHY'S HE DOING THAT, ANYWAY?
IT'S JUST A WASTE OF AN ERASER.
HUH...?
LOOKING CLOSER, THE SCRAPS
ARE SORTED BY COLOR?
THE USUAL WHITE, THEN BLUE... AND GREEN.
HOW DID HE GET THE COLORS TO CHANGE?
OH, THE ERASERS THEMSELVES ARE DIFFERENT COLORS!
HE WAS SWITCHING ERASERS.
ERASER SCRAPS, HUH.
I USED TO USE MY RULER TO KNEAD THEM INTO LUMPS.
RUBBING AN ERASER ON A CLEAN DESK MAKES CLEAN SCRAPS.
WHICH WILL MAKE FOR PRETTY SCRAP BALLS FOR SURE, BUT...
TOO MUCH EFFORT?
THEY'RE USELESS ANYWAYS.
Extravagant!

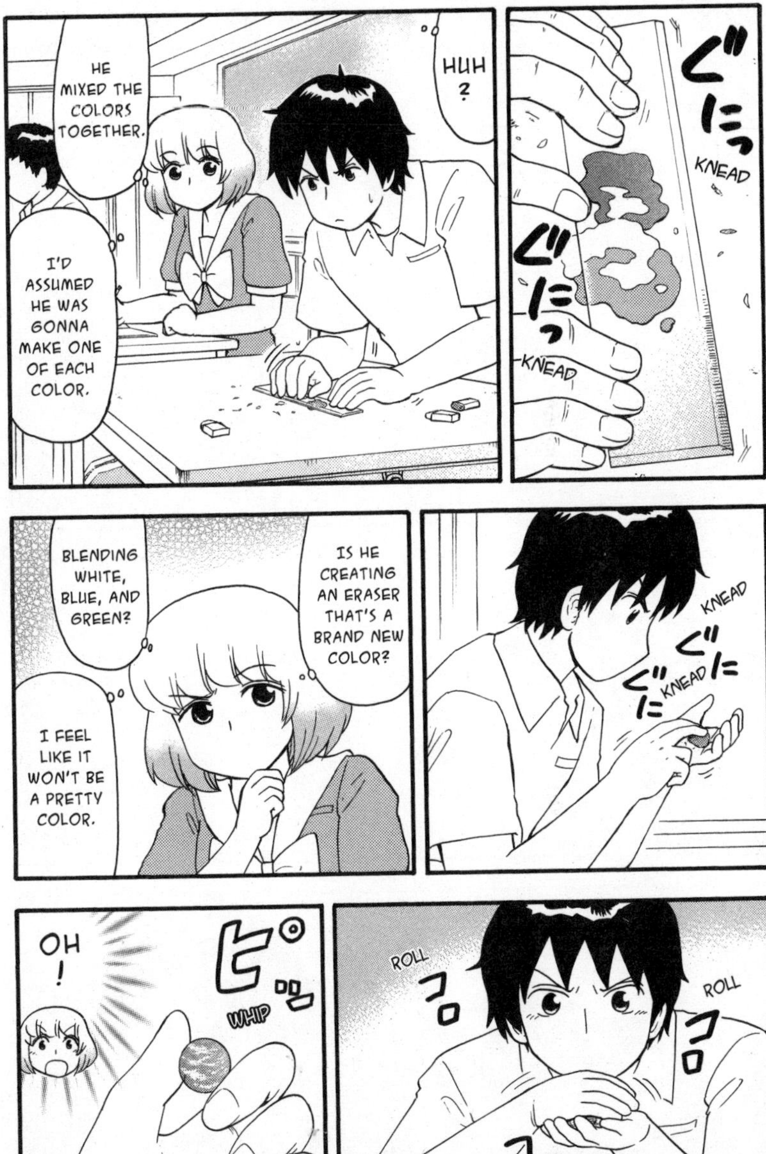
ぐにっ
KNEAD
ぐにっ
KNEAD
HUH?
HE MIXED THE COLORS TOGETHER.
I'D ASSUMED HE WAS GONNA MAKE ONE OF EACH COLOR.
KNEAD
ぐに
ぐに
KNEAD
IS HE CREATING AN ERASER THAT'S A BRAND NEW COLOR?
BLENDING WHITE, BLUE, AND GREEN?
I FEEL LIKE IT WON'T BE A PRETTY COLOR.
ROLL
コロ
ROLL
コロ
コロ
ROLL
WHIP
OH!

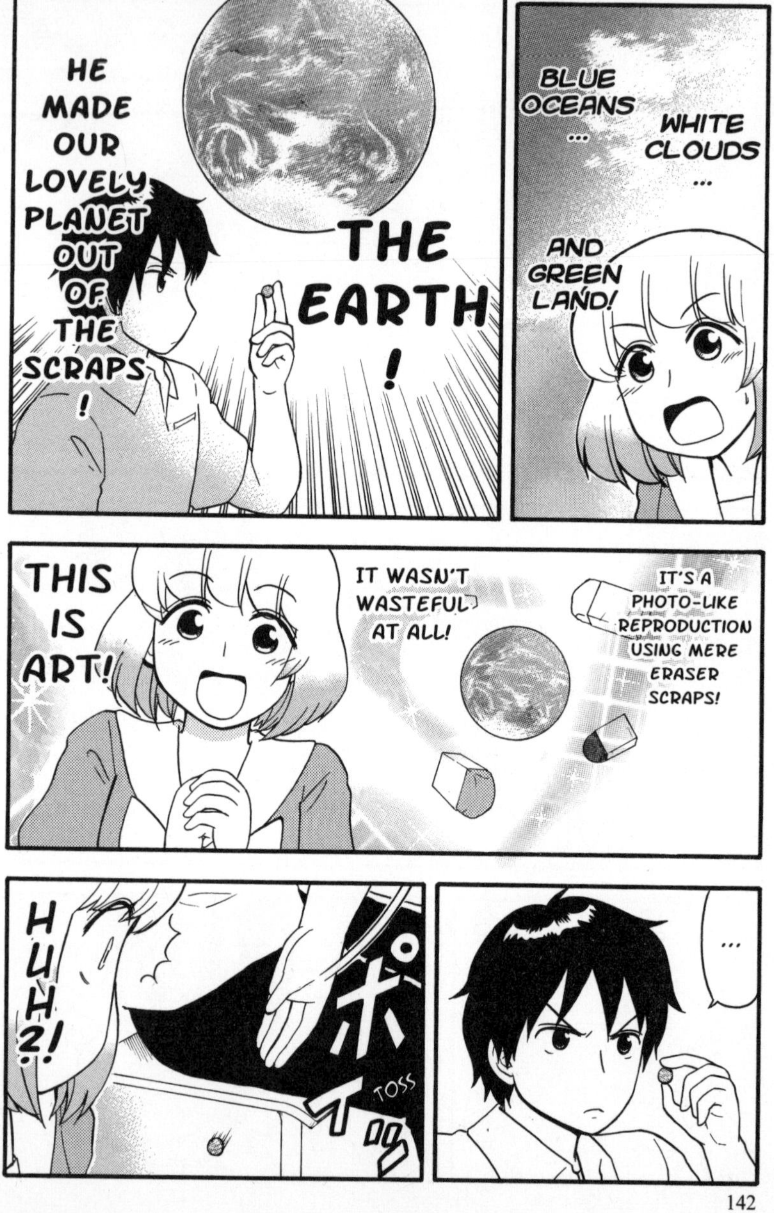
BLUE OCEANS ...
WHITE CLOUDS ...
AND GREEN LAND!
THE EARTH!
HE MADE OUR LOVELY PLANET OUT OF THE SCRAPS!
IT'S A PHOTO-LIKE REPRODUCTION USING MERE ERASER SCRAPS!
IT WASN'T WASTEFUL AT ALL!
THIS IS ART!
...
ポイッ
TOSS
HUH?!

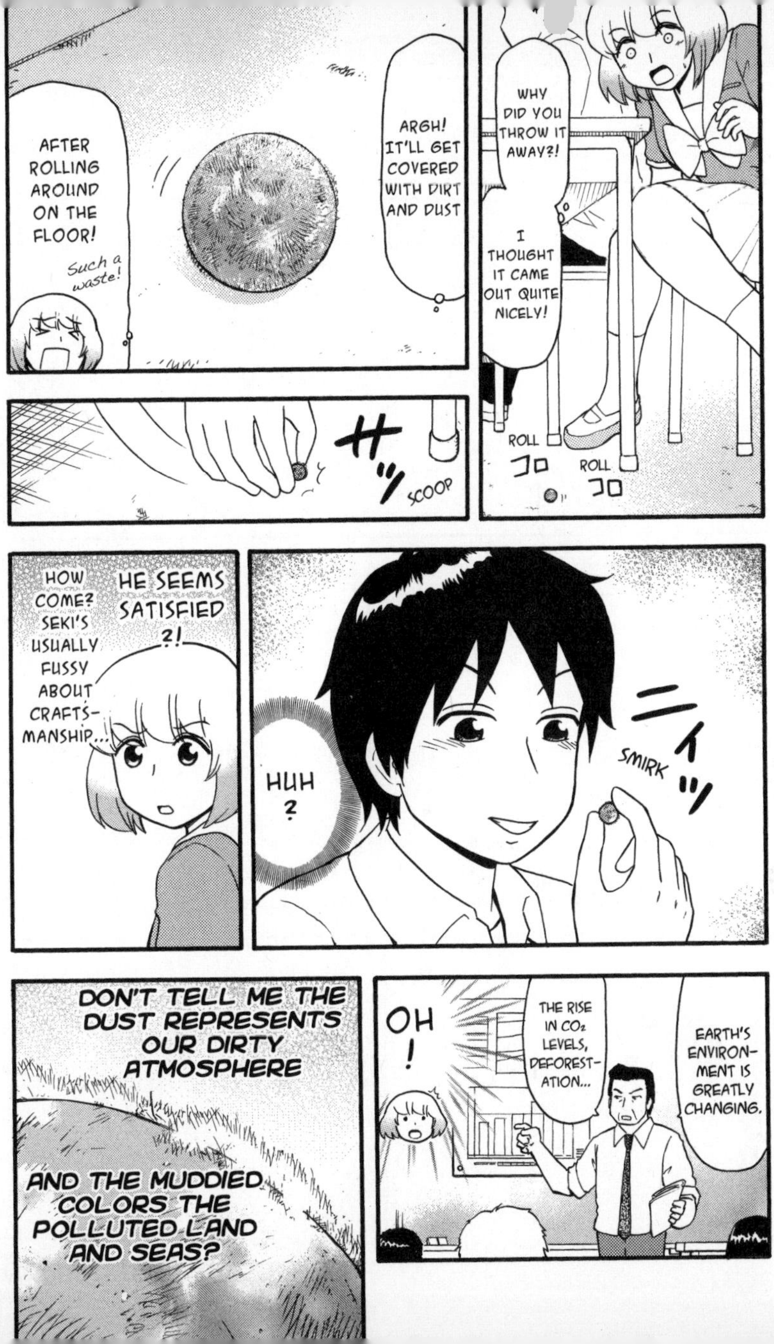
WHY DID YOU THROW IT AWAY?!
I THOUGHT IT CAME OUT QUITE NICELY!
ROLL コロ
ROLL コロ
ARGH! IT'LL GET COVERED WITH DIRT AND DUST
AFTER ROLLING AROUND ON THE FLOOR!
Such a waste!
サッ
SCOOP
HUH?
ニィッ
SMIRK
HE SEEMS SATISFIED?!
HOW COME? SEKI'S USUALLY FUSSY ABOUT CRAFTS-MANSHIP...
EARTH'S ENVIRON-MENT IS GREATLY CHANGING.
THE RISE IN CO2 LEVELS, DEFOREST-ATION...
OH!
DON'T TELL ME THE DUST REPRESENTS OUR DIRTY ATMOSPHERE
AND THE MUDDIED COLORS THE POLLUTED LAND AND SEAS?

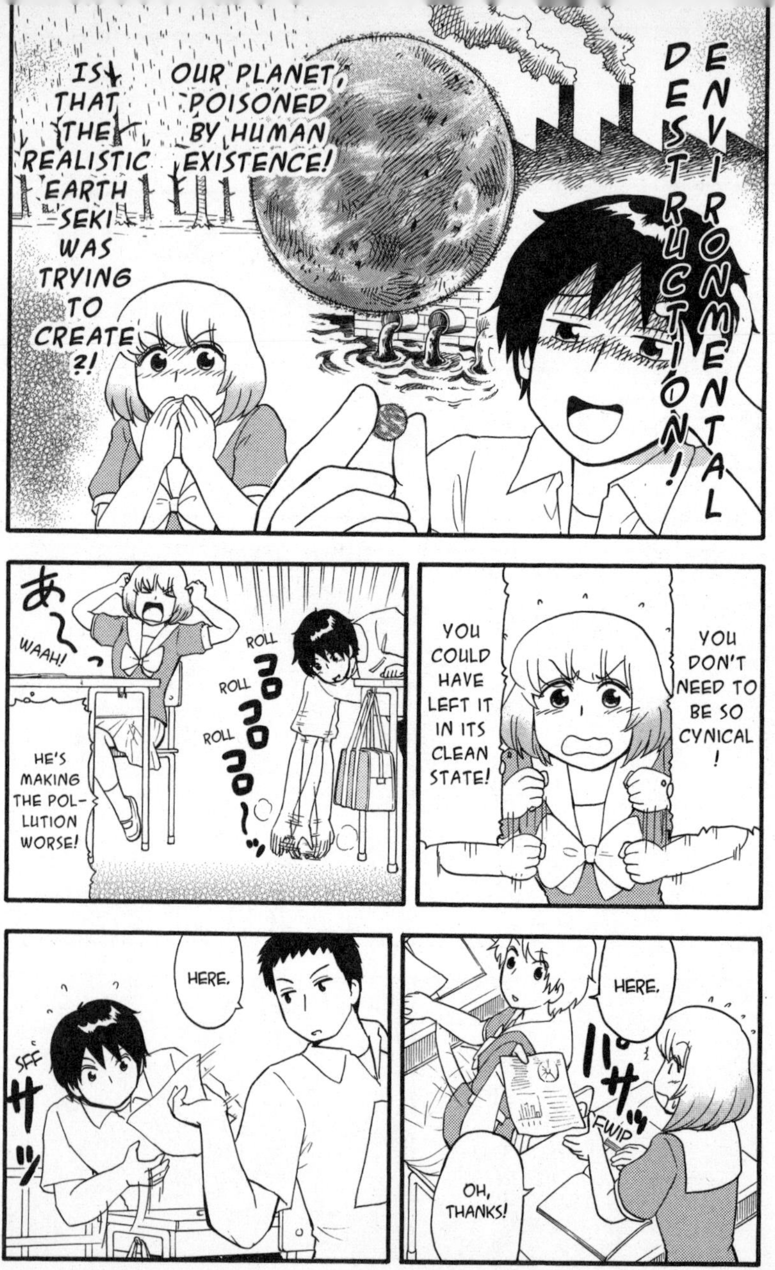

ENVIRONMENTAL DESTRUCTION!
OUR PLANET, POISONED BY HUMAN EXISTENCE!
IS THAT THE REALISTIC EARTH SEKI WAS TRYING TO CREATE?!
YOU DON'T NEED TO BE SO CYNICAL!
YOU COULD HAVE LEFT IT IN ITS CLEAN STATE!
あ〜
WAAH!
コロ
ROLL
コロ
ROLL
コロ〜ッ
ROLL
HE'S MAKING THE POLLUTION WORSE!
HERE.
パサッ
FWIP
OH, THANKS!
HERE.
サッ
SFF

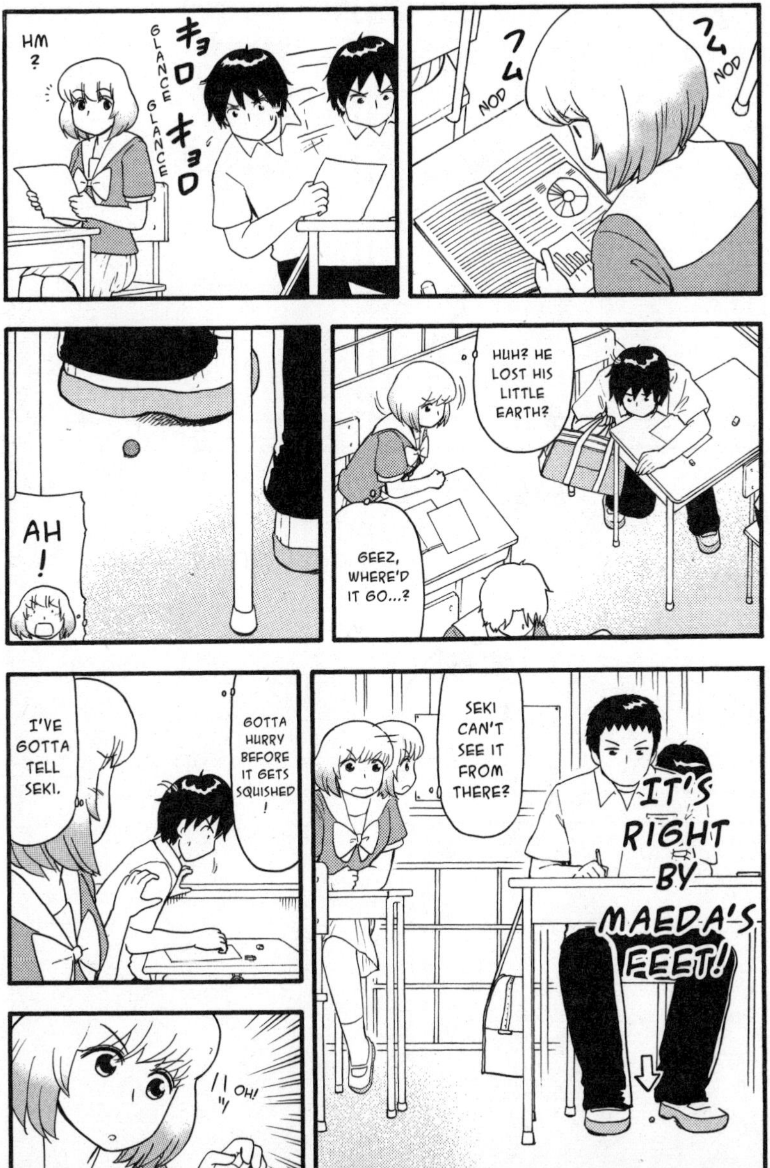
フム
NOD
フム
NOD
キョロ
GLANCE
キョロ
GLANCE
HM?
HUH? HE LOST HIS LITTLE EARTH?
GEEZ, WHERE'D IT GO...?
AH!
SEKI CAN'T SEE IT FROM THERE?
IT'S RIGHT BY MAEDA'S FEET!
GOTTA HURRY BEFORE IT GETS SQUISHED!
I'VE GOTTA TELL SEKI.
OH!

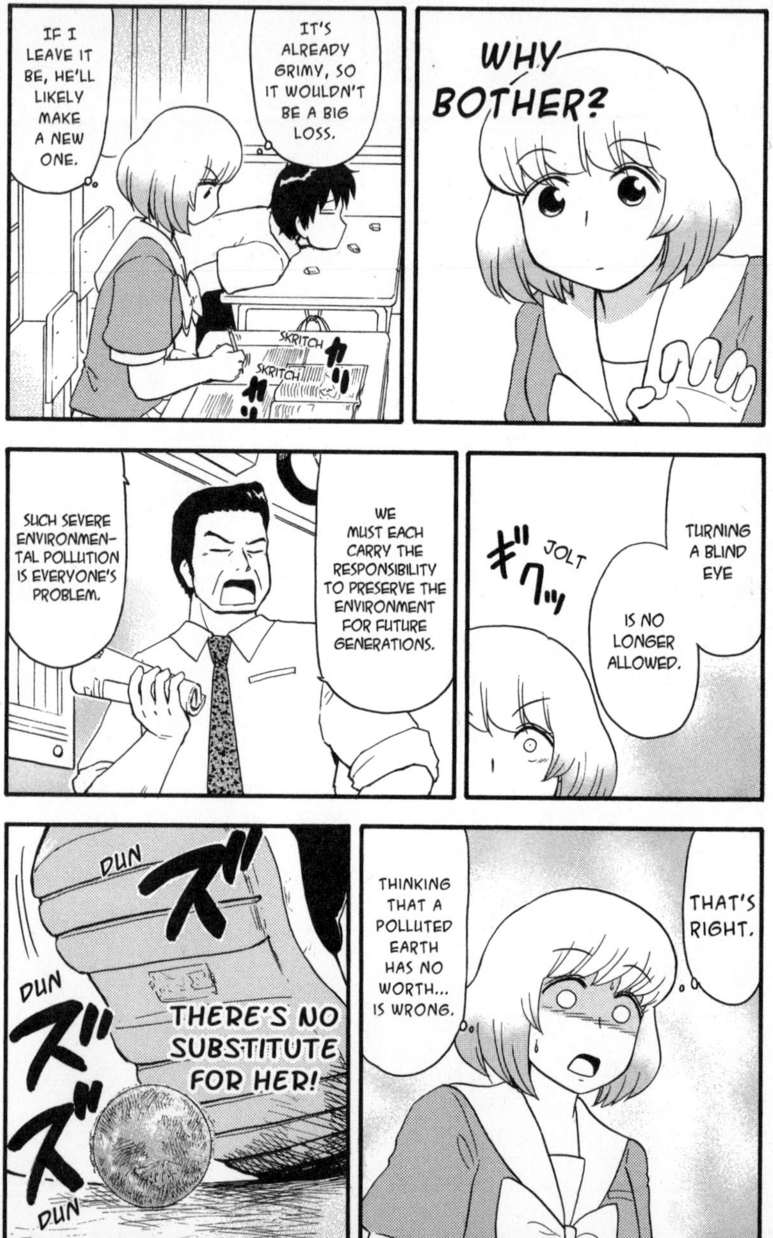
WHY BOTHER?
IT'S ALREADY GRIMY, SO IT WOULDN'T BE A BIG LOSS.
IF I LEAVE IT BE, HE'LL LIKELY MAKE A NEW ONE.
SKRITCH
SKRITCH
JOLT
TURNING A BLIND EYE
IS NO LONGER ALLOWED.
WE MUST EACH CARRY THE RESPONSIBILITY TO PRESERVE THE ENVIRONMENT FOR FUTURE GENERATIONS.
SUCH SEVERE ENVIRONMENTAL POLLUTION IS EVERYONE'S PROBLEM.
THAT'S RIGHT.
THINKING THAT A POLLUTED EARTH HAS NO WORTH... IS WRONG.
DUN
DUN
THERE'S NO SUBSTITUTE FOR HER!
DUN

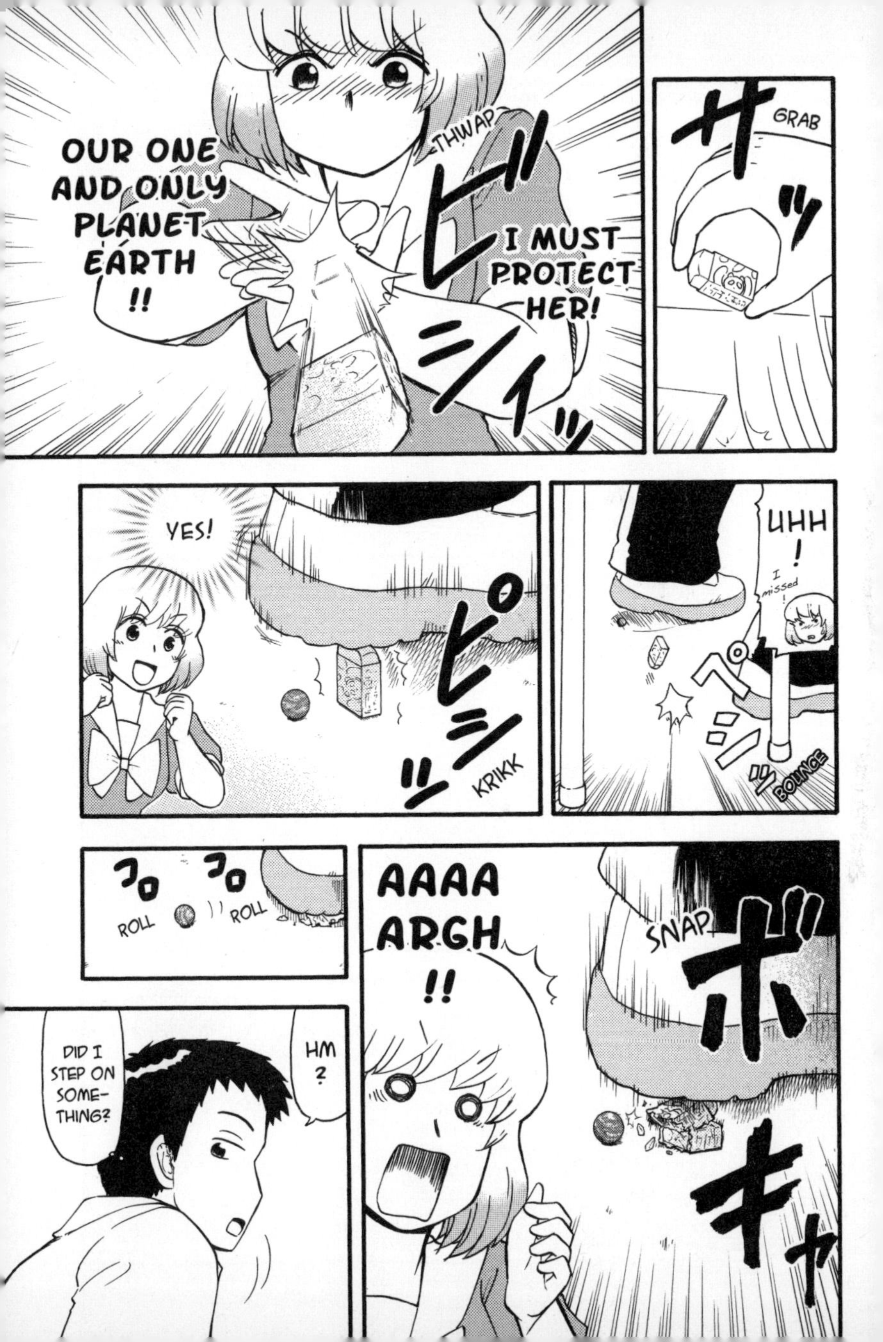

GRAB
THWAP
I MUST PROTECT HER!
OUR ONE AND ONLY PLANET EARTH !!
UHH!
I missed!
BOUNCE
YES!
KRIKK
SNAP
AAAA ARGH !!
ROLL
ROLL
HM?
DID I STEP ON SOME-THING?

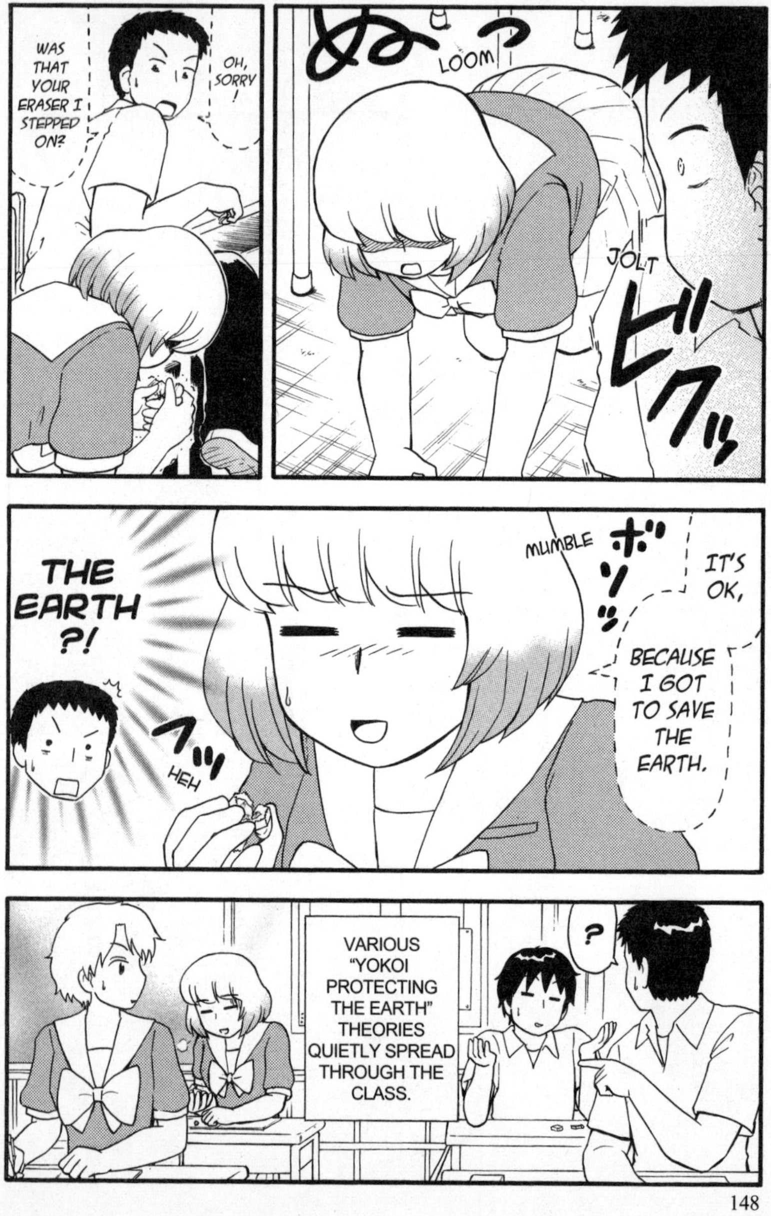
ぬっ
LOOM
JOLT
ビクッ
WAS THAT YOUR ERASER I STEPPED ON?
OH, SORRY!
MUMBLE
ボソッ
IT'S OK,
BECAUSE I GOT TO SAVE THE EARTH.
ヘッ
HEH
THE EARTH ?!
?
VARIOUS "YOKOI PROTECTING THE EARTH" THEORIES QUIETLY SPREAD THROUGH THE CLASS.

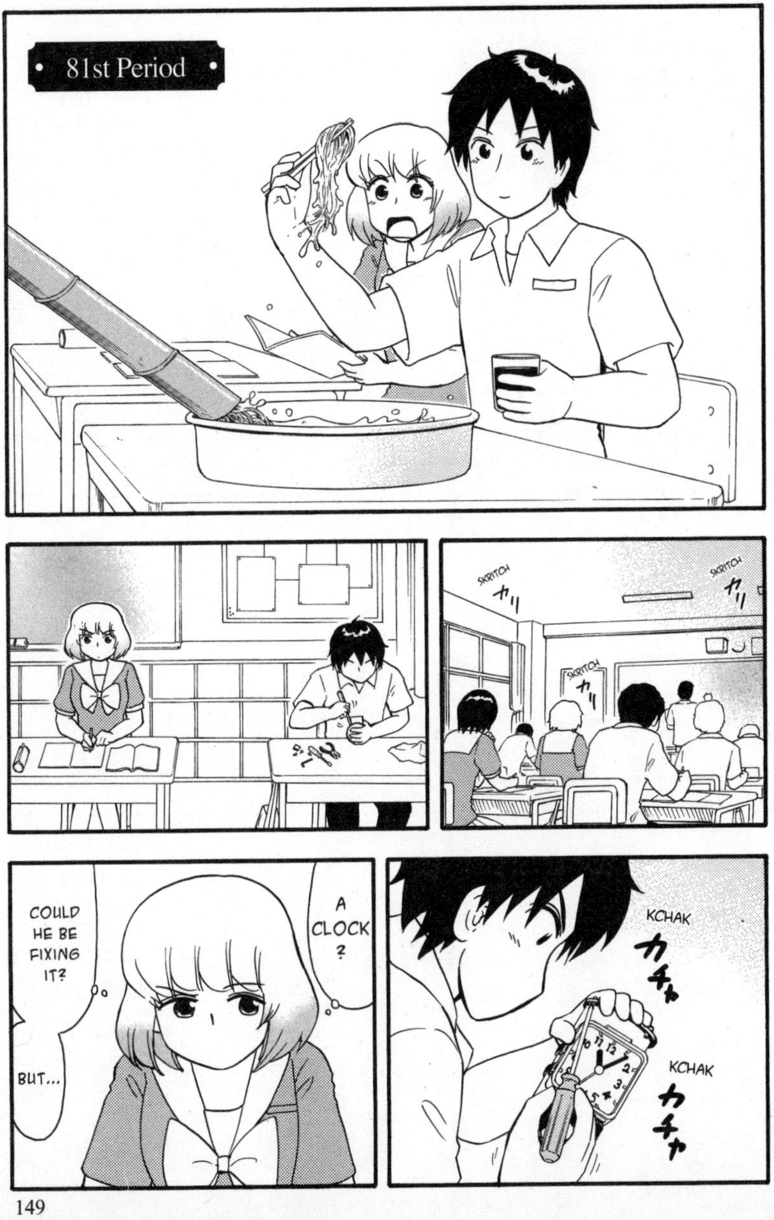
81st Period
SKRITCH
カリ
SKRITCH
カリ
SKRITCH
カリ
KCHAK
カチャ
KCHAK
カチャ
A CLOCK?
COULD HE BE FIXING IT?
BUT...

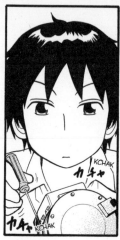

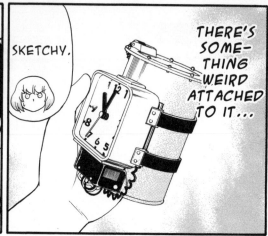

THERE'S SOME-THING WEIRD ATTACHED TO IT...
SKETCHY.
KCHAK
KCHAK
HE'S USING A LOT OF TOOLS.
MUST BE A PRETTY COMPLEX DEVICE.
SEKI CAN USE ALL THIS STUFF?
IS IT A DEVICE THAT OPERATES ON A TIMER?
BUT IT LOOKS QUITE A LOT LIKE
THOSE THINGS YOU SEE IN ACTION FLICKS...
A TIME BOMB!!
NAH, THERE'S NO WAY THAT THAT'S REALLY
A BOMB, THOUGH...
HA HA
KATNK

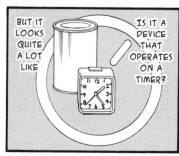

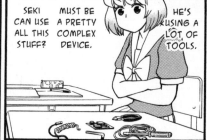

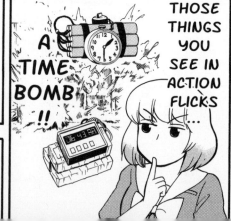

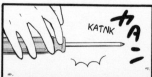

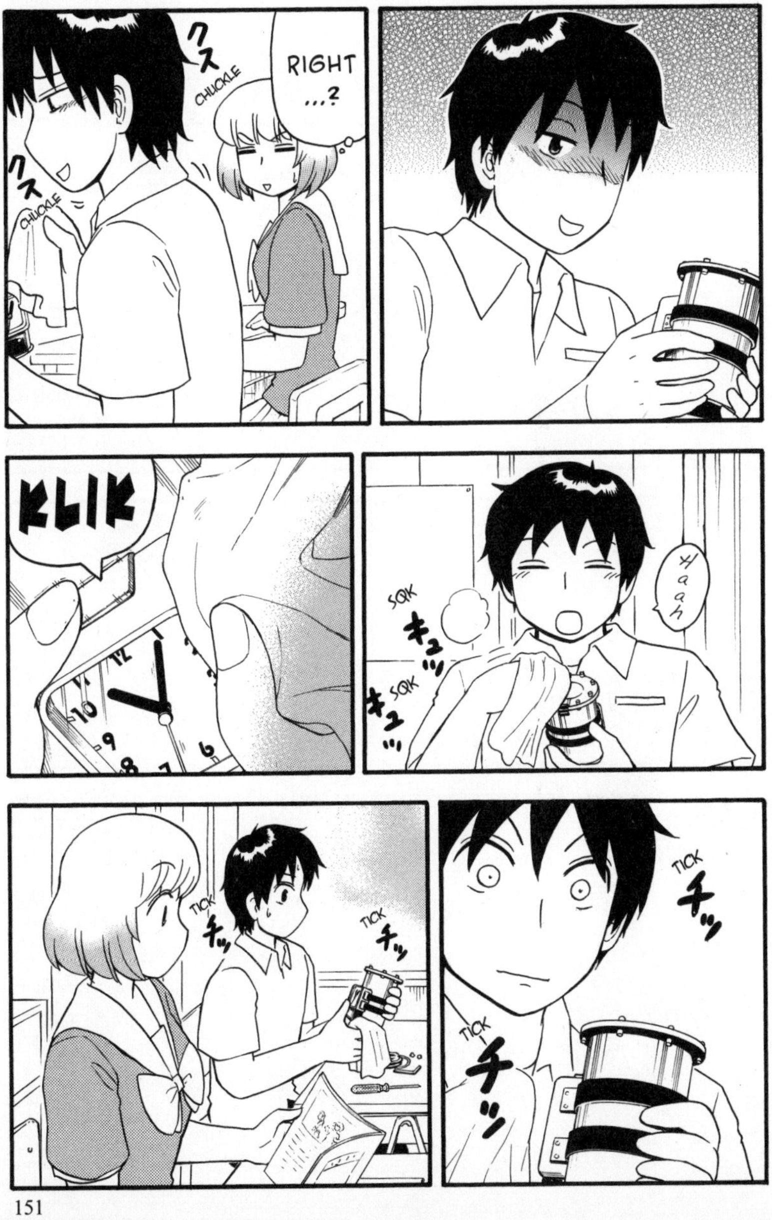

クス
CHUCKLE
クス
CHUCKLE
RIGHT ...?
SQK
キュッ
SQK
キュッ
Haah
KLIK
TICK
チッ
TICK
チッ
TICK
チッ
TICK
チッ

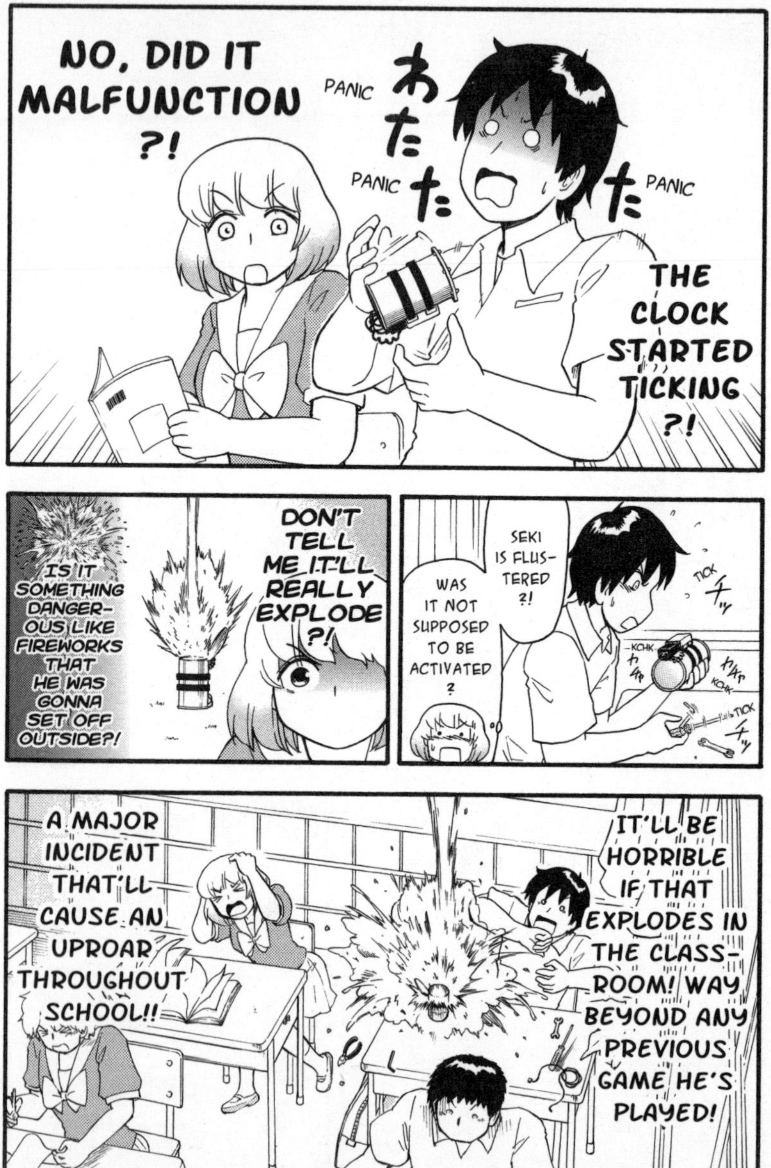
PANIC
わたた
PANIC
PANIC
THE CLOCK STARTED TICKING?!
NO, DID IT MALFUNCTION?!
SEKI IS FLUSTERED?!
WAS IT NOT SUPPOSED TO BE ACTIVATED?
TICK
KCHK
KCHK
TICK
DON'T TELL ME IT'LL REALLY EXPLODE?!
IS IT SOMETHING DANGEROUS LIKE FIREWORKS THAT HE WAS GONNA SET OFF OUTSIDE?!
IT'LL BE HORRIBLE IF THAT EXPLODES IN THE CLASSROOM! WAY BEYOND ANY PREVIOUS GAME HE'S PLAYED!
A MAJOR INCIDENT THAT'LL CAUSE AN UPROAR THROUGHOUT SCHOOL!!

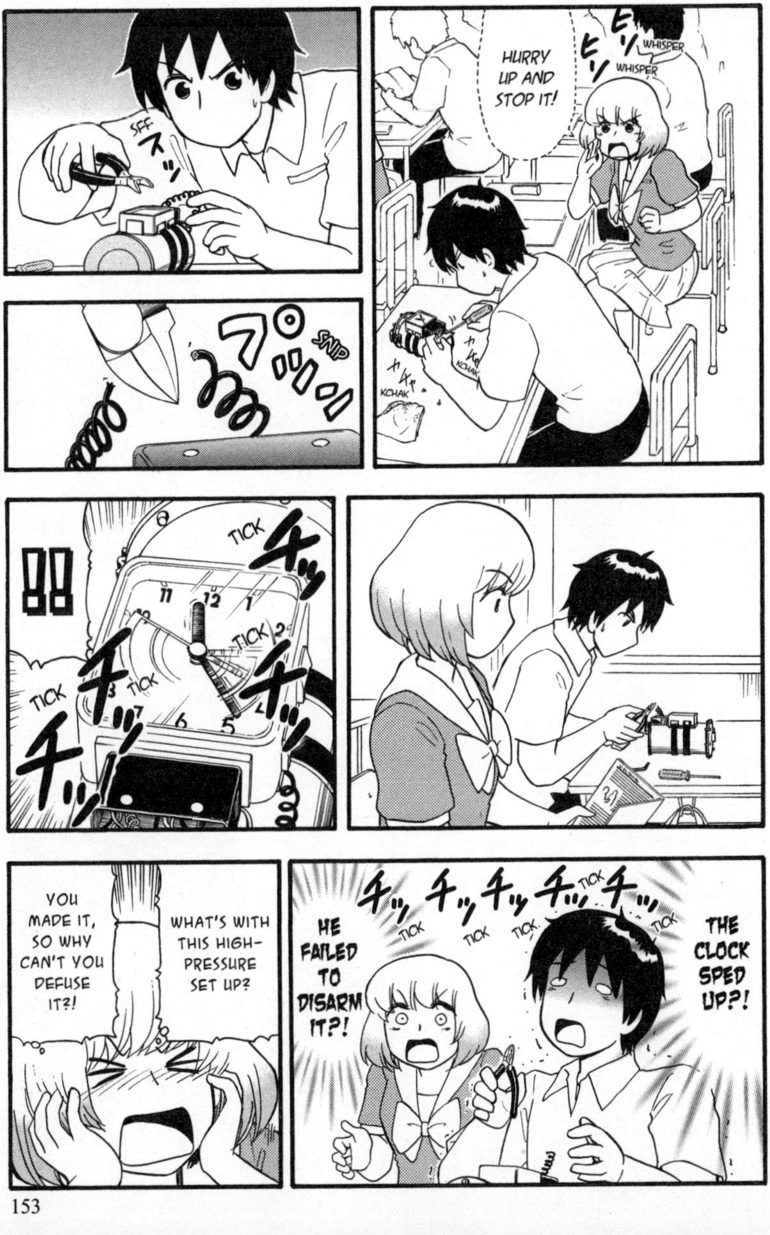
WHISPER
WHISPER
HURRY UP AND STOP IT!
KCHAK
KCHAK
SFF
SNIP
!!
TICK
TICK
TICK
TICK
THE CLOCK SPED UP?!
TICK
TICK
TICK
TICK
TICK
HE FAILED TO DISARM IT?!
WHAT'S WITH THIS HIGH-PRESSURE SET UP?
YOU MADE IT, SO WHY CAN'T YOU DEFUSE IT?!

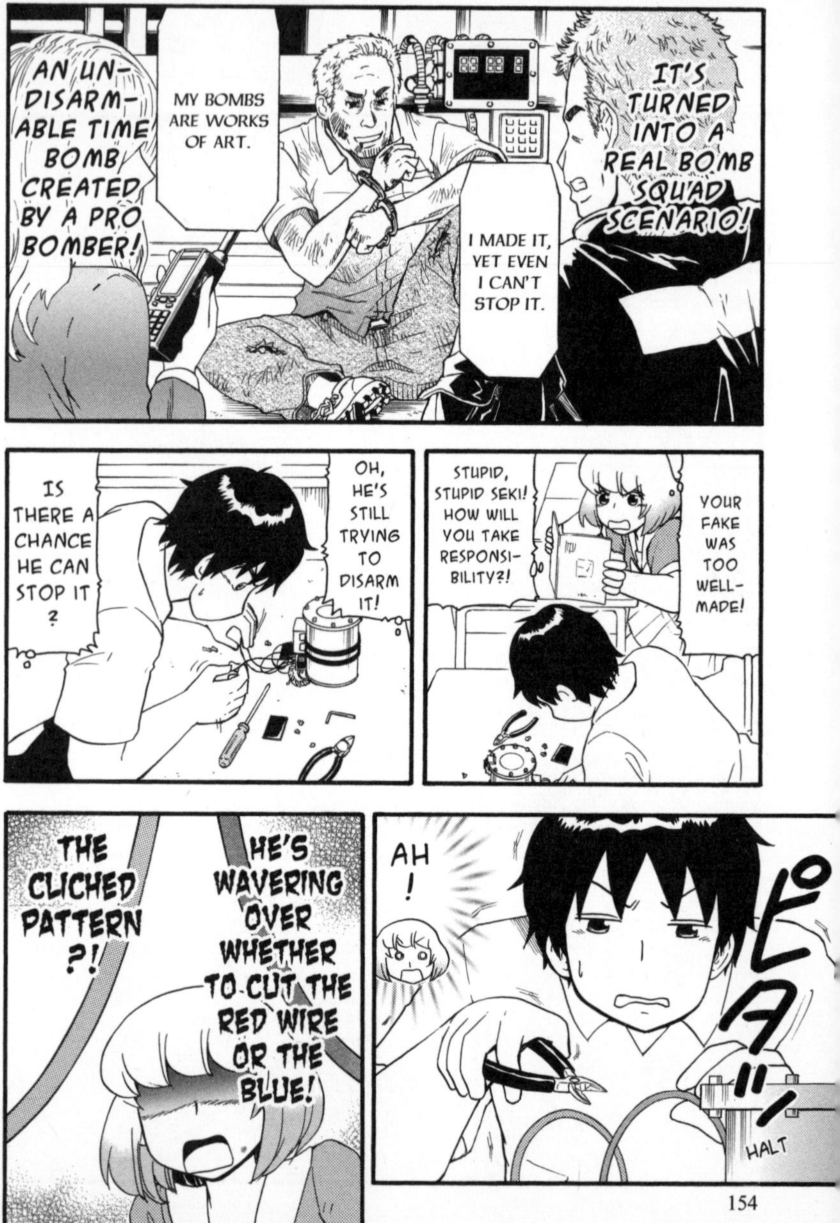
IT'S TURNED INTO A REAL BOMB SQUAD SCENARIO!
MY BOMBS ARE WORKS OF ART.
I MADE IT, YET EVEN I CAN'T STOP IT.
AN UN-DISARMABLE TIME BOMB CREATED BY A PRO BOMBER!
YOUR FAKE WAS TOO WELL-MADE!
STUPID, STUPID SEKI! HOW WILL YOU TAKE RESPONSIBILITY?!
OH, HE'S STILL TRYING TO DISARM IT!
IS THERE A CHANCE HE CAN STOP IT?
ピタッ
HALT
AH!
HE'S WAVERING OVER WHETHER TO CUT THE RED WIRE OR THE BLUE!
THE CLICHED PATTERN?!

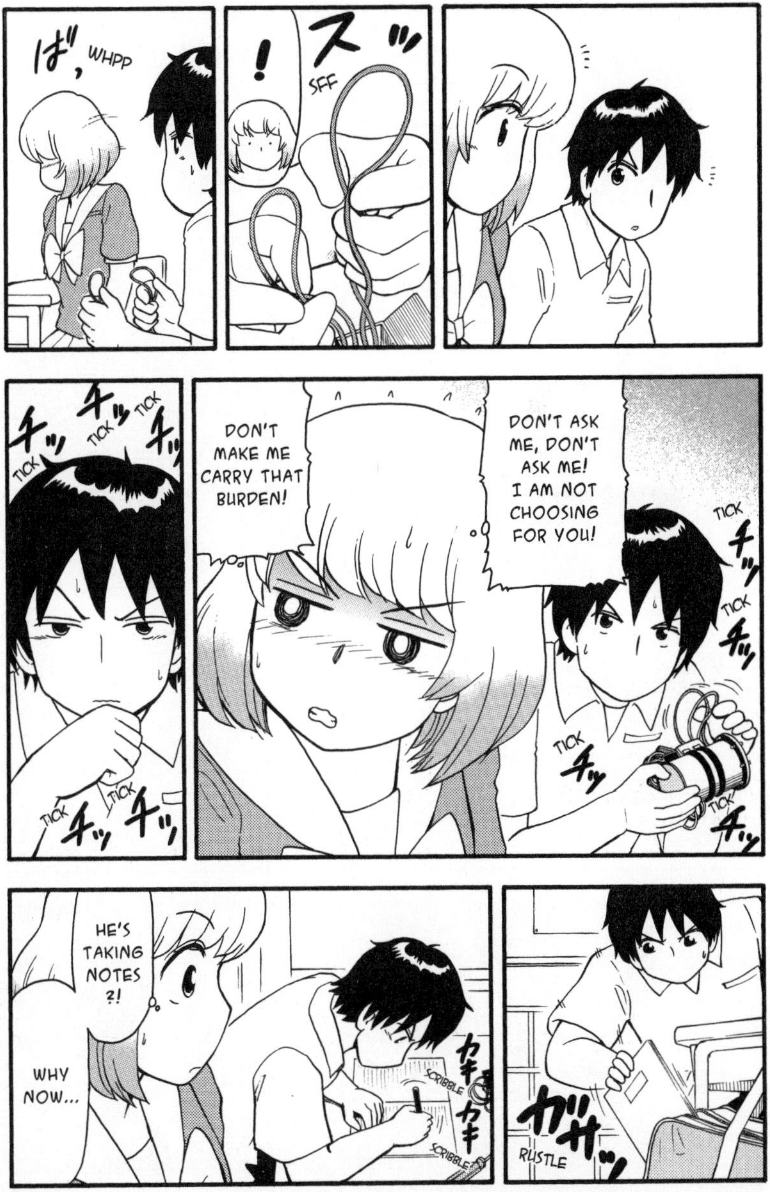
!
スッ
SFF
ばっ
WHPP
DON'T ASK ME, DON'T ASK ME! I AM NOT CHOOSING FOR YOU!
DON'T MAKE ME CARRY THAT BURDEN!
チッ
TICK
チッ
TICK
チッ
TICK
チッ
TICK
チッ
TICK
チッ
TICK
チッ
TICK
チッ
TICK
チッ
TICK
ガサッ
RUSTLE
HE'S TAKING NOTES ?!
WHY NOW...
カキ
SCRIBBLE
カキ
SCRIBBLE

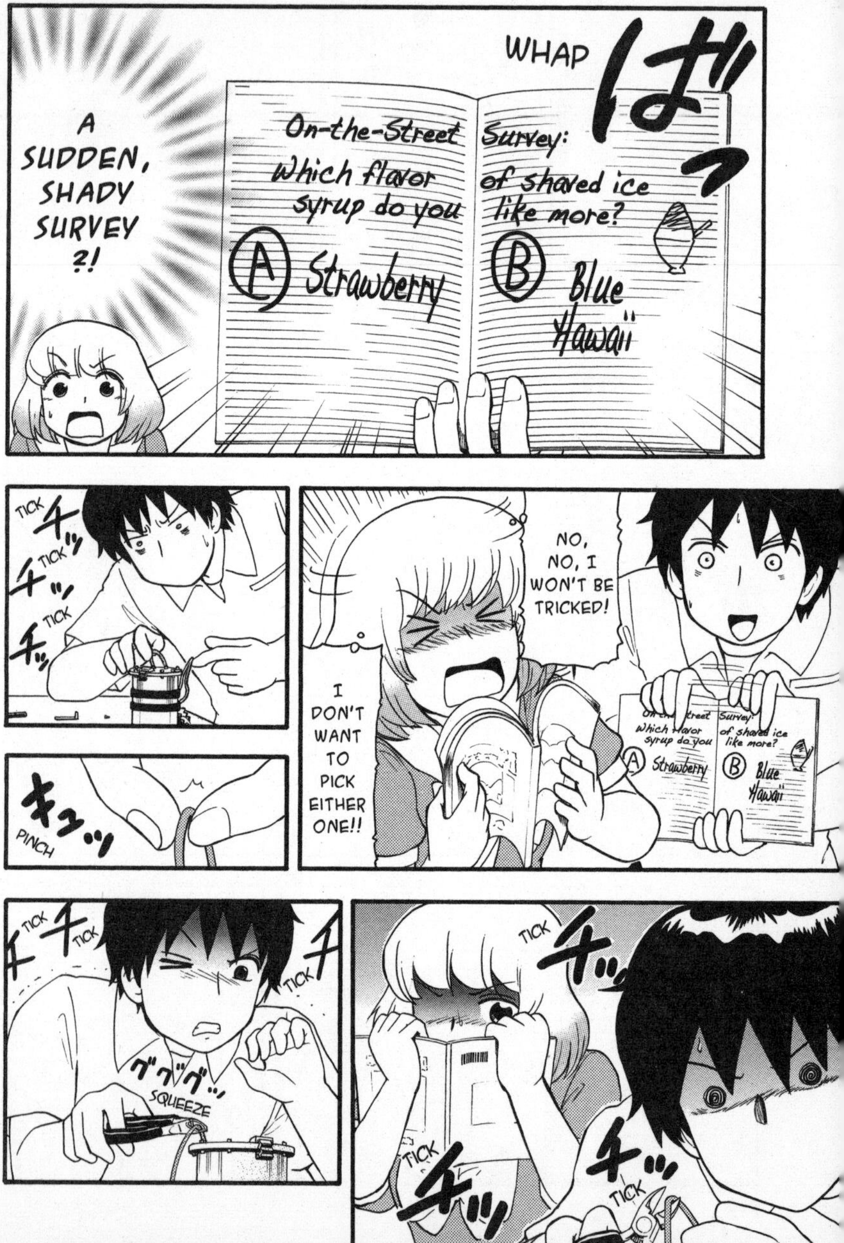
WHAP
ばっ
On-the-Street Survey:
Which flavor of shaved ice syrup do you like more?
A Strawberry
B Blue Hawaii
A SUDDEN, SHADY SURVEY ?!
NO, NO, I WON'T BE TRICKED!
I DON'T WANT TO PICK EITHER ONE!!
On-the-Street Survey:
Which flavor of shaved ice syrup do you like more?
A Strawberry
B Blue Hawaii
TICK
チッ
TICK
チッ
TICK
チッ
キュッ
PINCH
TICK
チッ
TICK
チッ
TICK
チッ
TICK
チ
TICK
チ
TICK
チ
グググッ
SQUEEZE

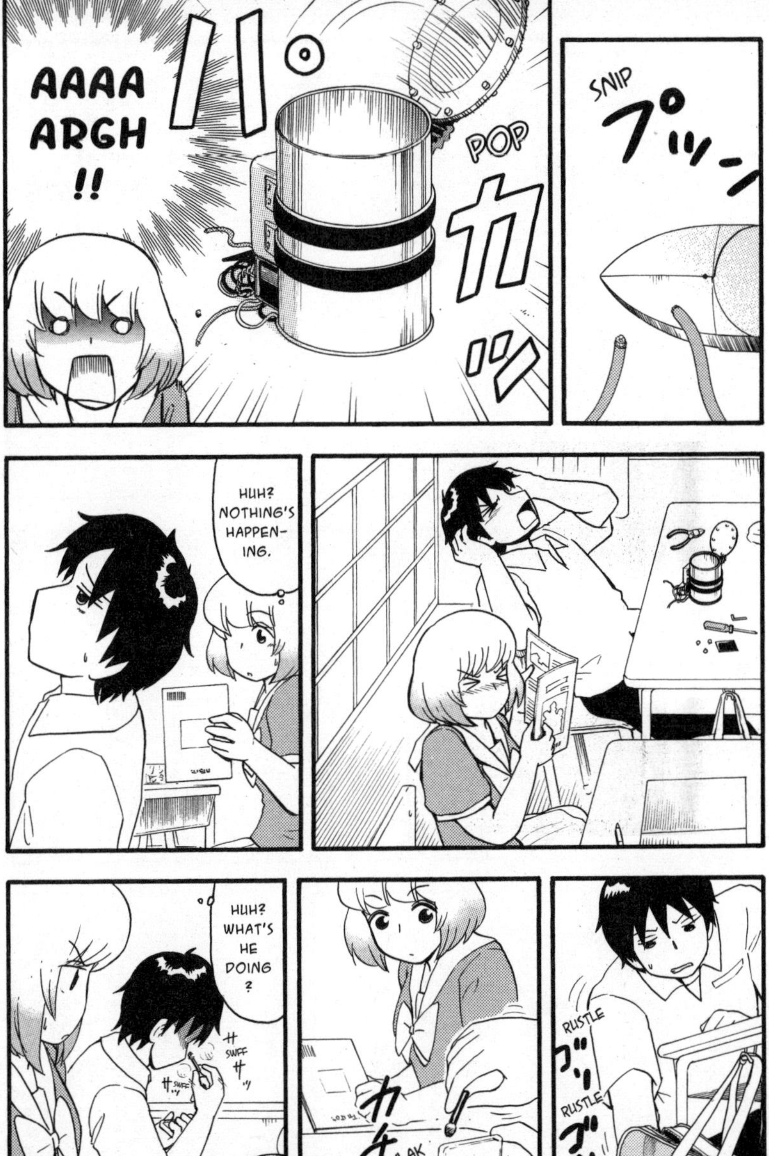
SNIP
プッン
AAAA ARGH!!
パ
POP
カッ
HUH? NOTHING'S HAPPENING.
RUSTLE
ゴソ
RUSTLE
ゴソ
カチャッ
KLAK
HUH? WHAT'S HE DOING?
サ
SWFF
サッ
サ
SWFF
ッ

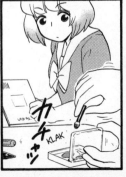

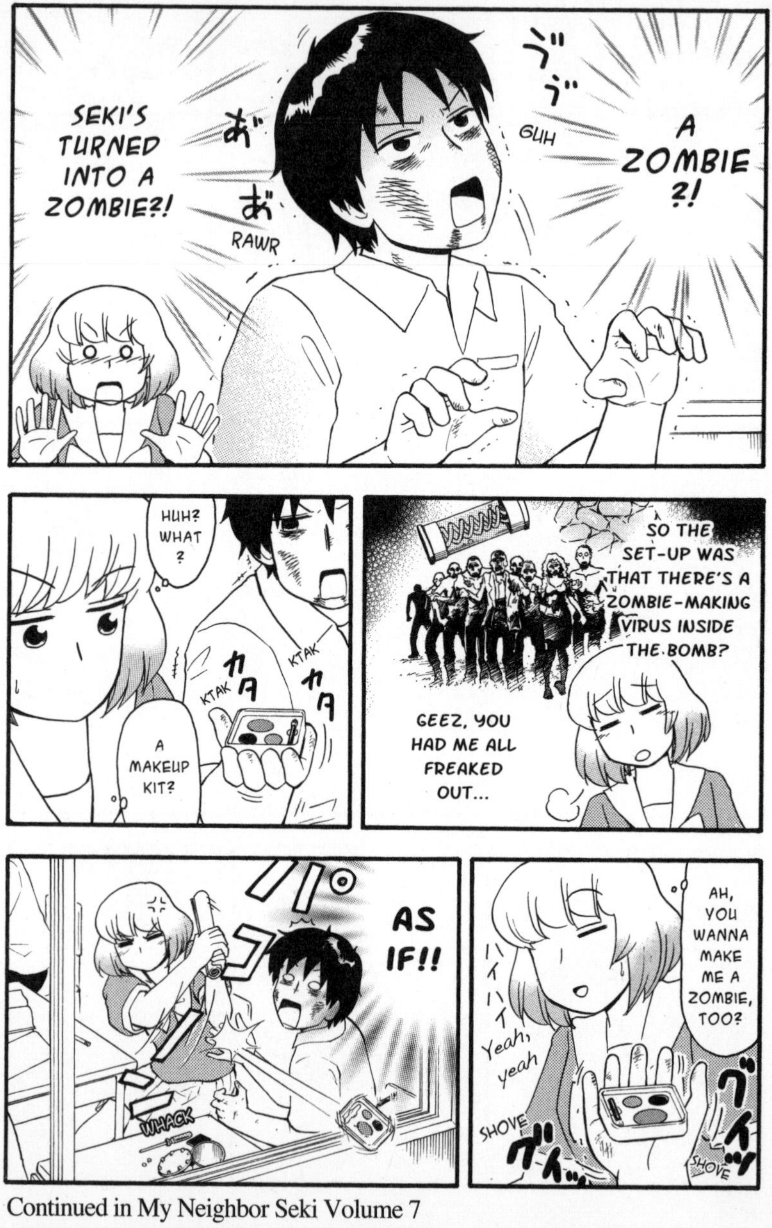
A ZOMBIE?!
ゔゔ
GUH
あ あ
RAWR
SEKI'S TURNED INTO A ZOMBIE?!
SO THE SET-UP WAS THAT THERE'S A ZOMBIE-MAKING VIRUS INSIDE THE BOMB?
GEEZ, YOU HAD ME ALL FREAKED OUT...
HUH? WHAT?
カタ
KTAK
カタ
KTAK
A MAKEUP KIT?
AH, YOU WANNA MAKE ME A ZOMBIE, TOO?
ハイハイ
Yeah, yeah
グイッ
SHOVE
グイッ
SHOVE
AS IF!!
パコ
WHACK

Continued in My Neighbor Seki Volume 7

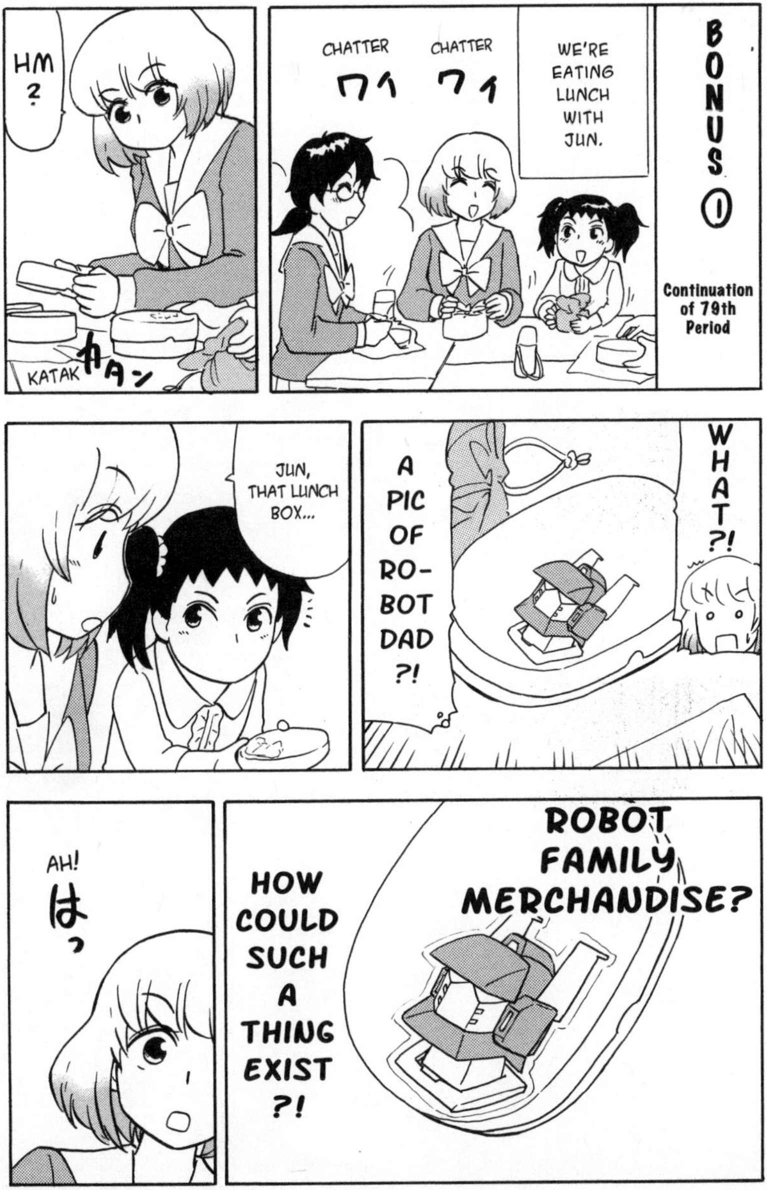
BONUS 1
Continuation of 79th Period
WE'RE EATING LUNCH WITH JUN.
CHATTER ワイ
CHATTER ワイ
HM?
KATAK カタン
WHAT?!
A PIC OF RO-BOT DAD?!
JUN, THAT LUNCH BOX...
ROBOT FAMILY MERCHANDISE?
HOW COULD SUCH A THING EXIST?!
AH! はっ

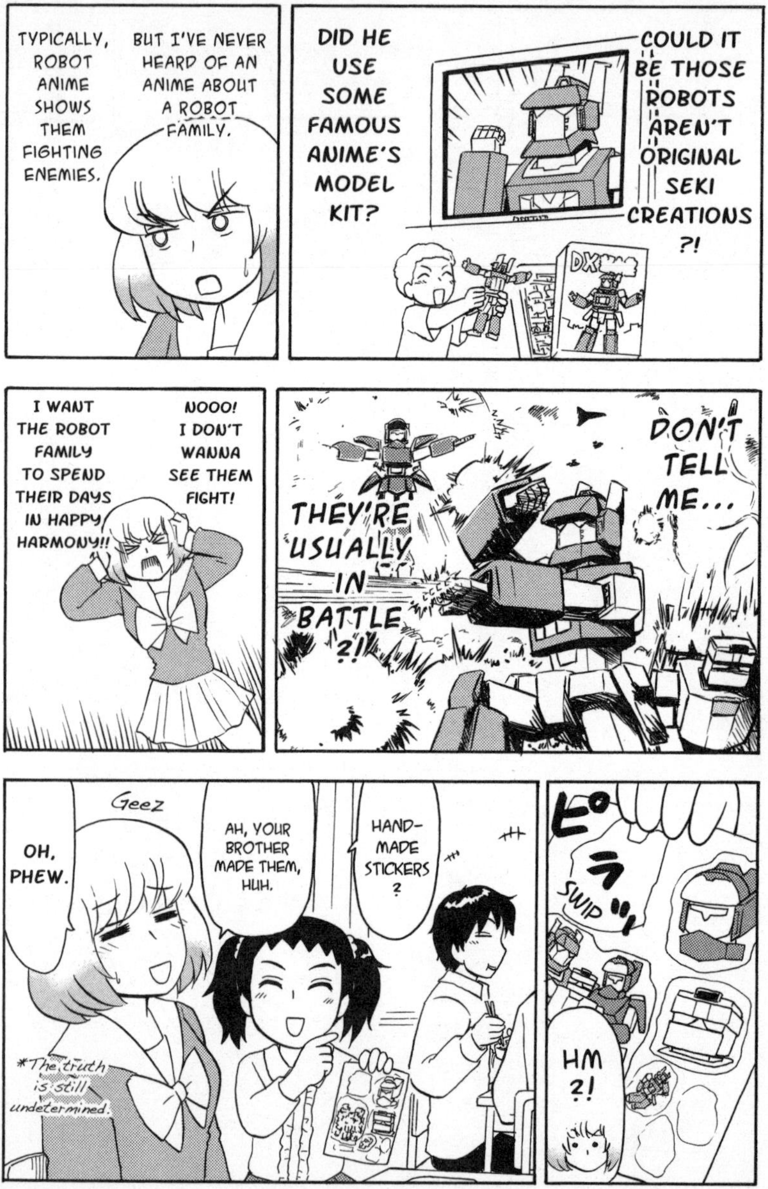
COULD IT BE THOSE ROBOTS AREN'T ORIGINAL SEKI CREATIONS?!
DID HE USE SOME FAMOUS ANIME'S MODEL KIT?
DX
BUT I'VE NEVER HEARD OF AN ANIME ABOUT A ROBOT FAMILY.
TYPICALLY, ROBOT ANIME SHOWS THEM FIGHTING ENEMIES.
DON'T TELL ME...
THEY'RE USUALLY IN BATTLE?!
NOOO! I DON'T WANNA SEE THEM FIGHT!
I WANT THE ROBOT FAMILY TO SPEND THEIR DAYS IN HAPPY HARMONY!!
ピ
ラ
SWIP
HM?!
HAND-MADE STICKERS?
AH, YOUR BROTHER MADE THEM, HUH.
Geez
OH, PHEW.
*The truth is still undetermined.

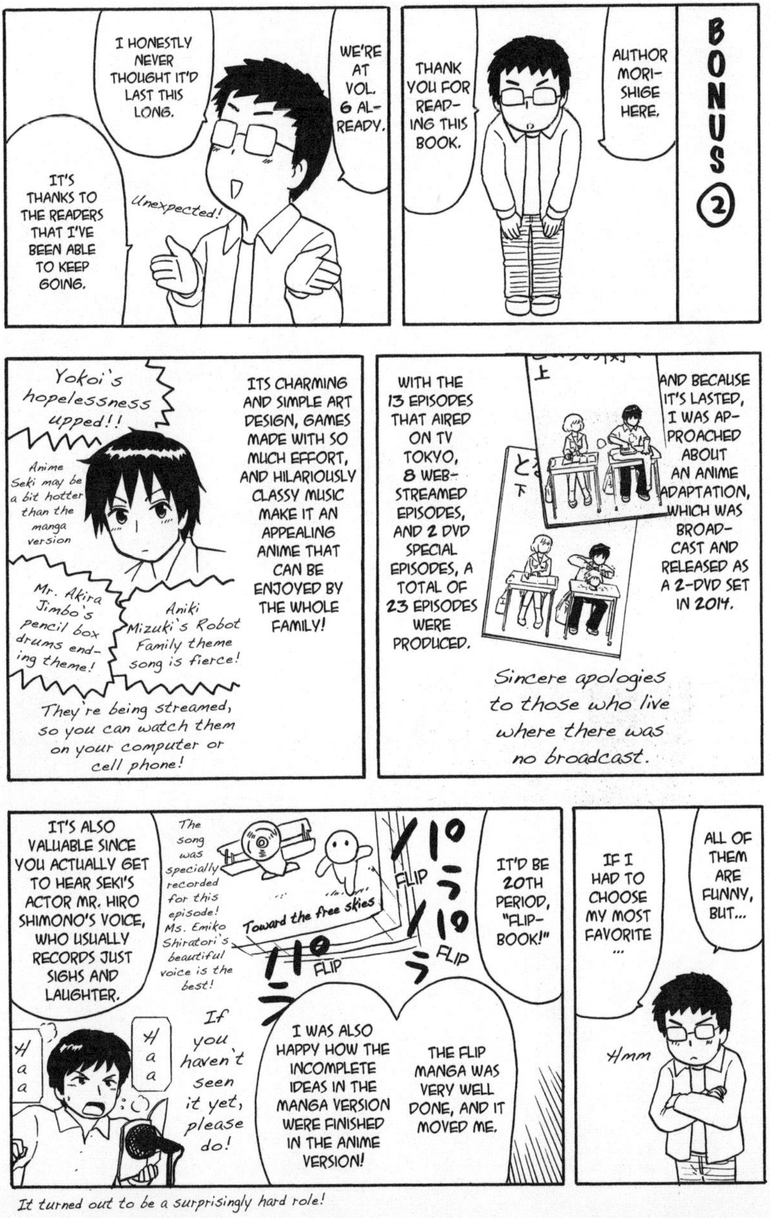
BONUS 2
AUTHOR MORISHIGE HERE.
THANK YOU FOR READING THIS BOOK.
WE'RE AT VOL. 6 ALREADY.
I HONESTLY NEVER THOUGHT IT'D LAST THIS LONG.
Unexpected!
IT'S THANKS TO THE READERS THAT I'VE BEEN ABLE TO KEEP GOING.
AND BECAUSE IT'S LASTED, I WAS APPROACHED ABOUT AN ANIME ADAPTATION, WHICH WAS BROADCAST AND RELEASED AS A 2-DVD SET IN 2014.
上
下
WITH THE 13 EPISODES THAT AIRED ON TV TOKYO, 8 WEB-STREAMED EPISODES, AND 2 DVD SPECIAL EPISODES, A TOTAL OF 23 EPISODES WERE PRODUCED.
Sincere apologies to those who live where there was no broadcast.
ITS CHARMING AND SIMPLE ART DESIGN, GAMES MADE WITH SO MUCH EFFORT, AND HILARIOUSLY CLASSY MUSIC MAKE IT AN APPEALING ANIME THAT CAN BE ENJOYED BY THE WHOLE FAMILY!
Yokoi's hopelessness upped!!
Anime Seki may be a bit hotter than the manga version
Aniki Mizuki's Robot Family theme song is fierce!
Mr. Akira Jimbo's pencil box drums ending theme!
They're being streamed, so you can watch them on your computer or cell phone!
ALL OF THEM ARE FUNNY, BUT...
IF I HAD TO CHOOSE MY MOST FAVORITE ...
Hmm
IT'D BE 20TH PERIOD, "FLIP-BOOK!"
FLIP
FLIP
FLIP
Toward the free skies
The song was specially recorded for this episode! Ms. Emiko Shiratori's beautiful voice is the best!
IT'S ALSO VALUABLE SINCE YOU ACTUALLY GET TO HEAR SEKI'S ACTOR MR. HIRO SHIMONO'S VOICE, WHO USUALLY RECORDS JUST SIGHS AND LAUGHTER.
THE FLIP MANGA WAS VERY WELL DONE, AND IT MOVED ME.
I WAS ALSO HAPPY HOW THE INCOMPLETE IDEAS IN THE MANGA VERSION WERE FINISHED IN THE ANIME VERSION!
If you haven't seen it yet, please do!
Haa
Haa
It turned out to be a surprisingly hard role!

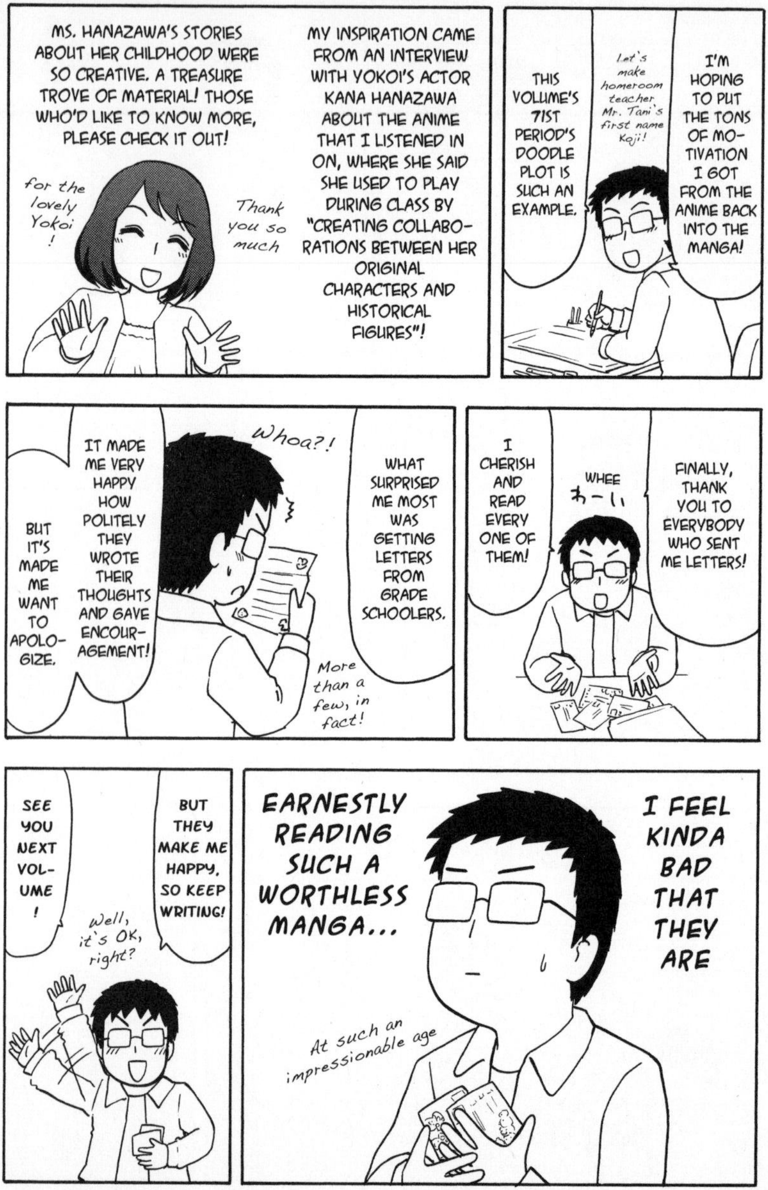
I'M HOPING TO PUT THE TONS OF MOTIVATION I GOT FROM THE ANIME BACK INTO THE MANGA!
Let's make homeroom teacher Mr. Tani's first name Koji!
THIS VOLUME'S 71ST PERIOD'S DOODLE PLOT IS SUCH AN EXAMPLE.
MY INSPIRATION CAME FROM AN INTERVIEW WITH YOKOI'S ACTOR KANA HANAZAWA ABOUT THE ANIME THAT I LISTENED IN ON, WHERE SHE SAID SHE USED TO PLAY DURING CLASS BY "CREATING COLLABORATIONS BETWEEN HER ORIGINAL CHARACTERS AND HISTORICAL FIGURES"!
MS. HANAZAWA'S STORIES ABOUT HER CHILDHOOD WERE SO CREATIVE. A TREASURE TROVE OF MATERIAL! THOSE WHO'D LIKE TO KNOW MORE, PLEASE CHECK IT OUT!
Thank you so much
for the lovely Yokoi!
FINALLY, THANK YOU TO EVERYBODY WHO SENT ME LETTERS!
WHEE
わーい
I CHERISH AND READ EVERY ONE OF THEM!
WHAT SURPRISED ME MOST WAS GETTING LETTERS FROM GRADE SCHOOLERS.
Whoa?!
More than a few, in fact!
IT MADE ME VERY HAPPY HOW POLITELY THEY WROTE THEIR THOUGHTS AND GAVE ENCOURAGEMENT!
BUT IT'S MADE ME WANT TO APOLOGIZE.
I FEEL KINDA BAD THAT THEY ARE
EARNESTLY READING SUCH A WORTHLESS MANGA...
At such an impressionable age
BUT THEY MAKE ME HAPPY, SO KEEP WRITING!
SEE YOU NEXT VOLUME!
Well, it's OK, right?

My Neighbor Seki

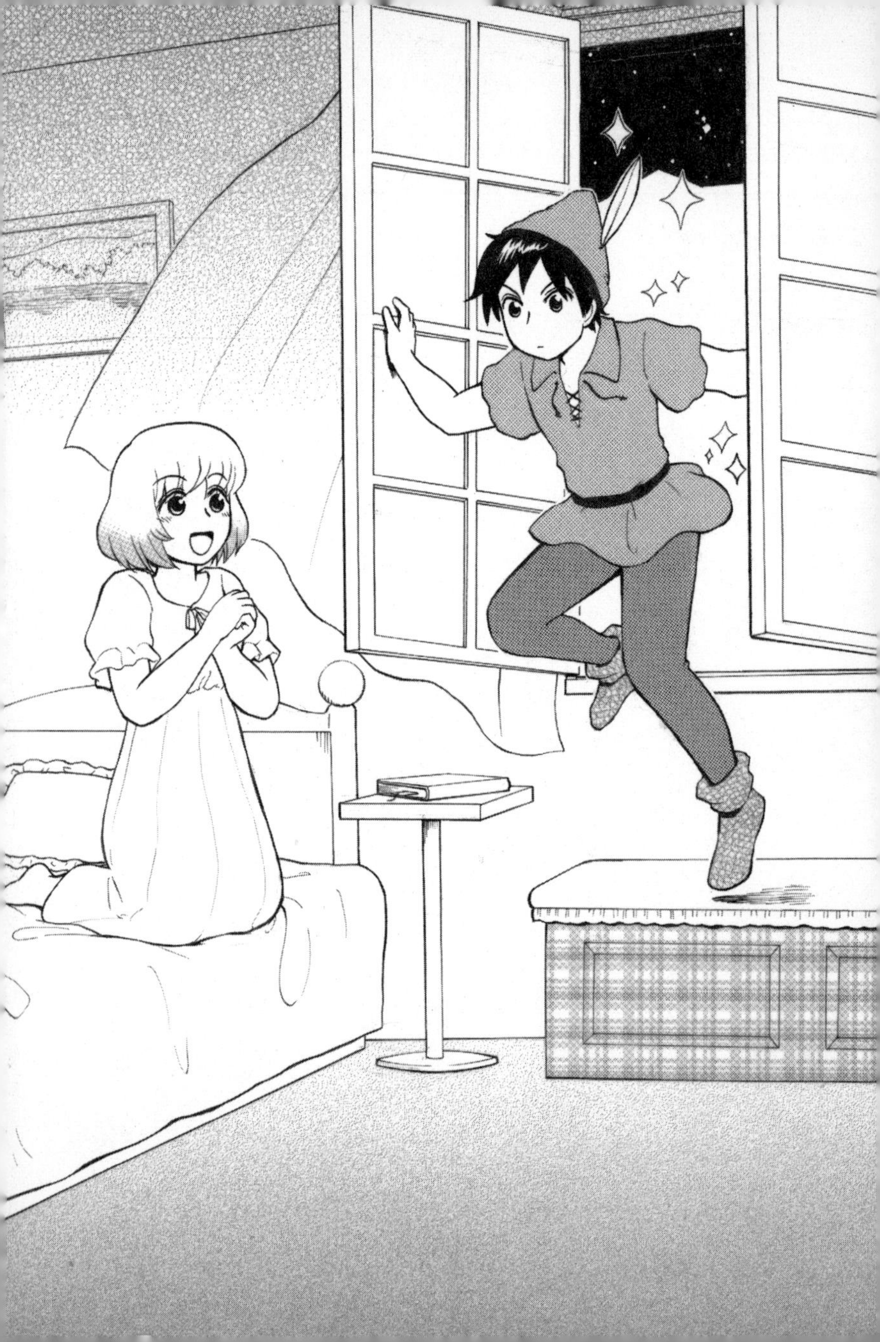